The French War
Against America

The French War Against America

How a Trusted Ally Betrayed Washington and the Founding Fathers

HARLOW GILES UNGER

WILEY

John Wiley & Sons, Inc.

Published by John Wiley & Sons, Inc., Hoboken, New Jersey
Published simultaneously in Canada

Photo credits: pages 9, 29, 36, 45, 47, 54, 69, 79, 100, 102, 111, 113, 136, 173, 198, and 223, Réunion des Musées Nationaux; pages 51, 88, 94, 119, 139, 155, and 239, Library of Congress.

For general information about our other products and services, please contact our Customer Care Department within the United States at (800) 762-2974, outside the United States at (317) 572-3993 or fax (317) 572-4002.

Wiley also publishes its books in a variety of electronic formats. Some content that appears in print may not be available in electronic books. For more information about Wiley products, visit our web site at www.wiley.com.

Library of Congress Cataloging-in-Publication Data:
Unger, Harlow G., date.
The French war against America : how a trusted ally betrayed Washington and
the founding fathers / Harlow Giles Unger.
    p.   cm.
Includes bibliographical references and index.
ISBN 0-471-65113-3 (Cloth)
1. United States—Foreign relations—France.   2. France—Foreign relations—
United States.   3. United States—Foreign relations—To 1865.   I. Title.
E183.8.F8U48   2005
327.44073'09—dc22   2004017100

Printed in the United States of America

10 9 8 7 6 5 4 3 2 1

To my dear friends
Gene and Lorraine Zaborowski
and
To my son,
Richard C. Unger

Contents

Maps and Illustrations   ix

Acknowledgments   xi

Introduction: The Seeds of Treachery   1

1   The War in the Wilderness   7

2   Shattered Glory   23

3   The Treacherous Alliance   39

4   "So Many Spies in Our Midst"   63

5   The French Invasion   87

6   Winners and Losers   115

7   The Appetite of Despotism   143

8   "Down with Washington!"   163

9   Toasts to Sedition   177

10 The War with France   193

11 "I Renounce Louisiana"   215

12 The American Menace   237

Notes   253

Selected Bibliography   271

Index   277

Maps and Illustrations

Maps

New France, 1664–1689   12
North America, 1713–1754   16
North America, 1763–1775   31
North America, 1783   127
Territorial growth of the United States from 1803   233

Illustrations

Louis XV   9
Duc de Choiseul   29
"Baron" Johann de Kalb   36
Louis XVI   45
Foreign Minister Comte de Vergennes   47
George Washington   51
Pierre Augustin Caron de Beaumarchais   54
Comte de Broglie   69
Marquis de Lafayette   79
John Adams   88
John Hancock   94
Admiral Comte d'Estaing   100
Comte de Rochambeau   102
Admiral Comte de Grasse   111
Surrender at Yorktown   113
Benjamin Franklin   119
Execution of King Louis XVI   136
Secretary of the Treasury Alexander Hamilton   139

Edmond Charles Genet   148
Thomas Jefferson   155
Maximilien Robespierre   173
Charles Maurice de Talleyrand Périgord   198
Napoléon I   223
James Monroe   239

Acknowledgments

First and foremost, my deepest thanks to André and Eva Mandel, my friends of nearly fifty years, for their ever-present support, enthusiasm, patience, and love. André's scholarly assistance proved invaluable in finding and translating French archival materials cited in this book—much of it in old, often archaic French. Always ready to help me in so many ways, he willingly undertook research chores, which made gathering background materials for this book quicker and more efficient.

Others who helped me compile the materials for this book include Peter Jaffe, of the rare books department of Argosy Book Store, New York; Louise Jones, librarian at the Yale Club of New York City; economist Jonathan Falk; and the librarians and research aides at the Bibliothèque Historique de la Ville de Paris and Bibliothèque Nationale de France in Paris. I am also most grateful to production editor Kimberly Monroe-Hill and copy editor Shelly Perron, who, despite growling authors like me, too often toil and suffer anonymously to ensure accuracy in books such as this and add much luster to their contents. Thank you.

And finally, my deepest thanks, as always, for the support and guidance of my friends, Edward Knappman, my literary agent, and Hana Lane, my editor, who together helped me travel roads I would never have discovered.

Introduction:
The Seeds of Treachery

NO ALLIED NATION infuriates Americans more these days than France and its relentless, often irrational campaign to deprecate almost everything American—American people, American culture, American politics, history, economy, business, and, above all, American foreign policy. The French government permeates almost every area of French life—schoolrooms, churches, books, newspapers, radio and television, theater, film, even museum exhibits and cultural events, and, of course, foreign affairs—with anti-American vitriol. In addition, the French disseminate propaganda far beyond French borders via the globe-engirdling Agence France Presse "news" network, which feeds media in the vast French-speaking world of the former French empire in West Africa, the Middle East, Indochina, Polynesia, and the Caribbean.

To many Americans, the incessant French assault seems particularly odious coming only decades after the United States sacrificed so many innocent lives and invested so much national treasure in the gallant rescues of France in two world wars—wars that France helped start and the United States sought to avoid.

Although obsessive French anti-Americanism has dismayed and dumbfounded a succession of American presidents, it would not have surprised our Founding Fathers: "They are not a moral people," John Adams warned Congress in 1782, knowing then that far from being our ally, France was, in fact, our enemy.[1] "It is not in their interest," declared Chief Justice John Jay, "that we should become a great and formidable people, and therefore they will not help us to become so."[2]

Contrary to what many Americans believe—indeed, contrary to what most of us learned in school—the French did *not* support the American Revolution to help create a free and independent new nation, but to try to restore French sovereignty over North America. As Adams and Jay pointed out, the French intended their financial and military aid to *prolong* the revolution and weaken *both* the English and Americans enough to permit French reconquest of Canada and territories lost fifteen years earlier in the French and Indian War. Although Adams and Jay foiled the scheme, French rulers would continue plotting for the next century to recapture North America—only to be frustrated and often humiliated by the upstart new nation they helped create. The fifty-year-old campaign of anti-Americanism since World War II is the residue of those frustrations.

Until the creation of the United States, the French had dominated the Western World for the better part of ten centuries—by God's will! Or so the French believed and, in many cases, still believe.

For centuries, French priests, parents, and teachers indoctrinated generations of French children that God chose France as the birthplace of nations when He designated Clovis, king of the Franks, to create the kingdom of France from disparate tribes. Clovis thanked God by converting to Catholicism in A.D. 696 and declaring the nation Catholic. Pope Athanasius II accordingly proclaimed France "the elder daughter of the church," and ordered the French clergy to serve the king in governing the nation. Thereafter church and crown remained inextricably linked, with Pope Stephan coming from Rome to the basilica of Saint-Denis near Paris to crown Pépin the Short in 751. He anointed him with holy oil, as the prophets had anointed the biblical kings of Israel, and he declared the French "the People of God."

French history texts for preadolescents write that God appointed Pépin's son Charlemagne the "great civilizer" to embrace all Europe within the French empire. Charlemagne's armies swept across the face of the Continent—Germany, Austria, Italy, Corsica, Sardinia, northern Spain, Denmark, and eastern Europe. In 800, Pope Leo III crowned Charlemagne in Saint Peter's in Rome and declared him "Carolus Augustus, crowned by God, great and pacifying emperor, governor of the Holy Roman Empire and, by the grace of God, king of the Franks and Lombards."[3] The kings of Spain ("His Most Catholic Majesty") and Britain ("His Most Britannic Majesty") paid homage to Charlemagne as "His *Most Christian* Majesty," king of all Christendom and protector of Christian sanctuaries in Jerusalem.

In the centuries that followed, the links between church and state grew stronger and molded the French into the most warlike people the world had ever seen. The ravages of the Huns had lasted little more than a century; the Mongols less than two centuries; the Mohammedans about three. Charlemagne's conquests marked the beginning of *eleven centuries* of French military terror in Europe, Africa, Asia, and North America.

After the French conquered England in 1066, French clerics ascended the Papal throne and sent French armies on seven Crusades of mass slaughter to seize the Holy Land and the Tomb of Christ from the Mohammedans. For the next two hundred years, French kings and their armies plundered the Levant of gold and silver treasure— ruthlessly butchering in the name of God. King Louis IX earned sainthood for leading the last two Crusades and carrying what he claimed was the Crown of Thorns to Notre-Dame Cathedral in Paris.[4] In 1309, King Philip IV tightened the French grip on the church by carrying off Pope Boniface VIII and the Papal court to France. During the so-called Second Babylonian Captivity, seven successive Popes governed the church as French vassals from a new Papal palace in Avignon, where they helped create a powerful French, or Gallican, Catholic Church that gave the French king spiritual as well as temporal control of France. Even after the papacy returned to Rome, the French Catholic Church remained independent of Rome, with the French king appointing all bishops—and, indirectly, all priests—in France, thus ensuring unquestioned church fealty to the French crown. The Gallican Church not only rejected papal infallibility, it subjected papal decisions to the approval of ecumenical councils and the French king.

Control of church hierarchy extended royal oversight into every parish in the nation and erased the lines between church and state:

clerical and secular rule were one; national glory became celestial glory; the glory of France *was* the glory of God. The Gallican Church instilled a degree of religio-nationalism in the French that no other nation would experience until, perhaps, twentieth-century Japan.

In the seventeenth century, Cardinal Richelieu directed national policy for Louis XIII, and Richelieu's protégé Cardinal Mazarin did the same for young Louis XIV. Together, cardinals and kings filled every church and school with zealously loyal priests to indoctrine generations of literates and illiterates that the French king was God's representative on earth by "divine right." French armies swept across the earth, as far east as India and westward over the Atlantic to the New World, where "New France" stretched across Canada to the Rockies, up to the Arctic Ocean and down to the Gulf of Mexico. At the center of the empire, Louis XIV—"Louis the Great"—built a palace-city at Versailles of such celestial size and splendor that visiting monarchs from the earth's most storied lands trembled as they approached and saw it loom over the horizon.[5] After proceeding through a maze of gilded antechambers, many grew faint as they walked the endless Hall of Mirrors to the foot of the golden throne to hear pronouncements of le Roi Soleil (the Sun King). Louis XV boldly proclaimed, "We owe our crown to God only," and Foreign Minister comte de Vergennes duly instructed the young king Louis XVI, "France has the right to influence all the world's important matters. Her king is comparable to a supreme judge, entitled to regard his throne as a tribunal established by Providence."[6] The deep French belief in God's immutable ties to France lies at the heart of what Americans (and most Europeans, incidentally) perceive today as (and fail to understand about) French "arrogance." Arrogance, however, is a normal characteristic (symptom?) of those who believe their systems of beliefs to be "God-given"—Christianity, Islam, Judaism, American democracy, the French "Enlightenment." All often assumed the right—and sometimes, the obligation—to impose those beliefs on others.

In the seventeenth century and first half of the eighteenth century, the French boot stomped across the European landscape in four wars to enforce French authority over the Continent. Finally, in 1756, the English cried "Enough!" and in the long brutal war that followed, the English humiliated the French and stripped them of New France and the rest of their empire. But the ink had not dried on the peace treaty ending the war before French king Louis XV, and his astute foreign minister, the duc de Choiseul, began plotting the reconquest of North America. His plan was to support an American revolution that would undermine English economic and military strength enough to permit French armies to return to New France unimpeded.

The plan not only failed, it inadvertently led to the end of monarchy in France. From the first, John Adams, John Jay, and George Washington recognized the folly of trusting the oldest, most despotic monarchy in the Western world to help overthrow a homologous monarchy and risk the spread of liberty in a world ruled by autocrats. Adams and Jay, as a result, negotiated a secret peace treaty with Britain that ignored French interests. In the end, the costs of the American Revolution to France exceeded those of England. Apart from the military and economic costs, she paid a huge political price. As French statesman Talleyrand (a bishop) warned, "The effect of political equality invites every citizen, regardless of class, to acquire wealth that rightfully belongs to the aristocracy and monarchy."[7] In fact, French troops and officers in the American Revolution succumbed to the effects of the political equality they experienced in the New World and, as British statesman Edmund Burke put it, "imbibed a love of freedom" that proved critical to the success of the French Revolution and destruction of the French monarchy.[8]

But the end of monarchy did little to diminish the centuries-old French belief in their "right to influence all the world's important matters" and give the law to other nations. As the following pages reveal, subsequent French rulers—monarchs, emperors, revolutionary leaders, and presidents of the French Republic—continued pursuing Choiseul's plot to recover sovereignty over North America for the next century, using every strategy they could devise—espionage, insurrection, attempted overthrow of the American government, naval warfare, armed invasion, and vile treachery.

1

The War in the Wilderness

FRENCH KING LOUIS XV was feeding his insatiable sexual appetite with one of his mistresses when word of a great French victory in the North American wilderness reached the royal bedchamber. Without interrupting his exertions, he grunted his approval and sent the bearer of the news scurrying away through a maze of gilded halls and antechambers to an office in a mysterious apartment of the sprawling palace at Versailles.

Le Secret du Roi, as the office was called, was the hub of a far-reaching network of spies the king had established in 1748 as a personal instrument for controlling national affairs after the War of the Austrian Succession. Eight years of inconclusive fighting had ended with the Treaty of Aix-la-Chapelle, which sent all combatants behind their original borders—but Louis had no intention of remaining there—and saw no reason for doing so.

"The French king is master and arbiter of Europe," his mentor, Cardinal Fleury, had told him when he was but an infant prince—a time when his great-grandfather Louis XIV, the Sun King, still ruled. "Our neighbors have everything to fear from us—we nothing from them. . . . The diplomatic object of this crown has been and will always be to enjoy in Europe that role of leadership which accords with antiquity, its worth and its greatness; to abase every power which shall attempt to become superior to it, whether by endeavoring to usurp its possessions, or by arrogating to itself an unwarranted

7

preeminence, or finally by seeking to diminish its influence and credit in the affairs of the world at large."[1]

To identify those who sought to diminish Louis's influence, le Secret du Roi sent spies everywhere, in and out of the palace, under and into every bed, to every table, and into every council chamber from St. Petersburg to London. Their reports told Louis what every friend and enemy of France was planning before they had even planned it. The reports generated rewards for loyalty to the French state and retribution for disloyalty and provided the king with the omniscience that sustained the omnipotence God had granted him and other French kings more than twelve centuries earlier.

Although he had succeeded the legendary Louis XIV, the latter had reigned so long—from 1643 to 1715—that his son and grandson died before him and left his five-year-old great-grandson as successor and heir to the world's greatest empire, stretching east across India and west across North America. A regent governed the empire until Louis XV reached the age of majority, but with little interest in royal responsibilities, he set out to discover the pleasures of bed and board—with emphasis on the former.

In the interest of royal succession, the regent arranged the king's marriage to the Polish king's twenty-one-year-old daughter when Louis was only fifteen. Louis couldn't stand the sight of her and limited his visits to brief encounters that kept her in labor most of the time, producing a procession of princesses in her apartment, while he labored in his apartment with an endless procession of mistresses. Collectively, they earned him the often misinterpreted sobriquet of "Louis le Bien-Aimé"—Louis the beloved.

The motives for that love varied. Some women offered him their bodies to win titles or influence for themselves or their families; others went to the king's bed by order of their husbands or sons seeking profitable land grants, government contracts, or other favors; still others—like Jeanne d'Arc—heard the voice of God commanding them to the arms of the king "crowned by God." But their motives meant little: when a woman or girl caught the king's eye, neither she, her parents, nor her husband dared reject the blessing of a royal command. And off she went to the king's bedchamber, where her pleas, tears, or shrieks of pain only excited the king's lust.

Louis XV, the French monarch from 1715 to 1774, pursued the pleasures of his palace while the great empire of his forbear Louis XIV disintegrated and fell into the hands of the British.

He was "a mindless man without a soul, without feeling," said the duc de Choiseul, who would serve Louis as foreign minister for twelve years. "He loved hurting [people] the way children love to make animals suffer . . . he enjoyed making [them] suffer whenever he could; I don't think anyone who ever knew him ever saw him show any benevolence since the day he was born."[2]

"If she's pretty and I like her looks," snapped the king, "I say that I want her, and that ends it!"[3]

During his early years on the throne, he left administrative duties to his mentor and surrogate father, Cardinal Fleury. Fleury died in 1743, just as the beautiful twenty-two-year-old Jeanne-Antoinette Poisson, daughter of a minor bourgeois financier, captured the king's heart, mind, and body. A star of influential Paris social salons, she had married a merchant king who made the mistake of presenting her at Versailles. Louis snatched her from her husband, showed her to the royal bed chamber, and, two years later, ennobled her as marquise de Pompadour—the name of a manor the king bought for her. He was so taken with his new lady, he created a new title for her—maitresse en titre (official royal mistress)—and ensconced her in her new office at a formal court presentation that gave her a standing and power never before accorded to royal mistresses. It was, said Choiseul "a scandalous presentation . . . that violated every rule of dignity and morality. Sovereign princes by nature almost always represent a lower form of life than the rest of mankind, but, of all European princes, the French Bourbons rank as the lowest and most despicable."[4]

By default, Pompadour became the king's prime minister. He enjoyed nothing more than riding to hunt at Marly, a palatial hunting lodge between Versailles and Paris, and happily left Pompadour to manage palace politics. She set about reshaping the realm, ruthlessly disgracing any woman who tried to replace her in the king's esteem and elevating to power men who submitted to her political and sexual demands. Neither the king nor his mistress saw fissures forming in the structure of the great empire that stretched across the earth beyond the palace gates.

The French military machine held most of continental Europe in thrall; powerful French armies had secured the wealth of India and West Africa's lucrative slave and ivory trades; and in North America,

New France (La Nouvelle France) stretched across a vast expanse from the Atlantic coast of Canada to the Rocky Mountains, from the Arctic to the Gulf of Mexico. Fur trader Samuel de Champlain had become "Father of New France" in 1608, when he claimed eastern Canada for France. Twenty years later, Cardinal Richelieu, who governed France as prime minister for the shy and sickly King Louis XIII, lusted to find as much gold and silver in Canada as the Spanish had in Mexico. He organized the Compagnie de la Nouvelle-France (the Company of New France) with one hundred shareholders from the oligarchy of landed aristocrats who controlled the nation's wealth and wielded power from palace corridors behind the throne room. Also called the Cent Associés (One Hundred Associates), or Cent Familles (One Hundred Families), they sent French adventurer René-Robert Cavalier Sieur de La Salle to penetrate the North American heartland in the 1670s.

After exploring the shores of the Great Lakes, La Salle traveled the length of the Ohio, Missouri, and Mississippi rivers, and on April 9, 1682, he reached the Gulf of Mexico. He found no gold or silver but invoked the so-called law of discovery by planting a post in the ground bearing the arms of France and proclaiming King Louis XIV sovereign over "Louisiana *and all the lands watered by its rivers and tributaries* . . . [including] the seas, harbors, ports, bays, adjacent straits, and all the nations, people, provinces, cities, towns, villages, mines, minerals, fisheries, streams and rivers comprised in the extent of said Louisiana [italics added]."[5] Barren of precious ores, however, and far from the Atlantic, Louisiana attracted few French settlers, although a few trappers and fur traders roamed as far west as the Rocky Mountains.

In contrast, most British colonists came to North America to settle. Although British territory was limited to a pathetically narrow strip of coastal land on the Atlantic Ocean—about one hundred miles wide and nine hundred miles long—the English king and Board of Trade allowed anyone to call the land his own if he cleared, planted, and drove four stakes in the ground to mark the corners. By the early 1700s, 400,000 English colonists had flocked to North America, compared to only 18,000 French, and by midcentury, the English had burst the boundaries of their settlements and pushed westward into the wilderness—and into inevitable conflict with their

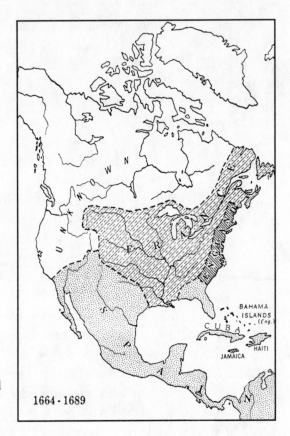

New France after the original
European explorations in
North America.

1664 - 1689

ancient European enemies, the French. Too few to repel the British, the French dispensed a mixture of artful rhetoric, brandy, and promises of fresh human scalps to enlist Indian warriors to their side.

"The difference between the king of England and the king of France is evident everywhere," French governor Ange de Menneville Du Quesne harangued the Indians. "Go see the forts of our king and you will see that you can still hunt under their very walls. . . . The English, on the other hand, drive away the game. The forest falls before them as they advance, and the soil laid bare so that you can scarce find the wherewithal to build a shelter for the night."[6]

Emboldened by brandy and thirsting for blood, the Indians followed the French on barbarous raids on English frontier settlements, burning, slaughtering, and scalping while the French harvested furs from the storehouses of their hapless victims. The frequency and devastation of raids exploded into frontier wars whose intensity and savagery exhausted and bankrupted both sides. In 1748, the British and French ended the fighting and returned behind prewar boundaries—except in the undefined Ohio River valley and the lands between the Appalachian Mountains and Mississippi River.

Although La Salle had claimed the territory for France under the "law of discovery" a century earlier, the British called the law—and the claim—absurd. With the 1748 cease-fire, therefore, British trappers and traders crossed the Appalachians into the disputed wilderness, fished and hunted with abandon, and raised a settlement at Logstown, about one hundred miles south of Lake Erie, where the Allegheny and Monongahela rivers meet to form the Ohio.

Early in 1749, English king George II claimed the territory for Britain and granted 200,000 acres near Logstown to the Ohio Company, a speculative venture of Virginia plantation owners led by Thomas Lee and Lawrence Washington. Washington and his partners envisioned hauling furs over the Appalachians to the upper reaches of the Potomac and floating them downstream to Chesapeake Bay for shipment to England. The route would halve the time the French needed to carry furs across the Great Lakes and down the St. Lawrence River. King George promised Ohio Company investors 300,000 additional acres if they succeeded.

In November 1749, Lawrence Washington sent his trusted younger half-brother, George, with a team of surveyors to map company lands. The Washingtons were great-grandsons of "Colonel" John Washington, who arrived in America from England in 1657 to cash in on the craze for American sweet tobacco. Virginia's John Rolfe had developed a curing method that sharply reduced spoilage on Atlantic crossings and made tobacco so profitable that Virginia townsmen planted it in the streets to extract every penny from the rich Virginia soil.

After four years, though, tobacco exhausted soil nutrients; the land had to lie fallow for twenty years to recover. Rather than wait, planters moved west onto virgin lands that teemed with game, offered a wealth in furs, and made land speculation a passion for every plantation owner. By the time George Washington was born, his family had accumulated 12,000 acres on the northernmost Virginia cape and was firmly entrenched in the Virginia "aristocracy." Unlike European aristocrats, who inherited or purchased their noble status, Virginia's aristocracy worked their way to wealth and power as daring entrepreneurs, risking life and limb on treacherous Atlantic crossings and plunging into the American wilderness to create the world's largest, most productive plantations. Their wealth and vast properties raised them to community leadership as sheriffs, legislators, and militia officers.

Although Washington's father died when George was only eleven, his twenty-five-year-old half-brother, Lawrence, took on the task of raising and educating the boy. A daring horseman and former officer in the British marines, Lawrence had received a brilliant education in England and passed it on to his young half-brother. By the time George was sixteen, he had mastered most academic skills and social graces. In addition to literature, geography, history, and advanced mathematics, he learned law, business, and surveying, all of which were essential to men of property. More than six feet tall by then, he displayed a thoughtful, kindly personality that belied his enormous physical strength. Galloping after Lawrence over the Virginia hills, George grew into a superior horseman and expert marksman, and he developed a keen eye for spotting not only the secret lairs of game but the potential value of undeveloped lands. By the time he approached twenty-one, he had earned commissions for nearly two hundred surveys—and renown for his ability to identify potential travel routes, prospective town sites, and natural resources. In 1749, his brother sent him west to survey Ohio Company lands.

To the French, the Ohio Company was both an economic and military threat. English settlements in the Ohio valley would not only capture part of the French fur trade, they would sever Louisiana from Canada and hamper French military and trade operations. To halt British incursions, the French began building forts along a north-south axis from northern Michigan to Illinois and down the Mississippi River to New Orleans. In 1754, Canadian governor Du Quesne sent 1,500 French troops to Fort Niagara to occupy the southern shore of Lake Erie and seize British settlers as hostages. Three French forts sprang up at twenty-five-mile intervals from Lake Erie south to Venango, on the banks of the Allegheny River. From

Venango, the troops marched to Logstown (now Pittsburgh) and burned it to the ground.

Enraged by French atrocities, Virginia governor Robert Dinwiddie dispatched George Washington—by then a frontier-wise twenty-year-old major in the Virginia militia—to warn the French to release English prisoners and withdraw—and provide restitution to Logstown property owners—or face war. Along the way, he learned that three Indian nations had allied themselves with the French; he countered by befriending an Oneida chief with the unlikely name of Half-King, who pledged allegiance to the English because the French had "killed, boiled and eaten his father."[7]

Washington finally met the French at Venango, where the officers in charge graciously shared their table before summarily rejecting Governor Dunwiddie's ultimatum. La Salle, they insisted, had claimed the territory for France "in the name of God," before any Englishman had set foot on its soil.[8]

After Washington returned to Virginia, the governor called an emergency session of the colonial assembly, or House of Burgesses, to report an army of French and Indians advancing to the Ohio River to "build more fortresses."[9] He asked the burgesses to raise six companies of militiamen at a cost of £10,000 to expel the French from the Ohio valley. The burgesses howled in protest that he and Washington had contrived "a fiction and a scheme to promote the interest of . . . [their own] private company."[10] Nonetheless, the governor prevailed, winning pledges of financial or military aid from Virginia and subsequently five other states. New York, Maryland, and North Carolina promised 550 troops; Pennsylvania pledged £10,000 to finance the expedition. Massachusetts governor William Shirley said he would lead 600 militiamen to eastern Canada to force the French to fight on two fronts.

On April 2, Washington—promoted by then to lieutenant colonel—set out on his first military command with a lightly equipped vanguard of 159 troops. A second contingent of 400 Virginians were to follow with reinforcements and a wagon train of arms, ammunition, and foodstuffs. Three weeks later, Washington prepared to cross the Alleghenies when a scout brought word that more than a thousand French troops had seized control of the Ohio

valley and raised a fort at Logstown, which they renamed Fort Du
Quesne, to honor the governor of Canada. Before Washington could
fire a shot to stop them, the French had won the first battle in what
would explode into a savage seven-year war with England for global
economic and military supremacy—a world war that would engulf
four continents and slaughter millions.

Certain that reinforcements and supplies were on their way,
Washington ignored his lack of battlefield experience and crossed
the Appalachians to attack the new French fort. He made camp
thirty-seven miles south of Fort Du Quesne at Great Meadows, an
all-but-suicidal position in a hollow between two ridges. The naive
commander envisioned the ridges as protection for his men rather
than as perches for enemy troops. Behind him lay an impenetrable
marsh, which he thought would protect him from the enemy rather

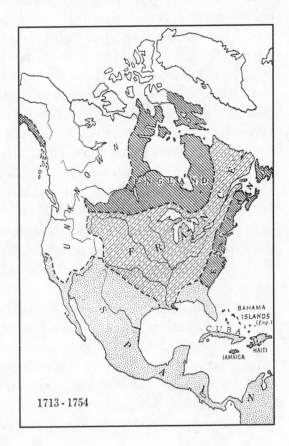

North America before
the outbreak of the
French and Indian War
in North America and
the Seven Years War in
Europe.

than block his escape. Two gullies on the fourth side of the meadow offered "natural entrenchments" from which his men could fire at oncoming enemy troops.[11]

Calling his makeshift encampment Fort Necessity, Washington awaited a French assault, and, on the evening of May 27, Indian scouts reported a column of fifty French troops encamped only six miles away. Washington determined to attack before the French awoke the next morning. Leaving half his force to defend Fort Necessity, he led the rest of his men, along with a handful of Half-King's Indians, toward the French camp. At eight o'clock the next morning, Washington's men surrounded the French, and he gave the order to fire—the first such order of his career. In an instant, musket balls flew past his head, eerily invigorating the young Virginia commander, who found "something charming in the sound" when he "heard the bullets whistle."[12]

Within fifteen minutes, the skirmish was over. Twenty-nine Frenchmen lay dead or wounded; the encounter claimed one English life and left two wounded. Some French soldiers began to flee, but seeing Indians at the rear, they threw down their arms, turned, and raced toward Washington's colonials. Behind them, Indians sprang from the woods onto the field of battle, crushed the skulls of the dead and wounded, and sliced off blood-soaked scalps as prizes of victory. All but one of the French survivors reached the safety of British lines. Before Washington could intervene, Chief Half-King had set upon the laggard—the French commander Sieur de Jumonville. As the helpless young man shrieked in pain, the Indian chieftain sliced his victim's forehead with surgical precision from left ear to right, then plunged his fingers beneath the skin at the incision and ripped the scalp off the Frenchman's skull. He displayed his trophy to his brothers, dancing about and howling triumphantly for exacting retribution on the French for eating his father's flesh. Shaken by the atrocity, Washington intervened before the Indians could attack other survivors, and he ordered an escort to march them eastward for transfer to Governor Dinwiddie's custody. A soldier's musket shot ended the dying de Jumonville's agony.

Washington's triumph was short-lived. Instead of recrossing the Alleghenies out of French reach to await reinforcements and resupply, he remained put, exhausting most of his foodstuffs by the end of the first week. Three days later, 180 Virginia militiamen, untrained in shooting anything but game, brought new supplies to feed the camp and a letter from Dinwiddie promoting Washington to full colonel. A week later, on June 14, 150 militia from North Carolina arrived, but to Washington's astonishment, they came unarmed. Not long after, a scout brought word that 800 French troops and 400 Indian warriors were preparing to attack. Half-King and his 80 Oneidas deserted.

At dawn on July 3, the crack of a musket shot pierced the loud chatter of rain. As the echo resounded across the encampment, Washington's troops grabbed their muskets and raced to the trenches, only to stare vacantly into an opaque screen of rainfall. By morning's end, the deluge engulfed the trenches and transformed the ground into a mire that sucked soldiers' legs so deep they could extricate themselves only by surrendering shoes and boots to the mud. As noon approached, Indian war whoops heralded the emergence of three columns of French troops on the ridges. They darted to within six hundred yards of Washington's men—but still too far for colonial muskets to respond. After an opening volley, the French suddenly broke ranks and scattered into the trees before opening fire again.

"They . . . kept up a constant galling fire upon us," Washington reported, "from every little rising, tree, stump, stone and bush." They raked the entire camp with musket fire, slaughtering livestock as well as troops. By the end of the day, every horse, cow, and animal in camp lay dead. The French had stripped the British of all sustenance and transport. By then, what Washington called "the most tremendous rain that [could] be conceived"[13] had soaked his men's cartridge boxes, firelocks, and powder and rendered them all but impotent. As their answering fire dissolved into silence, they heard a cry from enemy lines: *Voulez-vous parler?* With 30 men dead and 70 wounded, Washington's force was down to 165. He had little choice.

The ensuing "parley" yielded a water-soaked document of capitulation offering safe passage across the Alleghenies to English territory if Washington accepted responsibility for *l'assassinat qui a été fait sur un de nos officiers*—"the assassination of one of our officers." The French demanded two English captains as hostages until the British returned the French prisoners they had seized after the earlier confrontation. The note was signed "Sieur de Jumonville," the brother of the officer whom Half-King had slaughtered.

As midnight approached on July 3, 1754, Washington faced a useless massacre of his helpless little force unless he signed the capitulation. "I went out and was soundly beaten," he admitted.[14]

De Jumonville heralded his victory as the humiliation of a cowardly killer. "We made them consent to sign a document that they had assassinated my brother in his camp," he boasted. "We retained hostages as security for French prisoners who were in their power; we made them abandon the [French] King's country; we obliged them to leave their cannon, nine pieces; we destroyed their horses and cattle."[15]

His words found their way into colonial as well as London and Paris newspapers, smearing Washington with the blood of the young French officer. Although Washington suffered no personal recriminations for his military humiliation, the failure of the colonies to unite in common defense forced British leaders to reorganize the military in America. "Washington and many such may have courage and resolution but they have no knowledge and experience," wrote the Earl of Albemarle, titular governor of Virginia, and British ambassador to France. "Officers and good ones must be sent to discipline the militia and to lead them."[16]

In February 1755, Major General Edward Braddock led two regiments of regulars to America—nearly 1,500 in all. Named commander in chief of His Majesty's forces in North America, Braddock also brought £10,000 and 2,000 muskets to recruit colonial troops to support his regulars. A month after his arrival, he invited Washington to join his staff as a personal aide: Washington combined experience in frontier warfare with a surveyor's skills to plan effective routes for the army to travel westward through the wilderness.

By the beginning of July, Braddock's army stood on the banks of the Monongahela and began the twelve-mile advance to Fort Du Quesne. With the river protecting their rear, they marched inland through a clearing in the woods in traditional linear fashion, four columns wide—two columns on foot in the center, flanked by a column of cavalrymen on either side. "The British gentlemen," wrote a colonial officer, "were confident they would never be attacked . . . until they came before the fort—yea, some went further and were of the opinion that we should hear the explosion of the French fort blown up and destroyed before we approached it."[17]

At mid-afternoon on July 9, shots rang out from the trees on a ridge at the right. The British formed their line to return fire, but an explosion of bloodcurdling whoops rent the air. A mob of bare-chested French troops and naked Indians materialized, fired a staccato of shots, and raced back into the trees. Dozens of British troops dropped to the ground, dead and wounded. Before stunned survivors could return fire, the French and Indians were gone. The British fired at the forest, only to hear a crescendo of whoops at the rear. Before they could turn, another band of savages had emerged, fired, and vanished. In and out, they sprang from the left, right, front, rear . . . appearing, disappearing, reappearing . . . and firing . . . always firing . . . with the incessant chorus of fearsome whoops. They were everywhere . . . nowhere . . . never forming lines to fight by European rules of linear warfare. Confusion gripped British ranks as the hail of musket fire leveled their comrades. Survivors fired hysterically, haphazardly at invisible targets in trees, never knowing where to aim or if their shots hit home; certain only that they were helpless to protect themselves, that they, too, would fall an instant later. Their officers on horseback charged back and forth, shouting useless commands—trying to reform columns as if maneuvering in Flanders fields. All-too-easy targets in the open ground, officers and horses toppled like toys while terrified troops raced in circles or curled up on the ground sobbing. But the hideous howls of the unseen enemy and crackling musket fire went on. The British clustered into a frenzied, shapeless mob, helpless amid the stream of deadly musket balls. One officer who had survived Fort Necessity tried to lead his men in a charge at the woods on the right—only to be raked with fire from the rear by his own comrades, who thought they were deserting.

Conspicuously tall in his saddle, Washington felt musket balls slice through his hat and uniform; shots felled two of his horses but left him uninjured, and he remounted horses of dead comrades and tried to rally his men. Braddock was less fortunate. A ball shattered his arm, smashed through his rib cage, and lodged in his lungs. One by one, other officers fell onto the blood-soaked ground as they tried to rally troops. Ironically, the much maligned Virginia militiamen with experience in frontier warfare "were the only troops who seemed to retain their senses," according to Washington. Despite previous orders from Braddock not to do so, the Virginia soldiers "adopted the Indian mode and fought each man for himself behind a tree."[18]

The slaughter lasted three hours; more than 700 of the 1,370 British regulars lay dead or wounded. Twenty-six of the eighty-six officers were killed and thirty-seven were wounded. French casualties amounted to seventeen dead or wounded; the Indians lost about a hundred fighters.

Washington was astonished that he had survived. "By the all powerful dispensations of Providence," he wrote, "I have been protected beyond all human probability or expectation; for I have had four bullets through my coat and two horses shot under me, yet I escaped unhurt, although death was leveling my companions on every side of me."[19]

As French and Indian forces tightened their circle, surviving British troops abandoned their gear and fled to the river's edge, swimming, fording, and thrashing their way across, beyond the reach of musket shot. "They behaved with more cowardice than it is possible to conceive," Washington wrote. "They broke and ran as sheep pursued by dogs."[20] Seeing the futility of trying to restore order, Washington saw to his wounded general and, with the help of another officer, lifted Braddock into a cart and pulled it across the river. On the opposite bank, he found two hundred troops ready to rally about him. Braddock ceded command, and the Virginian led the troops to an easy-to-defend eminence about a quarter mile from the river to await their fate with their dying general. Instead of pursuing, however, the Indians remained across the river, hopping about the killing grounds like vultures, plundering wagons and dead—and methodically scalping—ignoring the agonizing shrieks of the wounded as they sliced and ripped hides off living heads as well as dead.

"The groans, lamentations and cries of the wounded for help," Washington wrote in his grief, were "enough to pierce the heart of adamant."[21] But what he called "the shocking scenes" about him near the Monongahela River were outdone a few miles away at Fort Du Quesne, where Indians returned with their booty of soldiers' caps, canteens, bayonets, belt buckles, and bloody scalps. A prisoner at the fort described what followed:

> I beheld a small party coming in with about a dozen prisoners, stripped naked, with their hands tied behind their backs and their faces and parts of their bodies blackened—these prisoners they burned to death on the bank of the Allegheny River opposite to the fort. I stood on the fort wall until I beheld them begin to burn one of these men: they had tied him to a stake and kept touching him with fire brands, hot irons &c and he screaming . . . the Indians in the meantime yelling like infernal spirits.

On the walls, the French troops watched and cheered their Indian allies, then raised their glasses of brandy and toasted their king.[22]

British general Edward Braddock died five days later. To prevent Indians from desecrating the general's body, Washington buried him in an unmarked grave, then ordered wagons to roll over it while men trampled the ground to leave the site indistinguishable from the rest of the road. A few days later, Washington led survivors to the safety of Fort Cumberland: only 23 officers and 364 soldiers of the original 1,370 returned.

2

Shattered Glory

THE CRUSHING DEFEAT of Braddock not only reinforced French control over most of New France, it ensured the fealty of native tribes. Convinced of French invincibility, Indian warriors swooped across the western frontiers of Maryland and Virginia with their French allies, burning farms and settlements, murdering or kidnapping scores of men, women, and children. As survivors streamed into Williamsburg with harrowing tales of savagery, the Virginia House of Burgesses tried to recruit 4,000 militiamen to defend the frontier—but the story of slaughter at the Monongahela crushed the will of potential recruits to fight.

With no organized opposition, French and Indian attacks gained intensity and spread along the entire length of the Alleghenies, from Fort Cumberland to the North Carolina border. As colonists fled eastward, the few British troops still on the frontier fell back. By autumn of 1755, the Indians had pushed eastward to within seventy-five miles of Alexandria and Mount Vernon. Throngs of settlers fled before their advance, bringing ever more horrifying tales of atrocities. On one farm, the Indians had scalped a man, woman, and small boy; on another they had driven stakes through the heads of living captives before scalping them and throwing their bodies into the fire.

The French and Indians tightened their vise around British colonies in the north as well. About 3,500 French troops and assorted bands of Indians had overrun northern New York, including

Lake Champlain and Lake George, north of Albany. Although winter slowed their advance, they renewed their campaign in April 1756, overrunning most back settlements in Virginia. "Desolation and murder still increase," Washington wrote Governor Dinwiddie from Fort Cumberland. "The Blue Ridge is now our frontier."[1]

Incensed by French outrages, Britain declared war on May 17 and embarked on a seven-year military adventure that would expand into a global conflict for control of the world's natural resources. Until then, Europeans had fought largely to determine succession to various thrones. From the beginning of their existence, European royals had intermarried to extend their realms—then warred with one another over inheritance of kingdoms—much as peasants fought over inheritance of land. At the beginning of the eighteenth century, France, England, and other countries wasted eleven years of war to put relatives on the Spanish throne, then five more years over the Polish throne, and another eight years for Austria's throne. After the slaughters, their treasuries emptied, they stopped fighting long enough to sign the Treaty of Aix-la-Chapelle in 1748 and return behind the same boundaries that existed before they started fighting a half century earlier. But it was an uneasy peace, with each king suspicious of his neighbors and desperate to refill his treasury to fight the next, inevitable conflict.

By then, kings were financially dependent on a new class of rich, clever commoners—la haute bourgeoisie. Made up of brilliant entrepreneurs, the haute bourgeoisie accumulated fortunes as intermediaries—borrowing idle cash and treasure from the church at low interest rates and lending the funds at outrageously high rates to kings for their wars. When kings learned they could lower lending rates by chopping off bankers' heads, the latter wisely turned to merchant banking. Instead of seeking cash repayments for royal loans, they accepted franchises and land grants that cost kings less out-of-pocket cash and enriched both bankers and monarchs from trade in colonial resources.

By the mid-eighteenth century, merchant bankers emerged as a new class of pseudoaristocrats, with fortunes built on fish, lumber, ore, spices, tobacco, rice, sugarcane, precious metals, and, of course, slaves to harvest those products. As their fortunes increased their influence at court, they added noble names to their own, sometimes of-fering daughters and dowries to titled profligates with costly châteaux and mistresses to maintain, or a rich son willing to assume the debts of a titled father-in-law in exchange for his daughter's title and own-ership of the family château. As marital ties reinforced commercial ties at court, the new class of entrepreneurs convinced sovereigns that commercial wars would be more profitable than dynastic wars. The War of the Austrian Succession, therefore, was the last conflict for a throne. Thereafter, monarchs would fight for colonial resources and the sea lanes that carried them to market.

By 1750, overcultivation, overhunting, and overfishing had badly depleted Europe's natural resources, and to fight famine at home and replenish national wealth, Europe looked to virgin fields, forests, and waters on far-off continents. The first such war—the Seven Years War—began as a two-nation, Anglo-French conflict in the North American wilderness, but it quickly evolved into a global conflict that would demand total military and economic commit-ments by England, France, Austria, Prussia, Russia, and a kaleido-scopic mix of allies and enemies who fielded more than a million troops on four continents and thousands of ships on the seas be-tween. The costly slaughter—the worst in the history of man at the time—changed the map of the world, leveled thousands of towns and villages, killed and maimed more than a million soldiers and civil-ians, and bankrupted a dozen nations. Called the Great War for Em-pire by some historians, it not only cost France her empire—then the world's largest and richest—it continued to rage or smolder alterna-tively for more than two centuries and eventually shattered the world's other great empires.

Fighting did not begin in Europe until 1756, by which time the French and their Indian allies were threatening to overrun the British colonies in North America. By mid-May, most of Washing-ton's militiamen had deserted and left him without an effective fight-ing force to defend the borders of Virginia. British secretary of state William Pitt organized an expeditionary force to go to Washington's aid. "Two Generals are appointed for America," Governor Dinwiddie wrote Washington, "and it's thought they will bring over two Bat-talions."[2]

The British did not arrive until the end of June 1757, and it took a year to integrate colonial militiamen with British regulars and prepare for battle. With Colonel George Washington in command of 900 Virginia militiamen, the 7,000-man army set off across the Alleghenies in the summer of 1758 and encamped about ten miles from Fort Du Quesne. British commander General John Forbes dispatched an advance party of 800 Highlanders and colonials to survey French and Indian strength at the fort. Arriving at midnight and seeing no campfires nearby, they inched ever closer—until an explosion of musket fire set the woods about them ablaze; the fort gates opened, and French troops poured onto the open ground, firing as they ran, then pivoting right and left and disappearing into the trees under protective Indian fire. Within minutes 300 British officers and soldiers lay dead, with the rest of their numbers in flight, many screaming in agony from painful wounds or shock from their first encounter with unconventional frontier warfare.

As he watched survivors struggle into camp, Forbes ordered his entire army to prepare to march to Fort Du Quesne, but before they could assemble, a scout galloped into camp shouting that the French and Indians were advancing. Forbes ordered Washington and Captain George Mercer to lead five hundred men each in diverging paths to encircle the enemy. In the dark, the two companies mistook each other for the enemy and fired. While the enemy vanished into the night without losses, thirty-nine colonial troops fell dead or wounded from friendly fire.

Exasperated by the disastrous incompetence of his subordinates, Forbes ordered the rest of his army to march on Fort Du Quesne. The French anticipated his move, however, and when the British arrived at the junction of the three rivers, the enemy had vanished. Forbes found nothing but smoldering embers where Fort Du Quesne had stood. Five years and two months had elapsed since Washington had warned the French to leave the fork of the Ohio River, and they finally had. What Forbes and Washington did not—could not—know was that the French had exhausted their ammunition and were in full retreat northward following British capture of a central supply and communications link between Fort Du Quesne and Montreal.

The retreat from the West climaxed a disastrous summer for the

French in North America. Earlier, a fleet of twenty-three British ships of the line and ten frigates had surrounded Cape Breton Island, a rocky eminence guarding the entrance of St. Lawrence Bay. As cannon fire from the big ships pounded the fortifications, 12,000 British and colonial troops stormed ashore, captured the fortress of Louisbourg, and took 6,000 French prisoners.

With the western frontier in English hands and Fort Pitt rising over the ashes of Fort Du Quesne, twenty-seven-year-old Colonel George Washington resigned his commission and retired from the military. Although the Seven Years War would rage in Europe for six more years, the North American phase, or French and Indian War, would soon end. In the summer of 1759, 11,000 British troops under Major General Jeffrey Amherst recaptured Lake George, while an armada of nearly 150 ships landed 10,000 troops along the St. Lawrence at the foot of the cliffs beneath Quebec. On the night of September 12, Major General James Wolfe led 4,500 of them up the steep incline, and at dawn, they poured over the top onto the Plains of Abraham behind the city. After five days of combat, Quebec capitulated. A year later, Montreal surrendered to General Amherst, completing the British conquest of Canada. While King Louis XV played in bed at Versailles, more than half his North American empire fell into enemy hands.

"A few acres of snow," scoffed French philosopher François-Marie Arouet, pen-named Voltaire.[3] But others, including soon-to-be foreign minister duc de Choiseul, saw the loss of Canada as an intolerable humiliation—especially at the hands of an Englishman. "Mr. Pitt," said a Choiseul aide, "seems to have no ambition other than lifting his nation to the summit of glory and reducing France to the lowest degree of humiliation."[4]

As gloom choked the atmosphere at Versailles, the king's ministers met in extraordinary session and, for several hours, awaited the king's instructions. A royal attendant, Robert Damiens, went to gain his master's attention from sexual play but gained more royal attention that he sought. As the king howled his rage, guards dragged Damiens to the palace gates, tied his limbs to four horses, and goaded the beasts with whips until they bounded forward and ripped the shrieking servant apart.

Assuming that his least favored ministers had sent the man to interrupt the sanctity of his sensual sport, Louis dismissed two of them, including his minister of foreign affairs. For replacements, he turned to his trusted royal mistress, Pompadour, who urged appointment of Étienne François, duc de Choiseul as foreign minister.

Like the sons of many noblemen, Choiseul had pursued a military career that took him across the face of Europe and earned him the rank of general by the time he was forty. Profligacy forced him to share his noble lineage with the daughter of a wealthy bourgeois financier, who gave Choiseul a huge dowry for a title and an open-ended contract to finance army purchases. Choiseul and his father-in-law signed the marriage contract when the bride-to-be was only twelve—not unusual at the time, although most men waited until their brides reached child-bearing age to consummate their marriages. Choiseul refused to wait and raped his child-bride on their wedding night, injuring her so savagely that she could never bear children.[5]

His wife's huge dowry—he called her "my little gold ingot"—permitted Choiseul to retire from the military and make his appearance at court, where he compensated for his short stature, trumpet nose, and thick lips by cloaking himself in costly clothes and whispering sensually to women he hoped to lure to his bed. His skills at court earned him a place in the king's inner circle of oligarchs—the ever-present Cent Familles, who controlled the wealth of France and wielded power behind the throne. After Choiseul warned Madame de Pompadour of a plot to reduce her influence on the king, she rewarded him with a night in bed and appointment as French ambassador to the Vatican, where he became a close confidant of the Pope. From Rome he went to the Austrian court, where he arranged a Franco-Austrian alliance that included the marriage of the future French king Louis XVI to Austrian archduchess Marie-Antoinette. His diplomatic triumph in Vienna—and the ministerial shake-up that followed the Damiens affair—earned him appointment as minister of foreign affairs in 1761 and the task of stemming the collapse of the empire.

He was too late.

By 1761, England had humiliated the French Army on four continents, decimated the French Navy and merchant fleet, and stripped

Duc de Choiseul. Louis XV's
foreign minister and a favorite
of Madame de Pompadour,
Choiseul devised the French
plot to recapture North
America in 1763 that French
governments would pursue
for the next century.

France of her colonies in North America, the West Indies, West
Africa, and India. The British Navy then set up an impenetrable
blockade of French ports that threatened the nation with mass starvation. With French troops exhausted and the royal treasury all but
empty, Choiseul saw little choice but to sue for peace.

"I could not reverse the destruction of our fleet by the British," he
explained, "or the English victory at Quebec or the loss of Guadeloupe. France faced enormous domestic problems: intrigues at court
. . . and a huge financial crisis with soaring military costs and falling tax revenues. [I] could not attack every problem at once. The
obvious first step was to make peace with England as quickly as
possible. . . ."[6]

Before opening peace talks, Choiseul lured the powerful Spanish
military and naval forces into the conflict, gambling that with Spain
and Austria at her side, France would have more leverage to wring
concessions from England in peace negotiations. In the summer of
1761, he went a step further, coaxing all Bourbon rulers—in Naples,

Sicily, and Parma, as well as Spain—to sign La Pacte de Famille, or Family Compact, with France, declaring that "whoever attacked one crown attacked the other."[7] As Choiseul had anticipated, the Pacte infuriated the British, who overran Spanish colonies in Cuba and the Philippines. Spain retaliated by occupying Portugal, Britain's ally.

By then, the war had exhausted every participant. Winners and losers alike faced national bankruptcy. Although Britain was the principal winner and emerged as the world's leading naval and colonial power, she doubled her national debt, and when the government tried raising taxes, antitax riots erupted in Britain and the American colonies.

France lost the most: the war cost her an empire and reduced her from a world power to an inconsequential and all-but-impotent little nation so mired in debt she stopped paying her troops and demobilized much of her military. Even more humiliating was her loss of influence and status. "Once the most powerful nation in Europe," a French minister lamented, "France became absolutely worthless, unrespected by her allies and scorned by the rest of the world."[8]

Early in 1763, France signed the humiliating treaty of peace with Britain and renounced all claims to New France. She ceded Canada and the Ohio River valley and most of the lands east of the Mississippi to England, along with most of her colonies in Africa and India. Although Pitt lifted the blockade of France, he ordered destruction of all fortifications at Dunkerque, the channel port nearest Britain, and put the city in the hands of a British commissioner, "without whose consent not a pier could be erected, not a stone turned."[9]

Choiseul salvaged one minor concession, however, when Britain agreed to let France cede Louisiana and the lands west of the Mississippi to Spain rather than England—thus leaving a large part of New France in the hands of a Bourbon monarch tied to France by treaty and royal blood. In the back of his mind, Choiseul was already planning the French recapture of New France.

The accumulation of British insults only hardened Choiseul's determination to retaliate against his nation's ancient enemy. "It took three years to negotiate the Treaty of Paris," Choiseul recalled, "during which time, I also worked on consolidating my personal power." His first step was to centralize control over the nation's scattered es-

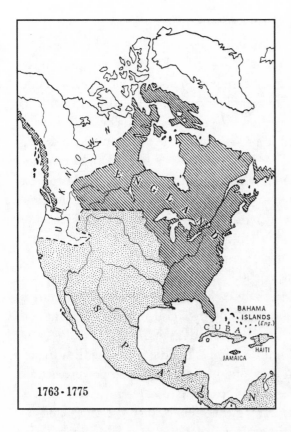

1763 · 1775

North America after the
British victory over France
in the Seven Years War.

pionage establishment. The king gave him full authority over the
post office, which provided access to all mail flowing in and out of
the palace and kept him "abreast of all intrigues at court. . . . The
king and I were most interested in reading the mail of everyone close
to the throne."[10]

Choiseul also expanded le Secret du Roi by merging it with military and naval intelligence in a new Bureau of Interpreters that sent
agents in the guise of interpreters to every French embassy and consulate and with every French diplomat or important figure traveling
abroad. To direct operations, Choiseul promoted forty-two-year-old
Edmé Genet, a renowned scholar and linguist. At the time, he had a
reasonable command of most European languages and grew fluent
in German and English during six years of diplomatic assignments in
Germany and London. While in London, he produced a brilliant
report on the British Navy that won the attention of both Choiseul

and the king. His subsequent reports on politics, finance, and commerce—especially Anglo-American commerce—lured political and military leaders and merchant bankers to his door, seeking counsel. His Versailles salon became a center for marshals, cardinals, and ministers from all parts of Europe. His talented oldest daughter, fifteen-year-old Henriette, was so knowledgeable in French poetry, so fluent in English and Italian, and so proficient on the guitar, piano, and harp that Choiseul appointed her reader to mesdames, the king's unmarried daughters. Two years later, when fifteen-year-old Marie-Antoinette arrived from Vienna to marry the king's grandson, she and Henriette became close friends, playing and singing duets, riding and amusing themselves together. When Marie-Antoinette became queen in 1774, she arranged a marriage to qualify Henriette as first lady of the bedchamber (essentially, the queen's social secretary) and keeper of the queen's moneys. Genet's two other daughters married prominent members of the royal household, and their collective ears became conduits of palace secrets to their father and his patron, Choiseul.

In April 1764, Madame de Pompadour died, leaving the king too despondent to focus on state affairs. In the ensuing power vacuum, Choiseul's authority reached its peak. He took over the ministries of war and navy, began rebuilding the French armed services, and formulated a strategy—a plot against America that would remain an integral element of French foreign policy for the next century and forever influence French relations with North America. Central to the original plot was the recapture of lost French territories in North America. He believed the key to success lay in weakening Britain militarily and economically.

"England is the declared enemy of your power," Choiseul lectured the king, "and she will be so always. Many ages must elapse before a durable peace can be established with this state, which looks forward to the supremacy of the four quarters of the globe."[11]

In 1764, Genet's Bureau of Interpreters reported growing unrest in England and the colonies. An avalanche of tax increases had swept 40,000 Englishmen into debtor prisons and provoked antitax riots by thousands of workers. Fearing the riots might swell into full-scale rebellion, Parliament lowered taxes at home but compensated by imposing new taxes on the American colonies. Military garrisons there were costing Britain nearly £700,000 a year, and Parliament believed Americans should pay for their own military protection with a stamp tax.

The prospect of new taxes provoked immediate protests. "Our trade will be ruined," cried Boston's John Hancock, arguably America's richest merchant banker.[12] The equally wealthy plantation owner George Washington seconded Hancock: "They have no right to put their hands in my pockets."[13] The fiery Boston orator and attorney James Otis charged that the tax would "deprive the colonies of some of their most essential rights as British subjects, and . . . particularly the right of assessing their own taxes."[14]

When Parliament ignored the protests, angry colonists threatened to hang stamp agents; they blocked the discharge of stamps from ships at American ports and all but ended commerce with England. Faced with bankruptcy from the sharp drop in trade, British merchants demanded repeal. "England . . . has discovered with surprise," Choiseul crowed "that . . . [her] colonial possessions in America . . . are the sources of power which she enjoys. . . . It is there that England finds the outlet for her manufactures."[15]

The tax protests convinced Choiseul that colonial America might break from the mother country and weaken Britain enough to permit the French to invade and recapture Canada. "The revolution that will inevitably occur in America," he told the king, "will enfeeble England enough to eliminate her as a threat to France and Europe."[16]

In 1766, Choiseul ordered Edmé Genet to send a naval officer-turned-spy—Sieur Pontleroy—to America to evaluate colonist dissatisfaction and determine whether French arms and money might help incite rebellion. At the same time, he asked the commanding general of the army, Charles François, comte de Broglie, to draw up a plan to invade England. Before de Broglie's elevation to military command, he had spent eight years as one of the French king's key diplomats and masters of international intrigue. Indeed, when the Seven Years War ended, the king appointed de Broglie director of le Secret du Roi, which position he held until Choiseul folded the agency into the Bureau of Interpreters under Edmé Genet, and de Broglie returned to his army command.

After a few weeks in America, Genet's spy reported that a deep economic depression had left New Englanders ready to rebel against the Stamp Act. In Boston, James Otis had pledged to "set the province in flames," while Samuel Adams, a failed merchant but master propagandist, was "spitting venom" and haranguing discontented workingmen along the docks. In Virginia, Pontleroy listened at the assembly room door in the House of Burgesses as the fiery Patrick Henry shouted defiance that "the inhabitants of this colony are not bound . . . to any law . . . other than the laws or ordinances of the general assembly [of Virginia]."[17]

As November 1 approached for the Stamp Act to take effect, antitax rioting spread across the colonies. Rioters sacked and burned the Massachusetts governor's mansion in Boston and almost hung the governor's aide. A mob in Newport, Rhode Island, set up a gallows for the tax collector, while New York rioters hung effigies of the governor and his three aides. At every port, angry waterfront crowds prevented the British from landing boxes of stamps, and, rather than face mob retribution, officials charged with distributing stamps resigned in nine American colonies and the Bahamas. Representatives of eight colonies—Connecticut, Delaware, Maryland, New Jersey, New York, Pennsylvania, Rhode Island, and South Carolina— approved a "Declaration of Rights and Grievances of the Colonists in America"—the first such joint action in colonial history.

To Pontleroy's astonishment, however, colonial representatives also expressed "glory in being subjects of the best of kings" and called their connection with Great Britain "secure" and, indeed, "one of the great blessings. . . ." Although they vigorously opposed the Stamp Act, they rejected rebellion, insisting that "the inhabitants in the colonies have the most unbounded affection for his majesty's person, family and government, as well as for the mother country, and that their subordination to parliament is universally acknowledged."[18]

The declaration convinced Pontleroy to advise Choiseul to abandon thoughts of encouraging American rebellion. It was sound advice. Less than five months later, in February 1766, Parliament repealed the Stamp Act without a single stamp's having been affixed to a colonial document.

The following year, rioters in England forced Parliament to cut property taxes 25 percent. To compensate, Chancellor of the Exchequer Charles Townshend reiterated the need for colonists to pay British troop costs in America. The subsequent Townshend Acts imposed heavy duties on essentials from Britain and empowered courts to search and seize properties of suspected smugglers. Although Townshend died before he could see the havoc his legislation would wreak, Choiseul all but danced in delight at the new incitement to riot that the English had devised. "Before six months have elapsed," he chortled to the king, "America will be on fire at every point. The question then is whether the colonists have the means of feeding it without the aid of a foreign war . . ."[19]

Again, Choiseul turned to Genet's Bureau of Interpreters to take advantage of the turmoil. Among Genet's agents was the "Baron" de Kalb, a gallant Prussian officer and mercenary in the French Army during the Seven Years War. Born a peasant in Bavaria, Kalb was a bear of a man—brilliant, exceptionally learned, but, like most commoners, self-educated. He invented a baronetcy to bypass French Army rules against promotion of commoners to officers. His fictitious noble ancestor raised him to a captaincy and a job as General de Broglie's top aide for sensitive correspondence with the minister of war and high-ranking French and European leaders. During the Seven Years War, de Broglie sent Kalb on missions abroad that honed his diplomatic skills and gave him fluency in several foreign languages, including English. His success in negotiating the return of properties from French occupation forces to a group of wealthy German nobles earned him fees that made him independently wealthy. Kalb then married the daughter of a minor French nobleman, who added a big dowry to Kalb's fortune and some legitimate luster to his fictional baronetcy.

At the end of 1767, Choiseul sent him to America to "learn the intentions of the inhabitants . . . ascertain whether they are in need of good engineers and artillery officers . . . find out what quantities of munitions of war and provisions they are able to procure . . . examine their resources in troops, fortified places, and forts . . . discover their plan of revolt, and the leaders who are expected to direct and control it . . . and [determine] the strength of their purpose to withdraw from the English Government."[20]

Kalb sent back an even more discouraging report than Pontleroy. He arrived in Philadelphia in early January and found Americans "at bottom . . . little inclined to shake off English supremacy with the aid of foreign powers. Such an alliance would appear to them to be fraught with dangers to their liberties." Although resentment against British rule was rising, he said, many Americans remembered the savagery of French and Indian raiders during the Seven Years War and despised the French more than the British. "In spite of their restive spirit," he concluded, "they all seem to be imbued with a heartfelt love of the mother country, from the leaders on down to the humblest citizen."[21]

Kalb predicted, however, that the colonies were "growing too powerful to remain governed from so far away much longer" and that "an independent state will *certainly come forth in time* . . . the open-ing of actual hostilities . . . can not be far distant . . ."[22] Kalb re-mained in America until the end of the year, mapping all strategic

"Baron" Johann de Kalb. A future hero of the American Revolutionary War, Kalb first went to America in 1767 as a French spy to determine how France could help incite rebellion against Britain.

lands and waterways in and about Philadelphia, New York, Boston, and Halifax. He traveled the length and breadth of Lakes George and Champlain and the entire Hudson valley. Before leaving each city, he recruited French agents to report regularly to the Bureau of Interpreters. After his return, the French network he organized in America generated a torrential flow of packets and envelopes to the Bureau of Interpreters in Versailles, with hundreds of articles from city newspapers, provincial journals, along with revolutionary placards and transcripts of sermons by discontented ministers.

As 1768 progressed, they reported a renewal of merchant boycotts of British goods and increasing tensions between colonists and the motherland. By the end of summer, fears of rebellion provoked the governor of Massachusetts to call the British fleet from New York. A few days later, a flotilla of warships sailed into Boston Harbor and landed 1,200 regular redcoated troops, who fanned out from the wharves "as if taking possession of a conquered town."[23]

In the months that followed, events in America inflamed Choiseul's passion for recapturing New France. He had rebuilt the French Navy to sixty-four ships of the line and fifty frigates, which, if added to the Spanish Navy, was equal in strength to the British fleet. He talked about the American question with everyone, saying the day was near when "France will have the chance to retake New France . . . the methods for reconquest are evident . . . the methods of helping the colonies and gaining control of their resources have been studied and debated by our ambassadors, by their special agents, by our secret agents . . . the path is clear."[24]

His constant prattle, however, began to weary fifty-five-year-old King Louis, who had found a new sexual playmate—the beautiful twenty-two-year-old Madame Jeanne Bécu, comtesse du Barry. An illegitimate daughter of a seamstress and a tax collector, Bécu landed in a Paris brothel at fifteen; the owner appropriated her for his own, then used her and other young girls to win favors at court by taking them to the king's summer palace in Compiègne, north of Paris, for the pleasure of the king's servants. The king saw her through a glass door dining with his valet, and wanted her. Although his valet warned that she had slept with so many servants she might transmit venereal diseases, the king snatched her away. To minimize scandal, he ennobled her by ordering her immediate marriage to Count Guil-laume du Barry, who had not finished uttering his oath of marriage before the king seized Madame's arm and led her back to the royal bed to consummate her wedding.

Choiseul despised Madame du Barry. He called her "contempt-ible scum and a danger to the king at his age and declining health . . . but we hoped she would prove nothing more than a passing fancy." [25] The king ignored his critics, and toward the end of April 1769, Choiseul witnessed what he called the king's "formal presentation at Court of a whore from the streets of Paris and her elevation to the rank of Royal Mistress." [26]

Early in 1770, rioting in Boston rose to fever pitch. On March 5, a screaming mob hurled rocks and missiles at British soldiers, who fired and killed six civilians and wounded six. When news of the Boston Massacre reached Versailles, Choiseul ordered Edmé Genet to prepare a *mémoire* on whether the British fleet in Boston had left the rest of the English coast vulnerable to a French invasion. Before he could present his plan to the king, Madame du Barry wreaked re-venge on the foreign minister for his insults by whispering in the king's ear that Choiseul was pocketing funds earmarked for the mili-tary. Although Choiseul gave the king an accounting of every sou he had spent—along with requisitions bearing the king's personal signa-ture—Louis fired Choiseul. Kalb immediately retired to his wife's country château, and the French plot against America slipped into the forgotten files of French Foreign Ministry archives.

But only temporarily.

Edmé Genet remained director of the Bureau of Interpreters and left his huge espionage network in place. From America, his agents sent reams of reports on discontent in council chambers, taverns, Masonic halls, and streets of colonial towns and cities. As materials accumulated, Genet realized a single spark would be enough to ignite conflagration and revive the French plot to recapture New France. He had only to await a minister willing to ignite it.

3

The Treacherous Alliance

WHILE TURMOIL ENGULFED MASSACHUSETTS, Virginia lazed on shores of relative calm, "in almost idolatrous deference to the mother country," according to Edmund Randolph, Virginia's first attorney general. "Being the earliest among the British settlements in North America . . . the sons of the most opulent families [were] trained by education and habits acquired in England. . . . To Patrick Henry the first place is due, as being the first who broke the influence of this aristocracy. . . . He was respectable in parentage, but the patrimony of his ancestors and of himself was too scanty to feed ostentation or luxury."[1]

Henry grew up in the Piedmont wilderness of western Virginia, with bare rudiments of formal education. One of eleven children of a Scottish immigrant, he went off to seek his living at fifteen and failed at everything. He was fired after a year as a store clerk; went bankrupt in a store he opened with his brother; and, all but destitute at eighteen, married a local tavern keeper's daughter with a dowry of three hundred acres, six slaves, and a house. But the land was barren, and his house burned down, leaving him, his wife, and their four children mired in debt.

Desperate for income, he borrowed some law books and practiced a rudimentary, albeit entertaining form of frontier law in his father-in-law's tavern. With a fragmented grasp of law, but an awe-inspiring gift for "talking a long string of learning," Henry mesmerized judges and juries with oratory, which was then the most common form of public entertainment in church, at court, or on the village green. "The music of his voice" and "natural elegance of his style and manner" held crowds spellbound.[2] After three years, his hypnotizing rhetoric had won him almost 1,200 cases and a seat in the House of Burgesses as a frontier hero. Though dressed in simple buckskin, he admired the glitter, pomp, and bearing of wealthy Tidewater plantation owners with whom he mingled in the House of Burgesses, and after his first wife died, he married Martha Washington's first cousin. She quickly transformed him into a Tidewater aristocrat with a dowry that included a 10,000-acre plantation, twelve slaves, and a resplendent carriage to take him to the House of Burgesses.

In contrast, burgess George Washington was no orator and found assembly proceedings tedious, although his status as a major landowner and planter obliged him to serve. Like most Tidewater burgesses, he was English in dress, conduct, and spirit and invariably voted as befit an Englishman, in the interests of his country, family, and burgeoning business enterprise. More concerned with attending his family, running his plantation, and increasing his land holdings than with participating in government, Washington often arrived in Williamsburg a few days late for the opening of the House of Burgesses, absented himself in midsession to look at lands for sale, and left before adjournment rather than miss Christmas with his wife and children. Although he had little political impact in Williamsburg, his physical stature and military bearing had a visual impact, according to his friend George Mercer, who had served with Washington in the West:

> He may be described as being straight as an Indian, measuring 6 feet 2 inches in his stockings, and weighing 175 lbs when he took his seat in the House of Burgesses in 1759. His frame is padded with well developed muscles, indicating great strength. His face is long rather than broad, with . . . blue-gray penetrating eyes . . . high round cheek bones and terminates in a good firm chin. . . . A pleasing and benevolent tho a commanding countenance, dark brown hair which he wears in a cue [sic]. His mouth is large and generally firmly closed, but from time to time discloses some defective teeth.

His features are regular and placid with all the muscles of his face under perfect control, tho flexible and expressive of deep feeling when moved by emotions. In conversation he looks you full in the face, is deliberate, deferential and engaging. His demeanor at all times composed and dignified. His movements and gestures are graceful, his walk majestic, and he is a splendid horseman.[3]

Despite his imposing presence, Washington preferred to let orators like Henry and Richard Henry Lee argue issues of the day. Washington's first direct involvement with affairs of state came in 1769, when Virginia legislators considered Massachusetts proposals for a colonies-wide boycott of British goods to force Parliament to stop taxing the colonies. "At a time when our lordly Masters in Great Britain will be satisfied with nothing less than the deprication [sic] of American freedom," Washington declared, "it seems highly necessary that something should be done to avert the stroke and maintain the liberty which we had derived from our ancestors; but the manner of doing it to answer the purpose effectually is the point in question."[4] Washington argued that a boycott would hurt the agricultural South more than northern states: the North had its own manufacturers of tools, textiles, and other essentials that Virginia had to import from England in exchange for tobacco. A boycott would leave Virginians with no sources of tea, paper, glass, paints, and other British products they needed and no market for their tobacco. Washington's argument won the day. A year later, the North had halved its British imports while Virginia had limited her support to menacing oratory, without curtailing imports.

Early in 1770, the Boston Massacre revived Virginia's interest in boycotts—until torrential spring floods of historic proportions sent forty-foot-high waves down the Rappahannock, James, and Roanoke river valleys. The floods swept away landscape, livestock, and crops, including 10 million pounds of tobacco, the sustenance of Virginia's economic life. Houses and outbuildings bounded downriver like flotsam; at least 150 people lost their lives. Economic losses exceeded £2 million and left hundreds of tobacco farmers penniless. With the lower Tidewater economy in a shambles, Virginians sought no quarrels with the mother country, and within days, as flood waters receded, Parliament extended a collective hand of reconciliation by removing duties on all exports to America but tea.

The floods of 1770 did not affect Washington and upper Tidewater planters. Unlike rivers to the south, the towering Potomac banks guided flood waters harmlessly into Chesapeake Bay and left adjacent fields subject to nothing more than a healthy downpour. By then, Washington was one of Virginia's wealthiest planters—perhaps the wealthiest—with heart and soul dedicated to business and family. He had married Martha Dandridge Custis in early 1759, after returning from the frontier war and resigning his commission in the Virginia militia. Both were twenty-seven, she a widow with a young boy and girl. Not only did Martha Washington provide the love, companionship, and family life her husband craved, she added 17,000 acres and a £20,000 dowry to his 12,500-acre Mount Vernon enterprise.

Washington had necessarily neglected his properties during his years of soldiering, but when he returned, he ordered a library of books on farm management and became an accomplished agriculturist and businessman by converting his ordinary, run-down plantation into a thriving, self-sufficient agricultural-industrial complex. In addition to planting a wide variety of crops, he installed a smithy, flour mill, distillery, fishery, and textile plant to convert crops into finished products that maximized profits by eliminating intermediary processors and distributors. By milling his own wheat and selling it directly to area bakers, for example, he reaped combined profits of grower, miller, and dealer.

After learning the extent to which tobacco depleted soil nutrients, he turned to less parasitic crops and converted them and other products of land and water into finished goods that yielded far higher profits. His fishery caught, salted, and sold 700,000 herring and 8,000 shad a year; his distillery converted the grains he grew into nearly 500 barrels of liquor annually; and his spinning and weaving activities converted hemp and flax from his own fields into thousands of yards of linen, cotton, wool, and other textiles. He manufactured his own bricks and shingles—first to expand his mansion, then to sell in nearby markets. All the while, he continued his obsessive quest for more land—either to improve and plant himself or to resell as demand from new settlers raised property values.[5] In 1772, when he turned forty, he had added more than 24,000 acres in the Ohio wilderness to his 33,000 acres under cultivation in the Virginia Tidewater. "Any person who neglects the present opportunity of hunting out good lands," he predicted, "will never regain it."[6]

Late the following year, however, events beyond Virginia began disrupting the smooth progress of Washington's life and fortunes. At the end of 1773, a Massachusetts mob protesting the British tax on tea boarded three ships in Boston harbor and dumped 342 chests of tea into the water. The "Boston Tea Party" not only outraged Britain, it angered many Americans, including Washington and other Virginians of his class, who agreed that those responsible deserved to be punished. In March 1774, Parliament ordered the port of Boston closed until the people of Boston paid for the lost tea and proved to the king "that peace and obedience to the laws shall be so far restored . . . that the trade of Great Britain may be safely carried on there, and his Majesty's customs duly collected."[7]

The Boston Port Bill was the first of four "Coercive Acts," which extended Parliamentary vengeance from Massachusetts to the rest of the American colonies and set off sparks where there were yet no flames of rebellion. In effect, the Coercive Acts ended suffrage and representative government in the colonies and made quartering of British troops obligatory in private homes. For Virginians such as Washington, the costliest of the new laws was the Quebec Act, which extended Canada's boundaries to the Ohio River and absorbed—in effect confiscated—huge tracts of land that had been part of Virginia and that Washington and other Virginians had purchased.

In early September, delegates from twelve colonies gathered at the first Continental Congress in Philadelphia to denounce the acts. After a month of futile debate, Boston silversmith Paul Revere galloped into town with electrifying news that Massachusetts had declared independence from Britain. The First Provincial Congress in Concord had assumed all powers to govern; it elected Boston merchant king John Hancock provincial president and authorized recruitment of "minute men" to "hold themselves in readiness [for battle] on the shortest notice."[8]

The news spurred the Continental Congress to action. It declared all parliamentary revenue acts since 1763 unconstitutional and labeled the Coercive Acts "unjust, cruel and unconstitutional."[9] It passed ten resolutions defining colonist rights to "life, liberty and property" and asserted the exclusive jurisdiction of elected provincial assemblies over taxation and internal legislation. Delegates agreed to end all trade with Britain, including the slave trade. After rejecting a last-gasp proposal for reconciliation with the motherland, delegates established a Continental Association of states that would reconvene on May 10 the following year, 1775, if Britain did not redress American grievances before then. Before adjourning, Congress rejected parliamentary authority and declared the king sole sovereign over American states.

The congressional proceedings stunned Versailles as much as London. In the four years following Choiseul's dismissal in 1770, the French court had paid scant attention to American affairs. The world was at peace, and Madame du Barry had kept Louis too occupied in bed to think about public affairs. He turned the task over to a new minister, René-Nicolas de Maupeou, who shelved Choiseul's scheme for restoring French glory and turned his attention to restoring national solvency. In May 1774, however, just before the Boston Port Bill took effect, Louis died. His only legitimate son had died ten years earlier, leaving his oldest grandson, twenty-year-old Louis XVI, to ascend the throne somewhat unsteadily. Compulsively taciturn, portly, and handicapped by a disability that impeded sexual arousal, Louis had little interest in society or sex. Although he had submitted to a marriage that Choiseul had arranged four years earlier to Austrian archduchess Marie-Antoinette, he was happiest alone in a quiet room, in a comfortable chair, studying history books and maps. Though round and ungainly, he was quite dexterous and enjoyed making delicate little metal trinkets.

His wife was the opposite—a wildly outgoing beauty, daughter of Austrian empress Maria Theresa and emperor Francis I, whose beautiful Schönbrun summer palace near Vienna had exploded with splendid balls and entertainment during her youth. Only nineteen when she became queen of France, Marie-Antoinette had chafed beside her impotent fat prince for four years. When the old king died,

Louis XVI. The grandson of his predecessor Louis XV, Louis XVI assumed the throne with "divine right" of absolute rule and originally had no intention of leading his nation to war or helping American commoners rebel against a kindred monarch.

she abandoned her husband to his maps and trinkets and staged a nonstop frenzy of balls, banquets, and theater galas that illuminated the skies over Versailles and Paris.

Louis XVI had little understanding of government or politics and turned for guidance to the venerable former minister comte de Maurepas, who urged him to appoint master diplomat Charles Gravier, comte de Vergennes, as foreign minister. A veteran ambassador who had served everywhere in Europe, Vergennes was a deft manipulator of men and events who had worked closely with Edmé Genet and the Bureau of Interpreters. As ambassador to Sweden, Vergennes orchestrated the coup d'état that restored absolute power to the pro-French king Gustave III and brought Scandinavia back into the French sphere of influence.

Described by some as difficult and dangerous, Vergennes was, above all, a nationalistic fanatic, as intent as Choiseul had been to restore French glory and power—and to punish England for the humiliations of the Seven Years War. "Placed as she is in the center of Europe," he told the king,

> France has the right to influence all the world's important matters. Her king is comparable to a supreme judge, entitled to regard his throne as a tribunal established by Providence. England is the natural enemy of France. . . . The invariable, most cherished purpose of her policies has been . . . the overthrow, humiliation and ruin of France. . . . All means to reduce the power and greatness of England . . . are just, legitimate, and even necessary, provided they are efficient.
>
> The humiliating peace of 1763 was purchased at the cost . . . of our commerce and colonies. It convinced the nations of the world that France was devoid of all resources and power . . . the nation that had been the most powerful in Europe had become absolutely worthless.
>
> One has but to read the Treaty of Paris . . . to understand how much that arrogant power [England] savored the pleasure of humiliating us . . . to understand how much indignation and desire for vengeance the word *english* [my italics] should inspire in every patriotic Frenchman.[10]

Foreign Minister Comte
de Vergennes. Louis
XVI's astute appointee
restored and put into
effect the duc de
Choiseul's plot to restore
French sovereignty over
North America.

Arriving in Versailles in August 1774, Vergennes strode into
Edmé Genet's office and dusted off Choiseul's plan to recapture
North America and de Broglie's scheme to invade England. He
poured over hundreds of documents from French agents in England
and America, including the secret proceedings of the Continental
Congress.

"They [the agents' reports] carefully outlined the course of the future American rebellion against England," he concluded, "including
the identities of all participants and a description of the moment
when the uprising in the American colonies would permit France to
retake them . . . the entire scheme had been laid out, the paths
cleared to success, with the names of colonist leaders ready to collaborate with France."[11]

The Massachusetts declaration of independence astonished Vergennes as much as it had the delegates at the Continental Congress.
The colonial revolution Choiseul had predicted was under way.

When the Continental Congress formed a Continental Association, Vergennes began developing his own master plan: France would secretly provide the rebellious colonies with money and arms to exhaust British military and financial resources and allow France to invade and reconquer Canada and the rest of New France.

At Vergennes's behest, Genet ordered French agents in America to bribe colonial leaders to collaborate with France by offering "personal considerations" and pledging French financial and military help for the rebellion. As the Continental Congress proceeded, French agents slipped into nearby taverns and dinner gatherings to excite American lust for independence with the promise of a fruitful alliance with France. One "French traveler"[12]—most likely the experienced Pontleroy—lured Patrick Henry into the French camp. Henry boasted that King Louis would furnish the colonists "with arms, ammunition and clothing; and not with these only, but he will send his fleet and arms to fight our battles for us; he will form with us a treaty offensive and defensive, against our unnatural mother. . . . Our independence will be established."[13]

In February 1775, England's Parliament declared Massachusetts in rebellion. Aware of French agitation in the colonies, it forbade the colonies from trading with nations other than Britain. The restrictions outraged Virginians. On March 23, 1775, Patrick Henry cried out in Richmond's St. John's Church, "We must fight!"[14]

> Our brethren are already in the field! Why stand we here idle? . . .
> Is life so dear, or peace so sweet as to be purchased at the price of
> slavery? Forbid it, Almighty God! I know not what course others
> may take; but as for me . . . Give me liberty or give me death![15]

A month later, seven hundred British troops marched from Boston to Concord to seize a rebel supply depot. Along the way they skirmished with farmers on Lexington green, killing eight Americans, wounding ten, and arousing the fury of the countryside. After failing to turn up the cache of Patriot arms, the British turned back to Boston—only to find woods and fields on both sides of the road swarming with Minutemen. As the Redcoats tried to leave Concord, Minuteman muskets claimed the lives of 12 British soldiers; the gauntlet of fire on the road back to Boston killed 73 more, and wounded 174.

The stunning colonist victory encouraged the Massachusetts Provincial Congress to raise an army of 13,600 men and appeal to neighboring colonies for 9,500 more to encircle and lay siege to British-held Boston, then virtually an island tied to the mainland by a narrow causeway called Boston Neck.

To win support for the rebellion, Patriot riders like Revere galloped across the colonies with news of the Minuteman victory, and newspapers embellished descriptions of the skirmish with imaginative tales of British atrocities. The British "pillaged almost every house," flashed the bold type in one journal. "It appeared to be their design to burn and destroy all before them . . . the savage barbarity exercised upon the Bodies of Our Brethren who fell is almost incredible. Not content with shooting down the unarmed, aged and infirm, they disregarded the Cries of the wounded, killing them without Mercy; and mangling their Bodies in the most shocking manner."[16] Tory newspapers reciprocated with equally bloodcurdling reports that Patriot soldiers had "scalped and otherwise ill-treated one or two of the men who were killed and wounded."[17] Patriot reports won the day in America, inflaming passions and provoking thousands of colonists to take up arms and rally behind the Minutemen near Boston.

The shots at Lexington resounded around the world, provoking consternation and anger in London—and smiles of satisfaction in Versailles that expanded into undisguised laughter at the vision of ill-clad farmers with outdated, muzzle-loaded muskets humiliating the vaunted British Redcoats. Choiseul had been prescient: America was on fire, and his forethought had emplaced French agents from Genet's Bureau of Interpreters near every leader of the American Revolution.

In Philadelphia, delegates at the Second Continental Congress could barely keep pace with accelerating events. Two weeks after the opening session, Congress declared the colonies in "a state of defense" and invited "fellow sufferers" in Canada to join the struggle. It embraced Patriot forces laying siege to Boston as a "Continental Army" and voted to raise six companies of riflemen from Pennsylvania,

Maryland, and Virginia to join them. It promoted Colonel George Washington to general and commander in chief, with "full power and authority" to command "all the forces for the defence of American liberty and for repelling invasion."[18] Washington accepted the post but refused compensation, insisting that service to the nation and liberty did not warrant monetary rewards. His willingness to serve and possibly sacrifice one of America's largest fortunes won universal acclaim and set him above the regional rivalries that threatened the unity of Congress and the colonies. It also freed him to make independent judgments and decisions—and reject approaches by Genet's French agents.

After Washington's appointment, Congress named the courageous Massachusetts leader Artemis Ward second in command. He had rallied the Minutemen at Lexington and was commanding the forces besieging Boston. As third in command, Congress picked the enigmatic Englishman Charles Lee, an eccentric Redcoat colonel who had fought with Braddock at Fort Du Quesne before returning to England to serve in the English war against Spain and then as a mercenary in Poland and Turkey. Unrelated to Virginia's famous Lee family, Charles Lee returned to Virginia in 1773, bought property, and, a month before the Second Continental Congress, materialized at Mount Vernon without invitation for a five-day stay that bored and irritated his host. Lee left with a dislike of Washington that the latter keenly reciprocated. Lee found Washington naive and shallow, while Washington thought Lee pompous and tedious and, indeed, grew suspicious of Lee's motives for joining the American uprising. Washington called Lee "the first officer in military knowledge and experience . . . in the whole army, [but] . . . fickle and violent. I fear in his temper."[19]

Before Congress could vote funds for the new army, the British commanding general in Boston declared martial law and proclaimed Americans besieging the city rebels and traitors—subject to summary hanging if taken prisoner. On June 17, the British spotted Patriots building a small fort at the top of Breed's Hill on the Charlestown peninsula, across the harbor from Boston. British ships landed 2,400 troops and laid a barrage on the hilltop as the Redcoats edged up the hill. A murderous rain of fire forced the British to retreat. A second

George Washington. Commander in chief of America's Continental Army, Washington was suspicious of efforts to implant French officers in the American military.

attempt to scale the hill met similar results. On the third attempt, the British threw off their heavy backpacks and charged up the hill with bayonets fixed. The firing from the top diminished and then ceased when the Americans ran out of powder. The British overran the hilltop, then assaulted and captured Bunker's Hill behind it. When they were done, 100 dead Americans and 267 wounded covered the two hilltops, but the assault cost the British 1,054 casualties, elevated their victims to martyrdom, and converted Bunker's Hill into a cause célèbre for proindependence colonials.

Two weeks later, on July 3, 1775, Washington arrived in nearby Cambridge to take command of the 14,500-man Continental Army, while Congress approved two resolutions that utterly confused Parliament and the king—and a few Americans as well. On July 5, an "Olive Branch Petition" expressed deep American attachment to King George III and hopes for restoring harmonious relations with Britain, but the following day, Congress issued a Declaration of the Causes and Necessities of Taking Up Arms and declared Americans ready to die rather than live enslaved.[20] The contradictory congressional declarations confused Vergennes and left English foreign minister Lord Rochford "puzzled . . . [by] what is going on in America."[21]

Late in August, King George ordered a massive force to America to crush the rebellion, and Vergennes told Genet to send a top-level, English-speaking agent—Archard de Bonvouloir—to America to determine congressional willingness to accept clandestine French aid. By the time de Bonvouloir sailed into Philadelphia, the Continental Army was in desperate want of arms, ammunition, and battlefield skills. With enough powder to issue only nine cartridges per man, Washington feared the British would break out of Boston and overrun the Americans. He sent a desperate plea to Congress: "I need not enlarge on our melancholy situation," he wrote to President John Hancock. "It is sufficient to say that the existence of the Army and salvation of the country depends upon something being done for our relief both speedy and effectual and that our situation be kept a profound secret."[22]

There was no way to maintain secrecy, however. Spies lurked everywhere. In early autumn, Brigadier General Nathanael Greene stunned Washington with a letter in cipher addressed to the British commanding general, describing the strength, equipment, and deployment of colonial forces. Its author was Dr. Benjamin Church, director general of hospitals, who had run out of medical supplies tending wounded Minutemen at Lexington and had galloped heroically into Boston alone to replenish them. Although captured by the British and held captive for several days, he said he had escaped and returned with fresh supplies to treat the wounded. In fact, he had gone to Boston to report rebel troop numbers and concentrations to the British commander. Without any American laws or precedents to deal with traitors, Washington ordered Church imprisoned indefinitely until Congress could deal with him.

Church was not the only spy in Washington's command. British, French, and American agents flocked in and out of Boston and Cambridge like sparrows. Most were tradesmen like Paul Revere, whose skills and tools were needed by both sides and whose common work clothes and stations in life made them seem unlikely candidates as spies. Although Tory spies reported Patriot ammunition shortages, summer and fall of 1775 passed without even a pretense of a British breakout. They had suffered heavy losses at Bunker Hill, and to avoid a repetition, British commanders decided to await winter to end the siege. Enlistment periods for Connecticut troops would end on December 7, and most other troops would quit the army on January 1 and leave too small a force to prevent the British from breaking out of Boston to put down the rebellion.

The British strategy convinced both Congress and French foreign minister Vergennes that the Americans could not win the war without foreign aid. While Congress prepared to solicit aid from England's avowed enemies in Europe, Vergennes tried to find ways to send aid secretly, without risking war with England. To devise the perfect plot, he turned to an old and sure friend of the court who had served his king and nation for twenty years as a top-level agent under deep cover: the master playwright Pierre Augustin Caron de Beaumarchais, whose *Barber of Seville* was playing to sell-out audiences in Paris, London, and other major European cities that summer of 1775.[23]

Beaumarchais did not start life expecting to be a playwright—or a spy. He was born Pierre Augustin Caron, the commoner son of an ordinary clock repairman. Even as a boy, however, he sensed his own genius, and when barely an adolescent, he outshone his father by inventing a remarkable new "escapement," the device that controls wheels and gears in watches and determines their size. Beaumarchais's revolutionary new mechanism permitted miniaturization of watches and gained him worldwide fame and fortune—and invitations to Versailles to make wristwatches and other miniature timepieces for the royal family. Wounded by a barrage of insults for his inferior dress, bearing, and education, he educated himself, and within a few years he not only dressed better than most courtiers, he outshone them in his vast knowledge of history, literature, philosophy, and music. He mastered the guitar and harp, then reinvented and simplified the inner workings of the harp to make it easier to play. It became the rage of French salons, and King Louis XV's daughters engaged him as their music master.

Beaumarchais combined royal connections with a quick wit and brilliant conversational skills to earn the confidence of—and

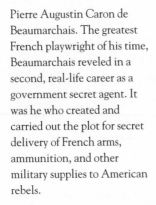

Pierre Augustin Caron de Beaumarchais. The greatest French playwright of his time, Beaumarchais reveled in a second, real-life career as a government secret agent. It was he who created and carried out the plot for secret delivery of French arms, ammunition, and other military supplies to American rebels.

profitable secret partnerships with—wealthy bankers at court. One banker gave him a silent partnership and taught him the skills of speculation in military supplies during the Seven Years War. He combined those skills with inborn cunning to earn a second fortune.[24]

Beaumarchais married twice—once to a lady with an estate, whose name, Boismarché, he corrupted to de Beaumarchais. He added it to his own name to feign noble ancestry as he edged unsteadily into the fringes of aristocratic society. His visits to the king's daughters at Versailles also generated a close friendship with the king's grandson, Louis XVI. When young Louis inherited the crown, with it came one of his grandfather's thorniest espionage problems in the person of Charles Geneviève de Beaumont, chevalier d'Éon. D'Éon was a skilled—indeed, deadly—swordsman and army captain, whose sweet, beardless face, suggestive body contour, and childlike voice left his gender in doubt—especially during his frequent masquerades in women's clothes as Mademoiselle Lia de Beaumont.

In 1755, d'Éon became a spy for Louis XV's Secret du Roi and went to England, where he became a double agent and demanded an annual bribe of 12,000 livres from the French court not to disclose state secrets. At Vergennes's (and the king's) behest, Beaumarchais went to London on the pretext of seeing the English production of *The Barber of Seville* and used his celebrity to tryst with Mademoiselle de Beaumont—d'Éon. After coaxing her/him to surrender compromising state papers, he wrote of his triumph to Vergennes: "Who would have believed that, to serve the king, I would have to court a captain of dragoons."[25]

While in London, Beaumarchais resumed a friendship he had formed with British foreign minister Lord Rochford when both had been in Spain ten years earlier. An intimate of George III, Rochford loved singing duets with Beaumarchais, who, between melodies, extracted British state secrets from his British devotee and sent them off to Versailles.

His successful, well-plotted schemes—on and off stage—made Beaumarchais the logical candidate to promulgate Vergennes's plan to send secret aid to American colonists. Beaumarchais responded with a script worthy of any of his popular stage productions. Called *La Paix ou la Guerre* (Peace or War), the plot provided for sending secret aid to America while enriching the king and national treasury at the same time. Beaumarchais proposed establishing a dummy corporation that would borrow 1 million livres from the king to buy surplus military supplies from the king's army, in effect, transferring funds on paper from the royal treasury through his company to the war ministry for redeposit into the royal treasury. Beaumarchais's company would then sell the military supplies to the Americans at a profit, accepting as payment tobacco, indigo, rice, and salt fish that could be resold in European markets for still more profits. Beaumarchais would then repay the original loan with interest while reaping a small fortune for the king (and himself, of course). Most French military supplies from 1763 were obsolete and deteriorating—all but worthless to the French Army, but of considerable value to Americans, who had almost no weaponry at all.

"Rather than ending the war between America and England," Beaumarchais explained, "this aid, if wisely administered, will serve to continue and nourish the war, to the great detriment of the English."[26]

Vergennes thought the plot brilliant; its goals matched his own, and he incorporated it into a policy proposal to the king called *Réflexions*:

> If the colonies are left to themselves, Great Britain will probably succeed in defeating and subjugating them . . . thus retaining the commercial benefits of her colonial trade, which sustains her domestic manufacturing and her merchant shipping fleet. She will, moreover, prevent the colonies from becoming independent enough to shift the balance of power in favor of some other state.

Vergennes listed the advantages of French assistance to the colonial rebels:

1. England's power will diminish while ours expands.
2. England's trade will decrease while ours increases proportionately.
3. As the war progresses, we may recover some of the territory the English took from us in America, such as the Atlantic fishing areas, the gulf of St. Lawrence, the Isle Royal [Cape Breton Island], etc. Not to mention Canada.[27]

Vergennes said reports from agents in America attested to the willingness and ability of Americans to bear arms, but they suffered from shortages of war materiel and currency to buy it from foreign nations. Moreover, they lacked a navy to prevent British reinforcements from landing. The Beaumarchais scheme, he said, would allow France to ship arms and supplies on private merchant ships to the West Indies, where Americans would buy the supplies *and the ships* and refit the latter for naval combat. The Americans would thus acquire arms for their land forces and a naval fleet at the same time. By laundering funds and military aid through a private company, he explained, France could disavow any ties to the transactions and at least delay a costly war while "preparing to strike a decisive blow against England at the appropriate time."[28]

In the meantime, Vergennes argued, "prolongation of the American war would be highly advantageous . . . inasmuch as it would be calculated to exhaust both victors and vanquished," leaving the former colonies dependent on France for money, trade, and military protection and England too weak to repel a French invasion of North America.[29]

As Beaumarchais, Vergennes, and Genet developed the plot, the British were devising one of their own: to recruit a Canadian force, invade New York, and seize control of the Hudson River Valley to New York—a strategy that would sever northeastern provinces from the rest of the colonies. Congress responded by ordering an assault on Canada, and in mid-November, some 1,000 Americans under Brigadier General Richard Montgomery captured Montreal. Meanwhile, Washington ordered the fearless Benedict Arnold to lead a second thrust northward through Maine to attack Quebec. A former apothecary-turned-militia-captain from Connecticut, Arnold had helped seize Fort Ticonderoga from the British the previous spring and destroyed Fort St. John at the head of Lake Champlain.

Arnold left Cambridge in early September with 1,100 volunteers, but trackless terrain in northern Maine so daunted his troops that more than 400 deserted, and he reached the St. Lawrence River in November with a force of only 650. Although Montgomery joined Arnold with 300 more men, the British were ready with a barrage of cannon fire. When the smoke lifted, the British had killed or wounded 100 Americans and taken 300 prisoners. Montgomery was dead, and Arnold had suffered a debilitating leg wound.

Arnold's plight in Canada spured a congressional effort to obtain foreign aid. At the end of the month, Achard de Bonvouloir arrived to confirm French willingness to send aid and welcome American merchant ships in French ports. He sent an optimistic report back to Genet and Vergennes on American prospects for victory. Writing with invisible ink—milk on the back of a fictitious invoice—he lauded the skills of American marksmen, the superiority of American rifles over British muskets, and the mastery of unconventional warfare that American officers had developed during the Seven Years War. He did not ignore American disadvantages: the nation had no navy and the troops lacked training, discipline, ammunition, food, clothing, and medical supplies. Moreover, Americans were far from united in support for the war: almost one-third remained loyal to Britain. British forces, on the other hand, were well equipped, well trained and disciplined, and had enough financial resources to hire foreign mercenaries. The British Navy controlled the coastline and offshore waters.

The British faced some disadvantages, however. As they demonstrated at Lexington, British troops were untrained in frontier warfare and unfamiliar with American terrain. And they were arrogant, inevitably underestimating the strength, skills, and will of Patriot fighters and unwilling to abandon traditional linear warfare to adapt to frontier conditions. In addition, the distance of supply lines from England could make it difficult to survive a long war of attrition.

Convinced of the efficacy of the Beaumarchais scheme, Vergennes wrote his counterpart in Spain to obtain another million livres for the project. He cited the Pacte de Famille and warned that if the English defeated the American rebels, they would almost certainly seize rich Spanish colonies in Florida and the Caribbean, as well as gold and silver stores in Mexico. By "keeping the flames of the American rebellion burning," Vergennes explained, Spain and France would keep the British too distracted to attack elsewhere.[30] Before turning over the funds to Beaumarchais, Vergennes warned the playwright that the two monarchs "shall have no further hand in the affair [because it] would compromise the government too much in the eyes of the English."[31] Vergennes urged Beaumarchais to obtain additional private investments from the wealthy aristocrats and merchant bankers among the Cent Families. To disguise the king's contribution, Vergennes made the king's million-livre check out to his fifteen-year-old son, who endorsed it over to Beaumarchais's company, Hortalez et Cie.

In August 1776, Hortalez et Cie opened for business in the huge Hotel de Holland, the opulent former residence of the Dutch ambassador. Clerks who scurried about the place spoke in hushed awe of their employer, the great Spanish banker Roderigue Hortalez. None had seen him, but all insisted they had heard him in discussions with Monsieur de Beaumarchais, who marched in and out of the banker's office throughout the day. Like Figaro himself, Hortalez was a larger-than-life character from Beaumarchais's magnificent imagination—

one that he exulted playing with an authentic Spanish accent. Beaumarchais was in his element at Hortalez et Cie, on a world stage, cloaked lavishly in renown, money, and intrigue, alone behind the closed doors of his office, talking aloud to himself—often arguing or laughing—in stentorian Spanish tones and replying to himself obsequiously in French.

Even Americans did not suspect Beaumarchais's connection to the French government. When Silas Deane, the naive congressman from Connecticut, approached Vergennes for two hundred cannons and enough arms and equipment for 25,000 men, Vergennes issued a stern rebuke that any aid would embroil France in war with England. In an antechamber near Vergenne's office, however, Edmé Genet whispered Beaumarchais's name into Deane's ear and gave him the address of Hortalez et Cie.

In the twelve months that followed, Beaumarchais sent eight shiploads of surplus arms, ammunition, and supplies from French royal arsenals to America, including two hundred field guns, thousands of muskets and kegs of gunpowder, and enough blankets, clothes, and shoes for 25,000 troops. Most of the initial Beaumarchais ships landed in Portsmouth, New Hampshire, and fortified General Horatio Gates's Northern Army, but did little to help George Washington's Continental Army in the middle states. During the seven years of his firm's existence, however, Beaumarchais purchased more than 21 million livres' worth of arms, ammunition, and military supplies for the United States, including more than 80 percent of the Continental Army's entire supply of gunpowder for the war. Deane would later tell Congress that "the United States are more indebted to him [Beaumarchais] on every account than to any other person on this side of the ocean." [32]

In fact, Beaumarchais found himself so swept up in the spirit of the American Revolution that he invested his own funds to buy and ship arms across the Atlantic. [33] Still bearing wounds of aristocrat insults inflicted when he was a young commoner, he harbored nothing but enthusiastic admiration for Americans, whom he saw as symbols of all men of high merit and low birth, like himself, struggling against oppressive aristocrats for liberty, equality, and opportunity. In addition to providing extravagant financial support for the American Revolution, he displayed his sympathies in penning Figaro's daring monologue in the last act of *Le Mariage de Figaro*, when he imagines himself confronting his noble patron, Count Almaviva, governor of Andalusia: "Because you are a great lord, you think you are a great genius. Nobility, wealth, honors, emoluments. . . . What have you done to earn so many advantages? You took the trouble to be born, nothing else."

The police imprisoned Beaumarchais for five days for his bitter criticisms of the ruling classes and banned performances of the play for three years. Public demand finally forced the Comédie-Française to stage the play in 1784, when it achieved the greatest success in the history of French theater and would later earn a listing in Flaubert's *Dictionary of Accepted Ideas:* "Figaro, Marriage of: Another of the causes of the French Revolution."[34]

Before the first French arms even left France, the British received secret correspondence from an agent in America with sketchy details of French plans to help American rebels. By way of protest, the British foreign minister showed the correspondence to the French ambassador in London, who sent a copy to Vergennes. "Monsieur [Major General Charles] Lee," it read, "asserts *sur son honneur* [his italics: 'on his honor'] that the Americans had received guarantees of military aid from France and Spain." Although Vergennes dismissed the charges as "absurd," he recognized that the British military had compromised the Continental army high command.[35]

Early on the afternoon of March 8, 1776, the British raised a flag of truce at their end of Boston Neck, and an officer and three civilians walked toward Patriot lines on the mainland with a letter to the American commander asserting the British Army's intention to evacuate the town and leave it undamaged "unless the troops . . . are molested during their embarkation or at their departure by the armed forces without."[36] By the end of March, they were gone, without a single loss of life on either side, and Massachusetts declared its independence of English authority. On April 12, North Carolina empowered its delegates in Congress to vote for a Declaration of Independence. On May 15, Virginia followed suit, and on June 7, 1776, Virginia congressman Richard Henry Lee resolved before Congress that the United Colonies "are, and of right ought to be, free and independent States."[37]

With Boston in American hands, Congress confidently opened all ports to trade from all nations but Britain. Washington, meanwhile, led his troops from Boston to defend New York, but within days of his arrival, an armada of more than five hundred British ships bounded across the horizon for a massive, three-pronged assault to crush the colonies in an irresistible military encirclement.

While the British fleet from Boston sailed to Halifax to defend Canada, the armada with fresh troops from Britain and Germany divided into two fleets: the smaller carried Major General Lord Charles Cornwallis and his troops toward Charleston, South Carolina, the largest port in the South and primary link in the vital tobacco and rice trade. The other fleet went to New York to establish the central British military command for North America and divide the New England states from the South.

The colonists countered with mixed results. Washington took command in New York and sent Major General Charles Lee to lead the defense of Charleston. Congress sent four battalions to Canada, but smallpox decimated their ranks, and the few who reached the St. Lawrence proved woefully inadequate. British ships arrived from Boston with reinforcements that sent the Americans reeling southward out of northern New York and left Lakes Champlain and George in English hands. To the distress of the American and French governments, French Canadians failed to take up arms against the British.

In the American South, Lee's forces had greater success. Although the British fleet pounded Fort Moultrie on Sullivan's Island at the entrance to Charleston Bay, the cannonballs embedded themselves in the soft palmetto logs of the fort's walls. Instead of destroying the walls, the solid cannonballs strengthened them and made them all but impenetrable. South Carolina cannons blasted the British fleet, and forced them to sail away ingloriously.

The victory in Charleston freed the south of British military presence for the next two years and so elated Congress that, on July 4, 1776, it approved a Declaration of Independence. In Versailles, Vergennes rejoiced as he gave the news to the king. He reiterated Choiseul's prediction that the American Revolution would sap Britain's military and economic strength and permit France to recover

North America. The time had come, he said, for France to put England "in her place."[38] A dispatch from the French ambassador in London agreed, predicting that American independence would undermine England's economy and eliminate her as "a source of anxiety" to France. "The [French] King," he predicted, "will once more become Europe's master and judge."[39]

4

"So Many Spies in Our Midst"

As JOHN HANCOCK scrawled his name beneath the Declaration of Independence, scores of French adventurers lined up outside the Paris quarters of Silas Deane, the Connecticut merchant and representative that Congress had sent to Paris to buy supplies and recruit military experts for the Continental Army. The Americans lacked engineers to construct—and demolish—bridges and fortifications; they lacked artillery specialists to direct cannon fire accurately; and they had no drill instructors to instill order and discipline among farmers and hunters who filled army ranks. With the exceptions of Washington and Charles Lee, few American officers had experienced wartime combat; most commanders were provincial political leaders, chosen by Congress because of their ability to recruit troops from their regions.

Deane had left Philadelphia for Paris in March 1776 on a circuitous route via Spain to avoid attention from British spies, but his lavish spending on personal accessories and his naively forthright inquiries at foundries, textile mills, and shipping companies on the way attracted swarms of spies and profiteers. In Paris, Dr. Barbeu Dubourg, a charming, elderly scientist who had befriended Benjamin Franklin and translated some of Franklin's works into French, showered Deane with hospitality and promises of introductions to every major figure at court. In fact, Dubourg only lurked about the fringes of Versailles society to intercept naive visitors, sell them counsel they

did not need, and forge letters of introduction they could have written themselves.

At the end of the month, Dubourg escorted Deane to Versailles
for what was to be a secret meeting with Vergennes. Astonished at
Dubourg's presence, Vergennes all but expelled the old meddler from
the palace before meeting privately with the American. When
Deane went to meet Beaumarchais the next morning, Dubourg clung
to his coattails, hoping to extract a share of profits from the American's arms purchases. As Deane wrote out orders for 100 cannons
and equipment for 25,000 men, Dubourg demanded a commission
and provoked an angry response from Beaumarchais, who wrote to
Vergennes:

> Monsieur le Comte.
>   I have to tell you that while we were together this morning,
> that unscrupulous chatterbox Doctor Du Bourg [*sic*] arrived with
> Mr. Deane, whom he follows everywhere. . . . He proposed assum-
> ing all responsibilities for trade between France and the Ameri-
> cans. . . . I wanted to slap him but repressed the urge and simply
> looked the other way each time he spoke. Can you not, Monsieur
> le Comte, deliver us of this dangerous, self-serving fellow. . . . For
> my sake and yours, I strongly recommend your taking appropriate
> measures to curb this man's indiscretions.[1]

Beaumarchais's warning came too late. Within hours of Deane's
meeting with Beaumarchais, Dubourg's busy tongue had spread the
news across Paris and set off a frenzy of jubilation. For centuries, hatred for Britain had festered in France, and in the fifteen years after
the Seven Years War, the French people had lived impatiently under
the humiliating terms of the peace treaty with England while meek
French monarchs acquiesced to a secondary role in a world they
should have ruled by divine right. Unarmed American farmers had
displayed more courage than kings, cried critics of the crown, and
demonstrated the vulnerability of the vaunted English Army.

The French laughed hysterically at the British humiliation at
Lexington, cheered America's Declaration of Independence, and,
with word of French aid to America, rushed en masse to Deane's
quarters on the place Louis XV (now place de la Concorde) to volun-

teer for the American Army. Exhilarated by their enthusiasm, Deane issued commissions as fast as he could write them. Adding to the madness was the arrival in France of King George III's younger brothers, the Dukes of Gloucester and Cumberland, both outspoken opponents of British repression of American colonists. Reaching Metz with news of America's Declaration of Independence, they dined with the comte de Broglie, commander in chief of the French northern army and former master spy to Louis XV. Dining with them were de Broglie's officers, including three of the king's young musketeers, the wealthy marquis de Lafayette; the vicomte de Noailles, Lafayette's brother-in-law and grandson of the French ambassador to London; and the comte de Ségur, Lafayette's relative by marriage, whose father was soon to be the French defense minister.

Gloucester's visit fired the imaginations of Lafayette and his friends. All were part of a small but growing class of educated young noblemen who had studied the radical social ideas of Diderot, Rousseau, Voltaire, and John Locke. They had all attended popular productions of Beaumarchais's *Le Barbier de Séville*, which satirized the venality and sexual perversity of the entrenched nobility and celebrated man's "natural rights." Adding to Lafayette's enthusiasm and that of other young officers was their active participation in Freemasonry, a brotherhood espousing the rights of man that had attracted thousands of the privileged in Britain and western Europe. In America, Washington had embraced Freemasonry, along with nine signers of the Declaration of Independence. Thomas Jefferson summed up Freemason philosophy so succinctly in the Declaration of Independence that it inspired young Freemasons like Lafayette to dream of fighting alongside Washington in America. "I gave my heart to the Americans," Lafayette declared, "and thought of nothing else but raising my banner and adding my colors to theirs."[2]

De Broglie saw the fire in the eyes of his young knights as an opportunity to further French interests—as well as his own—by sending French officers to take command of the American Continental Army and facilitate French recovery of New France. De Broglie took his plan to Vergennes; the foreign minister hesitated, insisting that de Broglie do nothing to provoke war with England. In fact, Vergennes was having second thoughts about whether French aid would sustain the American rebellion. The latest news from America was terrible.

The British had all but crushed Washington's Continental Army. Although the British had evacuated Boston and failed to capture Charleston, they controlled Canada and northern New York, and as Congress voted on independence, a huge British armada had landed more than 20,000 British troops and 10,000 German mercenaries unopposed on Staten Island, a Tory enclave at the entrance to New York Bay. Washington had barely 23,000 troops to defend Manhattan and Long Island and few generals to lead them. His pleas to Congress for more troops and officers went unheeded; Congress was out of money.

At the end of August 1776, British and Hessians sailed across New York Bay and stormed ashore on Long Island. Within days, they surrounded 5,000 American troops guarding Brooklyn, killed or wounded 1,500, seized 32 cannons, and, still worse, captured almost 250,000 pounds of precious livestock that would have fed the Continental Army for four months. Washington led the remnants of his force on a terrifying nighttime escape across to Manhattan. By morning, hundreds had deserted. "The check our detachment sustained," Washington lamented, "dispirited too great a proportion of our troops and filled their minds with apprehension and despair."[3]

The British captured two American commanding generals in Brooklyn. They immediately paroled General John Sullivan of New Hampshire to go to Congress with a proposal for peace. Benjamin Franklin, John Adams, and Edmund Randolph responded by meeting British commanders on Staten Island. Within hours, however, they stomped out of the talks after the British demanded revocation of the Declaration of Independence as a preliminary to a cease-fire.

A few days later, on September 15, British troops poured onto Manhattan island and sent American troops fleeing in panic in all directions. British buglers added to the humiliation by sounding a call to hounds at a fox hunt instead of the customary military charge. As Redcoats roared with laughter, Pennsylvania general Joseph Reed admitted, "I never felt such a sensation before. It seemed to crown our disgrace."[4]

Congress reacted to the disaster by appointing Pennsylvania's Benjamin Franklin and Thomas Jefferson to supplement Silas Deane's search for European aid. Jefferson declined the appointment, and Congress filled his place with Virginia's Arthur Lee, who was already in Europe. Washington, by then, had served as American commander in chief for a full year, but the fighting on Long Island and New York was his first major battlefield command, and it demonstrated his inexperience and shortcomings as a military leader. Some congressmen muttered about replacing him with a more experienced commander. He admitted to his brother:

> The difficulties which have forever surrounded me since I have been in the service, the effect of my own conduct, and present appearance of things, so little pleasing to myself, as to render it a matter of no great surprise [to me] if I should stand capitally censured by Congress; added to a consciousness of my inability to govern an army composed of such discordant parts, and under such a variety of intricate and perplexing circumstances; induces not only a belief, but a thorough conviction in my mind that it will be impossible unless there is a thorough change in our military systems for me to conduct matters in such a way as to give satisfaction to the public which is all the recompense I aim at, or ever wished for.[5]

The weeks that followed only added to Washington's defeats and despair. On every battlefield, the British not only outmaneuvered him but seemed to predict his strategy in advance. After abandoning Manhattan, he retreated northward to White Plains, where a British assault sent the entire American right flank fleeing in panic without firing a shot. A fierce British thrust cut the remaining Patriot force in two, with Washington forced to retreat westward across the Hudson River with part of his army, while General Charles Lee fled north to the Hudson valley highlands with 7,000 troops. By the end of November, desertions had reduced Washington's force to 3,000 men, and illness had rendered two-thirds of them unfit for duty. Facing annihilation by vastly superior British numbers, Washington sent urgent orders to Lee to cross the Hudson immediately to reunite

the divided army, but the ever enigmatic—and often insolent—
Englishman remained put while he considered the matter.

With the enemy fast approaching, Washington's men staggered
westward across New Jersey through sheets of icy autumn rains toward the Delaware River. And still no Lee. The British were only
steps behind as the Patriots crossed the Delaware to Pennsylvania on
December 11—and still no Lee. Only Washington's foresight in
commandeering small craft along the river prevented the British
from crossing and annihilating the Americans. British commander
General Sir William Howe posted troops at Trenton and Princeton
to wait for the river to freeze to cross on foot. Fearing the British at
Princeton would attack Philadelphia, Congress fled to Baltimore to
debate capitulation.

The French chargé d'affaires in London sent a gloomy report to
Foreign Minister Vergennes in Versailles: "The Americans can no
longer hold their ground. They have no choice but surrender."[6]
Rather than risk provoking war with Britain, Vergennes made a public retreat from his earlier position with an obsequious note to the
British ambassador to "share your joy at the satisfactory news of the
success of British arms [in] Long Island and New York . . . I beg Your
Excellency to accept . . . my sincere felicitations upon an event so
calculated to contribute to the reestablishment of peace in that part
of the globe."[7]

De Broglie, however, continued to implement the plot against
America. Alerted by Vergennes that the British had infiltrated
Washington's high command, he determined to do the same and
went to see Deane. He took with him his top aide, Baron de Kalb,
the English-speaking agent Choiseul had sent to America in 1767 to
assess colonist sentiment after repeal of the Stamp Act. De Broglie
convinced Deane that incompetent—perhaps even traitorous—military leadership was responsible for Washington's disasters. America
faced defeat, he said, unless she replaced her army high command
with experienced French officers and a veteran French commander
in chief to impose discipline on the army—and the Continental
Congress. America needed "a military authority . . . who would unite
the positions of a general and president . . . under the title of generalissimo, field marshal, etc."[8] Kalb then took over the discussion:

The beginning of Revolution in America is an event of the utmost importance to all the European powers, but especially to France, which would take any measure to bring about formal separation of the Colonies from the mother country which did not involve war with England. This is to be inferred from the aid already secretly furnished by France to the Americans. What is needed [now] is a military and political leader, a man with authority to suppress political divisions and unite the colonies, to attract people of all classes to follow him—not courtiers, but brave, efficient and well educated officers willing to put their entire faith in him.[9]

France, Kalb went on, had veteran officers, ready to convert the American Army into an efficient fighting force. Political dissensions among colonies had left Congress unable to respond to army requests for military supplies and troop payments. Kalb explained "the absolute necessity" of replacing Washington with a French

Comte de Broglie. The French Army general plotted to replace George Washington as commander in chief of America's Continental Army and become military dictator in the United States.

generalissimo—a military dictator, or *stathoudérat* ("stateholder"), with sweeping political and military powers. Such a commander "should have the power to choose his own subordinates, and, of course, he would select the best, who would be Frenchmen."[10]

De Broglie then promised Deane "a body of six thousand men, three hundred officers, thirty of them officers of artillery, and eighty-four pieces of cannon, all of them eight-pounders." He suggested that Kalb go immediately to Philadelphia to convince Congress of the urgency of appointing a French *stathoudérat* to lead the revolution.[11] Deane was ecstatic and in November 1776 wrote to Congress:

> The rage, as I may say, for entering into the American service increases, and the consequence is that I am crowded with offers and proposals, many of them from persons of the first rank. Count Broglie, who commanded the army of France the last [Seven Years] war, did me the honor to call on me twice yesterday with an officer [Kalb] who served as his quartermaster general the last war and has now a regiment in his service; but being a German, and having traveled through America a few years since, he is desirous of engaging in the service of the United States of North America. I can by no means let slip an opportunity of engaging a person of so much experience, and who is by every one recommended as one of the bravest and most skillful officers in the kingdom.[12]

Kalb, Deane added, "has an independent fortune, but being a zealous friend to liberty, civil and religious, he is actuated by the most independent and generous principles in the offer he makes of his service to the United States."[13]

Deane transmitted his enthusiasm for the project to Vergennes, who in turn gave de Broglie his cautious approval. If the plot succeeded, France would reap the benefits, but he warned of the diplomatic furor it would create if it became public knowledge, in which case the French government would disavow it as a rogue operation.

Deane was eagerly commissioning every French officer who approached him. All they had to do was express "sincere and unaffected . . . ardor to serve the cause of America."[14] Spies and scoundrels alike had only to pay the insidious Doctor Dubourg for the proper phrasing, along with letters from fictitious generals attesting to their character, rank, and experience. Deane exulted in his—and his nation's—good fortune in acquiring so many experienced, high-ranking officers. With Dubourg's enthralling tales of their credentials and military heroics spinning in his brain, Deane dispensed high-level commissions that committed Congress to catastrophically high salaries. In some instances, Deane sent the officers to their ships with travel fare and advances on their pay drawn from his own purse.

"The greater number of the first French who came to America," according to a priest who sailed with some of them, "were men crippled with debts and without reputation at home, who, announcing themselves by assumed titles and false names, obtained distinguished rank in the American army, received considerable advances in money, and disappeared at once."[15]

To quell British protests, Vergennes decreed that France would not protect Frenchmen captured by the British in America or on their way there, and he unexpectedly found himself forced to uphold his decree to avoid war. After a British frigate captured three French officers and two sergeants aboard a French cargo ship bound for America, Vergennes rejected their requests for repatriation: "Having left France without permission to serve the Americans, the representatives of the [French] king cannot involve himself in their situation."[16]

Washington was well aware that his disastrous defeats had not only diminished chances of foreign aid, they had substantially eroded American public support for independence. It was becoming impossible to recruit new troops; his veterans were deserting, and some of his top officers were insubordinate. To avoid formal charges of insubordination, Charles Lee reluctantly ordered his troops to march toward Washington's encampment on the Delaware River opposite Trenton. Along the way, however, Lee wandered off by himself to an inn, where a British patrol took him prisoner without a struggle.

As Washington nursed his injured pride in Pennsylvania, the majority of people in New York and New Jersey abandoned thoughts of independence to embrace king and country. Patriot officers and emissaries traveling through either state risked capture, imprisonment, and often harsh punishment in Tory hands. Washington knew he needed a dramatic act to restore public confidence.

In the dead of night on December 26, Washington led 2,400 troops through a blinding snowstorm across the ice-choked Delaware River. At 8 A.M. they reached Trenton and found the 1,400-man Hessian garrison still abed, dissuaded by storm from posting their usual dawn patrols.

Shocked awake to the reality of their plight, the terrified Germans scattered in disarray. *"Der Feind! Der Feind! Heraus! Heraus!"* they howled in panic. "The enemy! The enemy! Turn out! Turn out!"[17] Some tried to regroup at cannon emplacements at the head of King Street to repel the attack. Before they could get there, a young Virginia captain, William Washington, a distant cousin of the commander in chief, and his eighteen-year-old lieutenant, James Monroe, also a Virginian, charged through a hale of rifle fire and seized the weapons. Both men fell wounded but held fast until Washington's Continentals forced the Hessians to surrender. The chance arrival of a quick-thinking Patriot physician stemmed the flow of blood from Monroe's wound and saved the young man's life. Washington cited both Monroe and William Washington for conspicuous gallantry and promoted the former to captain and the latter to colonel. William Washington would later win promotion to general; Monroe, election to the presidency of the United States.[18]

Trenton cost only three American lives. Washington's men captured more than nine hundred Hessians, left thirty enemy dead, and may well have saved the Revolution by reviving American morale. Trenton proved to Congress and the American people—and even French foreign minister Vergennes—that Washington and his untrained army of citizen-soldiers, depleted though it was, had the skills and courage to defeat the world's most celebrated professional mercenaries and wrest America from English hands.

Washington's victory set off a wave of euphoria that temporarily bolstered troop morale and public support for the revolution. As winter progressed, army ranks began to swell instead of shrink, and Congress was confident enough to return to Philadelphia and respond to Washington's pleas to give troops twenty-dollar cash bounties and one hundred acres of land for long-term service.

Washington's victory also restored enthusiasm for the colonist cause in France. The stream of officers leaving for America turned into a torrent, and Edmé Genet began feeding handpicked agents into the stream. One of these, Adjutant General Colonel Philippe Trouson du Coudray, was an eminent French artillery officer who selected the munitions France sent to the American Army. When the first boatload of French officers was ready to sail, Genet talked Deane into commissioning du Coudray a major general in the Continental Army, with command of artillery and engineers. Congress confirmed the appointment when he arrived, but it provoked such a storm of protest from American generals that Congress rescinded the commission and made him inspector general of ordnance. Du Coudray inadvertently ended the controversy by drowning in the Schuylkill River before he could serve.

De Broglie, meanwhile, commandeered two frigates to carry Kalb and a junto of sixteen French officers to America to take control of the Continental Army. With Edmé Genet whispering in his ear, Deane appointed Kalb a major general—and promised him the highest salary in the Continental Army. Deane commissioned one other major general in Kalb's group, three lieutenant colonels, four majors, three captains, and four lieutenants.

"Men cannot be engaged to quit their native country and friends to hazard life in a cause which is not their own," he explained to Congress. "It is a universal custom in Europe to allow something extra." Enthralled by de Broglie's seductive pledges of victory, Deane also sent Congress de Broglie's proposal to replace Washington as commander in chief of the American Army.

> I submit one thought to you, whether you could engage a great general of the highest character in Europe, such for instance as Prince Ferdinand, Marshall Broglio [sic] or others of equal rank, to take the lead of your armies, whether such a step would not be politic, as it would give a character and credit to your military, and strike perhaps a greater panic in our enemies. I only suggest the thought, and leave you to confer with the Baron de Kalb on the subject.[19]

A week later, Deane sent Congress an amended list of officers, with a letter explaining the addition of the young marquis de Lafayette as another major general:

The desire which the Marquis de Lafayette shows of serving the troops of the United States of North America and the interest which he takes in the justice of their cause, make him wish to distinguish himself in this war. . . . I have thought I could not better serve my country than by granting to him, in the name of the very honorable congress, the rank of major general, which I beg the States to confirm to him. . . . His high birth, his alliances, the great dignities which his family hold at this court, his considerable estates in this realm, his personal merit, his reputation, his disinterestedness, and, above all, his zeal for the liberty of our provinces, are such as have only been able to engage me to promise him the rank of major general in the name of the United States.[20]

While the addition of Lafayette's name evidently delighted Deane, Kalb winced, and de Broglie did all he could to dissuade Lafayette from going, for fear the ebullient young man would compromise the junto. "I witnessed your father's death at the Battle of Minden," he told the boy, "and I will not be accessory to the ruin of the only remaining branch of your family."[21]

Lafayette was indeed the last living member of his line—a race of gallant French knights who had galloped to war for France since the start of the millennium. A Lafayette rode alongside Saint Louis in the Sixth Crusade of 1250 and Joan of Arc at the Battle of Orléans against the British, two centuries later. As de Broglie pointed out, Lafayette's own father had died during the Seven Years War and left his only son an orphan at the age of two. His father's death, however, made the young marquis arguably the wealthiest landowner in France, with close ties to the royal family and enormous influence at court. Deane saw Lafayette's enlistment as tantamount to enlisting a prince of France for America's struggle.

Far from meriting his rank as major general, Lafayette was only nineteen, with no military or political experience. Like all noblemen, he inherited and had to maintain a regiment to fight for the king, and, at eighteen, he spent the summer at de Broglie's military encampment in northeastern France, learning the bare essentials of military protocol and command. The evening with the duke of Gloucester at de Broglie's quarters inflamed his passion to fight beside the great American general Washington. When he learned of de

Broglie's plan to send officers to America, he signed up immediately and invited his two closest friends to join him—his brother-in-law the vicomte de Noailles and his relative-by-marriage the comte de Ségur. Lafayette later described his quest in his memoirs:

> Such a glorious cause had never before rallied the attention of mankind. Oppressors and oppressed would receive a powerful lesson; the great work would be accomplished or the rights of humanity would fall beneath its ruin. The destiny of France and that of her rival [England] would be decided at the same moment.[22]

By the time Deane's letter regarding Kalb reached Congress, flocks of French officers were landing in colonist-controlled ports along the East Coast. In Philadelphia, they milled about the doors of Congress, badgering members of Congress for high ranks and salaries and waving commissions signed by Deane; others presented forged papers or simply claimed that Deane had given them verbal assurances of employment in the army.

Congress sent some to Washington, who had long pleaded with Congress for more officers, but now complained of

> the distress I am . . . laid under by the application of French officers for commission in our service. This evil . . . is a growing one . . . they are coming in swarms from old France and the Islands. . . . They seldom bring more than a commission and a passport, which, we know, may belong to a bad as well as a good officer. Their ignorance of our language and their inability to recruit men are insurmountable obstacles to their being ingrafted into our Continental battalions; our officers, who have raised their men, and have served through the war upon pay that has hitherto not borne their expenses, would be disgusted if foreigners were put over their heads.[23]

As the invasion of French officers gained momentum, Washington feared they would seize control of his army and asked "what Congress expects I am to do with the many foreigners they have at different times promoted to the rank of field officers. . . . These men have no attachment nor ties to the country . . . and are ignorant of the language they are to receive and give orders in . . . and our officers think it exceedingly hard . . . to have strangers put over them, whose merit is not equal to their own, but whose effrontery will take no denial." [24]

Washington's most trusted comrade, the prescient Nathanael Greene of Rhode Island, now promoted to major general, called French officers "so many spies in our midst." [25] Although some were mere adventurers, many were indeed agents planted in the American Army by Genet to seize command of key battalions for integration into the French Army when it landed. Besides du Coudray, Genet sent an Irish-born French colonel, the comte de Conway, and a team of officer-spies to Deane to volunteer for duty. A former colonel in an Irish division of the French Army, Conway, like Kalb, had invented a noble heritage as the comte de Conway to gain entry into officers' ranks. The naive Deane took him at his word. "I have recommended several officers to your service," Deane wrote to Congress,

> but none with greater pleasure, scarce anyone with so much confidence of his answering great and valuable purposes, as the bearer, Colonel Conway, a native of Ireland, advanced in this [French] service by his merit. His views are of establishing himself and his growing family in America; consequently he becomes our countryman and engages on the most certain principles. This gentleman has seen much service; his principal department has been that of training and disciplining troops and preparing for action; and from his abilities, as well as from his long experience, he is considered one of the most skillful disciplinarians in France. . . .
>
> Colonel Conway brings with him some young officers of his own training which know well the English language and may be of immediate service in the same important department of discipline As Colonel Conway has been long in service . . . in this kingdom, I am confident you would not think it right he should rank under . . . an adjutant or brigadier general. I have advanced him . . . his expenses and appointments or wages and told him he may rely on your granting him one of the above ranks in the continental forces. Should the honorable Congress have a new body of troops, this gentleman might take direction of them to very great advantage. [26]

Although Congress agreed to commission the English-speaking Irishman a brigadier general, it recognized the validity of Washington's concerns about French officers and agreed to rein in Deane's ac-tivities. Although too late to halt Conway and du Coudray, Congress got unexpected assistance from young Lafayette, who unwittingly helped foil the de Broglie junto. Kalb and de Broglie's men were aboard ship at the port of Le Havre when a messenger galloped to dockside with a dispatch from Vergennes canceling the expedition. Lafayette's friends Noailles and Ségur were, like him, both minors, but as an orphan he was free to do as he pleased, while they needed permission from their parents to sail to America. Their requests ex-posed the Kalb expedition to all—including Lafayette's father-in-law, the duc d'Ayen, a close friend of the king and a nephew of the French ambassador to Britain.

D'Ayen was furious that Lafayette would abandon his pregnant wife, the duke's daughter, to fight and possibly die in a far-off war that had nothing to do with France. It was one thing for obscure soldiers of fortune to chase adventure across the sea, but quite another for three king's musketeers—three noblemen from France's oldest, most powerful families—to enlist in a rebellion by commoners against a fellow monarch with whom France was at peace.

Although young French knights and their ladies hailed the three as heroes, the British ambassador lodged a strong protest and threat-ened to break diplomatic relations. Vergennes was furious at La-fayette's impetuous, impolitic behavior; the prime minister, comte de Maurepas, called it "a hostile act that would most assuredly be against the wishes of the king" and moved to appease Britain by clos-ing French ports to American ships and banning sales of war materiel to America. Vergennes canceled de Broglie's departure, and the min-ister of war ordered the arrest "with plenty of publicity and severity" of any French soldiers who claimed the French government had or-dered them to go to America. Unconvinced of French sincerity, the British blockaded French ports to halt French arms shipments to America, and Vergennes had to stop clandestine French government aid to America. De Broglie recalled his officers to Paris, and Deane prepared to return home in disgrace.

Deane tried repairing the ruptured pipeline of French aid by jus-tifying his enlistment of Lafayette to Vergennes: "To gain a most gal-lant and amiable young Nobleman to espouse our cause and to give to the world a specimen of his nature and hereditary bravery, surely cannot be deemed criminal." [27]

Undeterred by the furor, Lafayette met secretly with de Broglie and proposed buying a ship and financing the expedition himself. Still ambitious for Washington's job, de Broglie agreed, and on April 20, 1777, Lafayette secretly set sail for America to fight for the rights of man—with no inkling that Kalb and other officers traveling with him not only scorned those rights, but planned to topple Lafayette's hero George Washington and raise the French tricolor over North America.

Despite government disavowal of the Lafayette expedition, Edmé Genet convinced Benjamin Franklin of the potential benefits of engaging Lafayette, and the venerable doctor urged Congress to welcome the young man:

> The Marquis de Lafayette, a young nobleman of great family connections here and great wealth is gone to America in a ship of his own, accompanied by some officers of distinction, in order to save our armies. He is exceedingly beloved and everybody's good wishes attend him; we can not but hope he may meet with such a reception as will make the country and his expedition agreeable to him ... we are satisfied that the civilities and respect that may be shown him will be serviceable to our affairs here, as pleasing not only to his powerful relations and to the court but to the whole French nation. He has left a beautiful young wife big with child and for her sake particularly we hope that his bravery and ardent desire to distinguish himself will be a little restrained by the General's [Washington's] prudence, so as not to permit his being hazarded much, but on some important occasion. [28]

When Lafayette and the others reached Philadelphia, Congress snatched the welcome mat from under their feet and all but slammed the doors in their faces. "It seems that French officers have a great fancy to enter our service without being invited," snarled Congressman James Lovell of Massachusetts. "It is true we were in need of officers last year, but now we have experienced men and plenty of them." [29]

Lafayette's Masonic affiliation, however, won him a chance to

Marquis de Lafayette. Caught up in the spirit of the American Revolution, he volunteered to serve without pay in the Continental Army under Washington.

confer with John Hancock, the president of Congress and a "brother" Mason. After reviewing the letter from Franklin and Deane, Congress relented, appointed Lafayette an honorary major general and agreed to let him serve with Washington as a volunteer without pay. Congress also reexamined Kalb's impressive military credentials and, because he could issue commands in English, appointed him a major general as well.

Kalb's appointment seemed to open the door for de Broglie, but to de Broglie's consternation, his longtime aide abruptly abandoned the project. In appointing him a major general, Congress had given Kalb a rank that would have remained forever beyond his reach as a commoner in Europe, and he was not about to forgo that honor to satisfy de Broglie's ambitions.

"If I return to Europe," he wrote to de Broglie, "it will be with the greatest mortification, as it is impossible to execute the great design [de Broglie's coup d'état] I have so closely come to subserve . . . the project is totally impracticable; it would be regarded no less as an act of crying injustice against Washington, than as an outrage on the honor of the country [America]."[30]

Kalb and Lafayette joined Washington just as American fortunes were again declining. Late in August, 15,000 British troops sailed up Chesapeake Bay and landed at Head of Elk (now Elkton, Maryland), about fifty miles southwest of Philadelphia. Although Washington spread his troops along Brandywine Creek to bar the way to the capital, a huge force of British soldiers worked its way around the American right flank and almost surrounded the entire Patriot Army. Although the Patriots managed to escape capture, 1,000 lost their lives, and Congress had to abandon America's capital city to the British and flee westward first to Lancaster and then to York, Pennsylvania. Early in October, Washington's attempt to counterattack met with another disaster in Germantown, near Philadelphia, where his two detachments lost their way in the fog and fired at each other. The British rushed into the melee and killed seven hundred of the confused Americans while capturing four hundred. In less than a month, Washington had lost the nation's capital and 20 percent of his army. Within two months, the British controlled the entire Delaware River basin as far north as Philadelphia.

Meanwhile, two British armies—one moving south from Canada, the other northward from New York—were about to end the Revolution by seizing the entire Hudson valley and isolating New England and eastern New York from the rest of the colonies. With the British already in control of coastal waters, they hoped New England would run out of arms, ammunition, and foodstuffs and have little choice but submission. They did not count on the flow of arms on the ships Beaumarchais had sent from France to Portsmouth, New Hampshire, where it found its way to the Northern Army commanded by the English-born general Horatio Gates at Albany. Before the two British armies could link up, American forces—now well equipped with French arms—outflanked and, after a series of skirmishes, surrounded the entire British Army that had come from Canada. On October 13, British general John Burgoyne surrendered to Gates, and a few days later, 5,700 surviving Redcoats laid down their arms and began a long, slow, humiliating march to internment near Boston to await repatriation, which would depend on British recognition of American independence.

Burgoyne's surrender had widespread repercussions on both sides of the Atlantic. The enormity of the defeat frightened Parliament into sending an emissary to discuss reconciliation with Franklin and Deane in Paris. They sent the Englishman packing with demands for nothing less than full independence and withdrawal of all British troops from American territory.

At Versailles, Edmé Genet warned Vergennes that if British efforts at reconciliation succeeded, Britain would almost certainly attack the French West Indies. By then, Genet had become an intermediary between Franklin and the French government, which had not officially recognized American independence and could not receive the good doctor at court. Instead, he became a regular at the weekly salon at Genet's home in Versailles and took the personable Frenchman into his confidence.

After Genet told Vergennes that the British had approached Franklin, the foreign minister asked his Spanish counterpart to help prolong the war in America: "Our primary interest," he explained, "is to separate the English colonies from their mother country forever and prevent any kind of reunion between them. England is our first enemy. The reason for French determination to join with America is the enfeeblement of England by depriving her of one-third of her empire."[31]

Spain, however, opposed American independence. "Spain believes the United States will very soon become her enemy," the Spanish foreign minister replied, "and rather than allow them to expand closer to Spanish territory, Spain will do everything in her power to drive the Americans back—especially from the banks of the Mississippi."[32]

Spain feared that a strong, independent American nation would not only seize the Mississippi River and lands to the west, but eventually threaten Spanish control over Mexico, the Spanish Caribbean, and perhaps even South America. Before recognizing American independence, he insisted that Americans withdraw behind the borders of the thirteen existing provinces and recognize Spanish dominion over Florida, the Gulf of Mexico, and lands west of the Appalachian Mountains to the Pacific Ocean. Vergennes accepted the Spanish conditions, and the two nations signed a secret agreement to support America's War of Independence against Britain, but to limit the power and territory of the new nation to a weak confederation behind the borders of the existing thirteen British provinces.

Without disclosing the French agreement with Spain, King Louis XVI recognized American independence on December 17, 1778, and, a month later, signed two treaties with the United States—one, a treaty of amity and commerce establishing free trade between the two nations; the other, a military alliance in which each nation pledged to defend the other's American territories and agreed not to negotiate peace with Britain independently. In June 1778, France and England went to war, with France expelling the detested English commissioner from Dunkerque; a year later Spain declared war on England but refused to recognize American independence and remained out of the American conflict.

In America, the stunning Gates victory at Saratoga and the equally shocking Washington defeats near Philadelphia provoked demands in Congress for Gates to replace Washington as commander in chief. Behind the scenes, the French government added its voice to the debate through its agent "comte de Conway"—now a brigadier general in the American Army. France had soured on Washington for at least three reasons: the failure of Arnold and Montgomery to capture Canada from the English; Washington's incompetent leadership at Brandywine and Germantown, which cost the Patriots their capital city; and Washington's outspoken antipathy for French officers enlisting in the American Army.

Kalb's initial reports reinforced French government determination to replace Washington: "As a General he is too slow, too indolent, and far too weak; besides, he has a tinge of vanity in his composition and overestimates himself. In my opinion whatever success he may have will be owing to good luck and to the blunders of his adversaries, rather than to his abilities. I may even say that he does not know how to improve upon the grossest blunders of the enemy. He has not yet overcome his old prejudice against the French."[33]

Throughout 1777, Kalb continued to send de Broglie and Vergennes detailed reports, but it soon became clear that Kalb's allegiance was shifting. Seduced by the honor of a major general's commission and by Washington's gracious respect, Kalb became a staunch American patriot and loyal subordinate of his American commander in chief, whom he began to describe as "the bravest and truest of men . . . amiable, kind-hearted and upright." Kalb's encomiums convinced Edmé Genet to replace Kalb with Thomas Conway as lead agent in the plot to replace Washington with a French generalissimo.[34]

From the moment Conway arrived in America, he had encouraged anti-Washington feelings in both Congress and the army high command, and a month after Saratoga, he enlisted the victorious Northern Army commander Horatio Gates into a cabal against Washington. Gates considered himself a superior military leader and strategist and lusted for Washington's post. Conway argued that the Gates victory and Washington defeats warranted Washington's replacement as supreme commander by a Board of War. To the delight of Genet and Vergennes, Congress agreed and appointed a Board of War to take supreme command, with Gates as president and the French agent Conway as inspector general and second in command.

Without consulting Washington, Conway convinced Gates and
Congress to authorize a winter invasion of Canada, led by the marquis de Lafayette, with Conway as his second. Congress agreed that
French-speaking officers were the most appropriate leaders for an invasion of French-speaking territory. Conway quickly appointed his
own cadre of French officers, whom he knew would support the cabal
against Washington.

Initially, the plan enthralled Lafayette. He called "the idea of
rendering the whole of New France free . . . too glorious." Expressing
his eagerness to expel the English from "the lands they have taken
from us [the French]," he told Congress his "consanguinity with the
Canadians and the name of Frenchman I am honored with" had convinced him to undertake the command, "if those measures are taken
which I think proper to succeed." To Conway's consternation, one of
those measures all but undermined his cabal against Washington. In-
tuiting at least part of Conway's scheme, Lafayette told Congress he
"would only accept the command on condition of remaining subordinate to General Washington," and that he would accept orders only
from Washington—not the Board of War.[35] Rather than risk a rift
with so popular a French hero, Congress agreed. Lafayette then replaced Conway's officers with twenty French officers loyal to Washington. In Lafayette's coup de grâce against the Conway cabal, he
appointed Baron de Kalb, by then a fierce Washington loyalist, as his
second in command, above Conway, to prevent the cabalist from assuming command if Lafayette died in action.

Though unaware of the French government's ties to the turmoil
engulfing the American military, both Kalb and Lafayette knew that
plotters were attempting to undermine Washington. "Many foreigners
who have failed to obtain commissions, or whose ambitious schemes
after having obtained them could not be countenanced, have entered
into powerful conspiracies," Lafayette wrote to his wife.[36]

Lafayette and Kalb suspected Conway and Gates, and Kalb was
first to identify a third conspirator—Quartermaster General Thomas
Mifflin. A prominent Philadelphia merchant before the war, Mifflin
had been an outspoken advocate of Valley Forge as the site for the
Continental Army's winter encampment of 1778. "The idea of win-
tering in this desert," Kalb wrote to de Broglie,

can only have been put in the head of the commanding general by an interested speculator or a disaffected man. If they are not traitors, they are certainly gross ignoramuses. I am satisfied that our present position . . . will offer none of the advantages expected of it. On the contrary, the army will be kept in continual alarms from being too near the enemy, and too feeble . . . the divisions are kept so far asunder, that we are practically split up into a number of petty detachments, isolated so as to be unable to support each other, and helplessly exposed to every assault. . . . The army contractors . . . have declared that the present location is the most convenient for them. . . . I do not know what is done in the clothing department; but it is certain that half the army are half naked, and almost the whole army go barefoot. Luckily we have an enemy to deal with as clumsy as ourselves.[37]

Early in February, Lafayette and Kalb went to take command of the 2,500-man Northern Army in Albany. When they arrived, they found none of the promised ammunition, provisions, or supplies for the Canadian expedition. Not only were the troops "unfit for duty," Lafayette learned that their commanders "had written, before my arrival, to General Conway, in the most expressive terms . . . that it would be madness to undertake this operation [in winter]. . . . I have been deceived by the Board of War."[38] Gates and Congress both apologized to Lafayette and agreed to transfer him and Kalb back to Washington's command, leaving Conway in the obscurity of Albany, where he could do no further damage to Washington and the war effort.

As Lafayette left Albany, the last vestiges of the Conway cabal and the plot against Washington collapsed when Mifflin resigned as quartermaster general after evidence surfaced that he had contributed to privations at Valley Forge by diverting troop supplies to his own warehouses. Mifflin's resignation and Conway's exile humiliated Gates and the Board of War; Gates resigned from the board and left for Albany to resume command of the Northern Army; and Congress restored Washington's authority as supreme commander. Late in April, Conway resigned, but his bitter denunciations of Washington goaded Washington loyalist General John Cadwalader to challenge the Irishman to a duel. Wounded badly and fearing imminent death, Conway wrote Washington a letter of apology. Although he recovered, he left the United States and returned to France, where the French government rewarded him by reinstating his officer's rank in the army and appointing him governor of French possessions in India.[39]

Although Conway's departure freed Washington's high command of French spies, it did little to rid his staff of British agents. In the spring of 1778, the British exchanged the captured Major General Charles Lee for a British officer of the same rank, and the English-born Lee returned to Washington's headquarters at Valley Forge. In June, he took command of a 4,000-man Patriot force with orders to attack the rear guard of the British Army, camped for the night at Monmouth, New Jersey, on its retreat from Philadelphia to New York. Lee delayed the attack so long that he sacrificed the element of surprise and permitted the British to regroup and counterattack. With Lee's forces retreating, Washington, exploding with rage, galloped to the front lines: "What is the meaning of this?" he shouted at Lee, then relieved him of command without waiting for a reply. Suspecting the Englishman of being a British spy, Washington ordered Lee to the rear and took command himself. At Lee's subsequent court-martial, Washington charged him with "disobedience of orders in not attacking the enemy . . . misbehaviour before the enemy . . . making an *unnecessary, disorderly and shameful retreat* . . . and disrespect to the Commander in Chief."[40] The court-martial found Lee guilty and relieved him of command for a year. Before he could return to service, Congress dismissed him from the army, and he died in disgrace in Philadelphia in 1782. Evidence later surfaced that his capture by the British had been planned by Lee and his captors in advance and that while a "prisoner," Lee had plotted with the British commanding general to defeat Washington's army. From the beginning, Lee had been a spy, planted in the Patriot high command to try to ensure British victory.[41]

5

The French Invasion

ON MARCH 20, 1778, the comte de Vergennes led Benjamin Franklin, Silas Deane, and Arthur Lee along the dazzling Hall of Mirrors in the Palace of Versailles. In the Peace Drawing Room at the south end, His Most Christian Majesty King Louis XVI sat on the elevated throne, resplendent in snow-white ermine and blue silk robes appliquéd with gold fleurs-de-lis—the colors and symbols of the once-glorious French empire. Within a week, Vergennes appointed his close, longtime aide, Conrad Alexandre Gérard de Rayneval, minister to the United States "to watch Congress carefully and warn Versailles if there were any indications they might opt for reconciliation with England." Once again, Vergennes had "a master of intrigue" near the seat of government in America.[1]

"The Count de Vergennes," wrote the ever-wary John Adams, "instructed Mr. Gérard by some means or other to penetrate into the Secrets of Congress and obtain from some of the Members or some of the Secretaries or Clerks, Copies of the most confidential Communications between Congress and their Ministers. . . . Mr. Jay . . . can tell the World, if he will, as he has told me, the Arts and Importunities even to rudeness and ill manners, which he employed with Mr. Jay to obtain his Instructions."[2]

With no ministers trained in espionage, Congress could only rely on the popular but doddering, seventy-year-old inventor Benjamin Franklin and the naive Connecticut merchant Silas Deane to serve as emissaries in France. The Conway cabal, however, left Congress so suspicious of Deane's commissioning activities that it recalled him and appointed the irascible John Adams of Massachusetts as a replacement. Compared to Franklin, Adams made a terrible impression in France. The French had hailed the arrival of the philosopher-scientist Franklin as "the embodiment of the Enlightenment, the ideal representative of the natural aristocracy" emerging from "the noble experiment in the New World."[3] In contrast, John Adams was "quite out of his element" in the French court. "He cannot dance, drink, game, flatter, promise, dress, swear with gentlemen, and talk small talk or flirt with the ladies." He was a "man of inflexible integrity," who, from the first, recognized the nefarious motives of the French for supporting the American Revolution.[4] "It has always been the deliberate intention and object of France," Adams maintained, "for purposes of her own, to encourage the continuation of the war in America in hopes of exhausting the strength and resources of [England] . . . and depressing the rising power of America."[5]

John Adams. The first vice president of the United States, Adams was the first of the Founding Fathers to recognize the nefarious motives for French aid in the American Revolution.

After Adams arrived in France, Edmé Genet tried luring the New Englander into his web, as he had Franklin and Deane, with a warm hand of friendship and hospitality. He took his fifteen-year-old boy, Edmond Charles, with him to Paris to visit the American, who had brought his own beloved son John Quincy, then eleven. Genet invited Adams to his home in Versailles to dine with his family; the handsome young Edmond Charles insisted on inviting Quincy, as intimates often called the boy to distinguish him from his father. Edmond was already fluent in English and a master of diplomatic skills. The youngest of five children and the only boy, he was as gifted as his father, who, from the first, groomed the boy to succeed him as head of French espionage. By the time Edmond was twelve, he had learned Latin, English, Italian, and German and studied the classics. His father schooled him in history and law; his older sisters taught him to play the harp and pianoforte; and, because his oldest sister was the queen's closest friend, he shared the royal family's riding, fencing, and dancing classes.[6]

When he met John Adams and Quincy, he was already working in the Bureau of Interpreters, translating simple foreign documents and learning the basic art and mechanics of politics, statecraft, diplomacy, and espionage. Each day brought brief encounters with spies, diplomats, and notables from England, Holland, Spain, Germany, Russia, Turkey, and other exotic lands, and he learned to charm them all with his enchantingly accented English, winning smile, and precocious social graces.

Though Adams grew genuinely fond of both Genets, the dandy mannerisms and laced shirt cuffs of French court figures repelled the crusty New Englander, who refused to wear court dress—or fawn before America's benefactors. Although not ungrateful for French aid, Adams insisted that France had as much to gain from an American victory as the United States. Adams argued that "were it not for America, to whom France should understand she was under the greatest obligation, England would be too powerful for the House of Bourbon."[7] Adams's remarks to Genet infuriated Vergennes, who said he would deal only with the warmly Francophilic Franklin on matters of common interest to the two nations. With nothing to do in Paris, Adams would return home a few months later.

Before the Adams run-in with Vergennes, England's Parliament still hoped to dissuade Americans from allying themselves with France by repealing the Tea Act and Coercive Acts and pledging never again to tax Americans directly. It even appointed a peace commission to negotiate reconciliation with Congress. But it was all too late. On March 28, the king of France sent a letter to the American Congress:

> VERY DEAR AND GREAT FRIENDS AND ALLIES: You will learn, undoubtedly with gratitude, the measure which the conduct of the King of Great Britain has induced us to take of sending a fleet to endeavor to destroy the English forces upon the shores of North America. . . .
>
> The Count d'Estaing, vice-admiral of France, is charged to concert with you the operations. . . .
>
> Moreover, we pray God that he will have you, very dear and great friends and allies, under his holy protection.
>
> LOUIS[8]

With the promise of French military support, Congress rebuffed Parliament's negotiators by limiting all discussions with the British to two points: United States independence and withdrawal of British troops from American territory. To demonstrate its resolve, Congress commissioned Captain John Paul Jones to lead a small naval squadron against the British. Sailing from the French west coast, he seized British ships and raided English ports, boldly landing at Whitehaven and spiking the guns of the fort before setting fire to ships at anchor and sailing back to France.

On July 6, 1778, General Vice Admiral Charles Henri, comte d'Estaing, and his fleet sailed into Delaware Bay with 4,000 marines to storm ashore near Philadelphia and restore the American capital to the Patriots. The French could not have picked a worse commander. A soldier by profession, he had no experience at sea and acquired his admiral's commission only because of his lifelong friendship with the king and the king's father. Instead of sailing directly to Philadelphia, d'Estaing lost time chasing British privateers in the Atlantic; by the time he arrived in Delaware Bay, the British had evacuated the city and consolidated their northern forces at more defensible sites in New York and Newport, Rhode Island. With no battles to fight near Philadelphia, d'Estaing sailed up the New Jersey coast to trap the British fleet in New York, but his ships drew too much water to cross the sandbars into the bay, and as the British fleet bobbed tantalizingly beyond cannon range, d'Estaing all but decided to abandon his American mission.

Washington proposed an alternative strategy, however: a joint attack with American forces against the 6,000-man British garrison at Newport, Rhode Island, to free New England of British troops. He sent Lafayette with 2,000 Continental Army troops to join 3,000 New Hampshiremen under General John Sullivan and 6,000 militiamen from Boston under Governor John Hancock. As the only high-level, bilingual officer, Lafayette would coordinate the two nations' forces.

D'Estaing agreed to sail to Newport, but he had lost enthusiasm for the American Revolution. Weeks at sea under short rations had killed some of his marines and left most of the rest too weak to fight. Bad timing at Philadelphia and bad luck at New York had only added to his men's deterioration. As he neared Rhode Island, his cautious eye saw nothing but a design for disaster on the navigation charts. Three narrow arms of the sea reached into Narragansett Bay to embrace two islands—desolate little Conanicut and the larger Rhode Island, with the British garrison on its southern tip at Newport. If he sailed into the bay to put his troops ashore, a British fleet could easily trap and annihilate them.

Although Lafayette tried to encourage cordiality between the elegant French count and the gruff, plainspoken Sullivan, they looked into each other's eyes and immediately despised each other. A rough-hewn, quick-tempered New Hampshire lawyer and virulent Francophobe (he bitterly recalled the French and Indian raids of his youth), Sullivan scorned European niceties of military protocol, and his sharp, direct tone offended the high-born count. At first, Lafayette managed to mediate differences and convince the two to agree on a joint assault against the British garrison at Newport. Before they could attack, however, a British fleet appeared on the horizon and d'Estaing sailed out to engage them.

Just as the titanic battle was about to begin, the skies darkened angrily; violent waves and winds gripped both fleets, tossing ships into the air, spinning them like tops, ripping sails, and snapping masts like so many twigs. The gale roared throughout the night. By morning both fleets lay crippled, barely able to steer, let alone battle. D'Estaing's flagship had lost its masts and rudder and bobbed about helplessly. A second man-of-war had lost two of its three masts, and a third had vanished over the horizon or under the ocean.

D'Estaing regrouped the ships he could find and bobbed slowly back to Rhode Island, his flagship in tow. When he arrived, he found an alarming shrinkage in Sullivan's force. Many troops had deserted after the French fleet sailed away, and the storm put thousands of others to flight. Hancock's 6,000-man militia had shrunk to 1,000, and, deeming the expedition against Newport lost, he, too, left the mud of the rain-soaked island and returned to Boston. Although Sullivan wanted to attack Newport, d'Estaing refused: "The same operation which was almost disastrous when we had our full strength," he argued, "would have been all the more imprudent to undertake with a weaker force."[9]

The Frenchman's refusal enraged Sullivan. He sent Lafayette and Greene to d'Estaing's flagship to urge him to change his mind. "If we fail in our negotiation," Greene quipped, "at least we shall get a good dinner."[10] As it turned out, they failed on both counts: Greene got too seasick to eat, and Lafayette could not change the admiral's mind; the French sailed off to Boston to get their ships repaired.

Sullivan was irate; he called d'Estaing's departure "destructive in the highest degree to the welfare of the United States of America, and highly injurious to the alliance formed between the two nations." To the diplomatic damage he inflicted, Sullivan added a general order to the army disavowing the alliance with France and predicting that d'Estaing's departure "will prove America able to procure with her own arms that which her allies refused to assist her in obtaining." Deeply injured by Sullivan's insults, d'Estaing prepared to write to his friend King Louis to abandon the alliance with America.[11]

Having fought the French twenty years earlier, Washington was as uncomfortable as Sullivan with French intervention in America, but he was aware that he would lose the war without it. He sent d'Estaing an abject apology—and Sullivan a stern reprimand. He also sent John Hancock an urgent plea to ensure the French fleet a warm welcome in Boston and speedy refitting.

In Philadelphia, Congress acted swiftly to repair the damage Sullivan had inflicted on the alliance. It resolved that d'Estaing "hath behaved as a brave and wise officer, and that his excellency and the officers and men under his command have rendered every benefit to these states . . . and are fully entitled to the regards of the friends of America." At Washington's urging, other American military leaders joined in praising d'Estaing and rejecting Sullivan's boorishness. "I could not have been more shocked by . . . the letter General Sullivan wrote to you," wrote the amiable Nathanael Greene of Rhode Island. "I beg your excellency not to judge other American generals by the tone of his letter. I can assure you with the greatest sincerity of the respect and veneration your reputation has inspired in them; permit me to add that no one feels this more deeply than I."[12]

At Washington's urging, Lafayette hurried to Boston to introduce d'Estaing to John Hancock, the popular state leader who had been Boston's leading merchant and shipbuilder before the war. Hancock interceded with the city's Francophobic shipfitters to repair the French fleet, and, in a symbolic gesture that all Boston witnessed, Hancock rode to harborside in his resplendent carriage to invite d'Estaing and Lafayette to a formal dinner at Hancock House, his stately mansion atop Beacon Hill. Dressed in purple velvet as brilliant as that of any European aristocrat, he boarded d'Estaing's flagship to deliver the invitations personally.

Later that day, Hancock sent his coach to bring his renowned French guests to dine with Boston's leading citizens in the glittering banquet hall at Hancock House. A servant in livery stood behind each chair to serve guests individually. The settings displayed the finest china, crystal, and silver, and Hancock's cellar yielded French wines as fine as any the count—or the marquis—had ever savored. Hancock climaxed the evening—and saved the alliance—by presenting d'Estaing with a magnificent portrait of Washington.

"I never saw a man so glad at possessing his sweetheart's picture," Lafayette wrote to Washington, "as the admiral was to receive yours." D'Estaing ordered his cannons to fire a royal salute as the portrait was

John Hancock. The first governor of Massachusetts, Hancock prevented a possible rupture of Franco-American relations by wining and dining French admiral d'Estaing at Hancock House, the stately mansion overlooking Boston.

hoisted aboard his flagship the next morning. He hung it above the mantel in his cabin, framed with laurel wreaths.

With the 1778 campaign at an end, Lafayette and d'Estaing worked out plans for winter and spring campaigns. Lafayette would ask Congress for 2,000 American troops to sail with French marines on d'Estaing's fleet in January to storm the British West Indies. In the spring, they would sail north to the St. Lawrence and attack the British in Quebec. Lafayette dutifully sent the plans to both Washington and Vergennes—only to have the American commander reject them out of hand. Washington feared French colonial ambitions as much as those of the English and suspected that d'Estaing would reclaim Canada for France and establish a state on the American border, with alien customs, morals, religion, and government.

Congress differed strongly; it feared the British far more than the French and argued that continued British presence in Canada would pose an ever-present military threat to the United States. Bribed by French agents to believe that France harbored no territorial ambitions in Canada, congressmen eyed Canada as a potential fourteenth member of the Confederation of American States, with a vast wealth of fish, furs, and forests to contribute to the new nation. Congress, therefore, overruled Washington and approved Lafayette's "Plan for Reducing the province of Canada"[13] the following spring. A few weeks later, Lafayette sailed home to France to obtain French military and financial aid to oust the British from North America.

Washington bridled at what he saw as congressional usurpation of his command over military operations. He went to Philadelphia to urge Congress to rescind its decision, arguing that France posed as great a threat to American independence as Britain. "France," he wrote, "[is] the most powerful monarchy in Europe by land, able now to dispute the empire of the sea with Great Britain, and, if joined by Spain, I may say, certainly superior, possessed by New Orleans on our right, Canada on our left, and seconded by the numerous tribes in our rear . . . so generally friendly to her. . . . It is much to be apprehended [that France would] have in her power to give laws to these states . . . it is a maxim founded on the universal experience of mankind that no nation is to be trusted farther than it is bound by its interests."[14]

In Boston, d'Estaing unwittingly reinforced Washington's argument with a "Declaration in the king's name to all former Frenchmen of North America," pledging French recovery of Canada from the English. "You were born French," he said, "you have never ceased to be French. . . . To all of you, my compatriots, a vast kingdom awaits you, with the same religion as yours, the same morality, the same language; a kingdom where you will rejoin your parents, your brothers, your old friends; a kingdom with inexhaustible wealth." D'Estaing went on to urge the "Priests of Canada to form an army to take an active role in government and to protect and expand religion."[15]

D'Estaing's frightening "Papist" proclamation convinced Congress that the French military had no intention of allowing Canada to join the American Confederation; they yielded to Washington and rejected plans to invade Canada. As it turned out, Vergennes also rejected the Canadian expedition: he feared that Canadians might opt for linkage with the American Confederation and create a nation powerful enough to overrun French and Spanish possessions in the Caribbean and Latin America. Moreover, the added cost of a Canadian campaign would be prohibitive. French expenditures in

America had already exceeded Vergennes's expectations, and instead of accruing to France's profits with increased trade, the war was threatening to bankrupt her. In addition to the costs of the d'Estaing disaster at Newport, France had loaned the Continental Congress 42 million livres—about $450 million today—and Congress had no hard currency to repay it. An invasion of Canada would spread French military and naval resources so thin as to render her vulnerable to British attack in the West Indies and, indeed, France herself.

With the Canadian project abandoned, d'Estaing sailed to the West Indies, and the British lost no time in profiting from the absence of French warships in American waters: they landed in Georgia, seized the port of Savannah, and marched overland to capture Augusta.

In the spring of 1779, Lafayette arrived home in France, where tales of his battlefield heroics had catapulted him to supereminence. Of all French officers who sought appointment in the Continental Army, he alone had served as an unpaid volunteer and won the complete trust of the xenophobic commander in chief. On his own initiative, Lafayette had charged into action at the sight of American soldiers fleeing in panic under enemy fire at Brandywine, near Philadelphia. He leaped into their midst, suffered a painful leg wound, and despite loss of blood, inspired them to regroup and led them to safety in a nearby wood before collapsing. His gallantry in subsequent encounters outside Philadelphia and in New Jersey earned the admiration of troops, commanders, and congressmen alike; his unswerving loyalty to Washington and the American cause earned their trust and love. After his singular diplomatic service at Newport, the comte d'Estaing noted that "no one is in a better position than [Lafayette] . . . to become an additional bond of unity between France and America."[16]

French ambassador Conrad Gérard agreed. "The prudent, courageous and amiable conduct of the Marquis de Lafayette has made him the idol of Congress, the army and the people of America," he wrote to Vergennes. "They all hold a high opinion of his military talents. You know how little inclined I am to adulation, but I would be less than just if I did not send you these universally acclaimed testimonials. . . . The Americans want him to return with the troops which the king may send."[17]

Although Vergennes had tried to prevent Lafayette's departure to America in 1777, he—and the king—welcomed the young Frenchman back to France as a national hero and the key link between Versailles and the United States. "I enjoyed the confidence of both countries and both governments," Lafayette explained in his memoires. "I used the favor I had won at court and in French society to serve the American cause and obtain every kind of help."[18]

Once in Paris, Lafayette met with Franklin, then went to Versailles with a plan to raid the British and Irish coasts with Scottish coastal raider John Paul Jones. The raids, he insisted, would force the British either to recall troops and ships from America or suffer the humiliation of constant French incursions on their homeland. Vergennes approved the plan at first and ordered the minister of war to prepare five ships for Jones and assign 2,000 raiders to Lafayette. In mid-May, however, just as the little fleet gathered in the port of Lorient in southern Brittany, Vergennes abruptly canceled the project. Spain, at last, was about to join the war, and instead of simple raids, France and Spain would launch a full-scale invasion of England, with an armada of more than a hundred ships under Admiral d'Estaing—again, d'Estaing—and an invasion force of 30,000 under General de Broglie.

Spain's entry into the war raised hopes in Congress that England might sue for peace rather than war against three nations on multiple fronts. It sent John Adams back to Paris to talk peace with British emissaries there, but he immediately renewed his diplomatic war with Vergennes when the foreign minister asked to see the New Englander's confidential instructions.

"The Count De Vergennes might imagine that I was so little read in the law of nations . . . and had so little experience in the world . . . that I would in all Simplicity and Naivete, send him a Copy of my Instructions," Adams fumed. "I had already reasons enough to suspect and indeed to believe, that the French Court, at least that the Count De Vergence [sic], would wish me to go to the utmost Extent . . . in contracting the Boundaries of the United States; whereas it was my unalterable Determination to insist . . . on an ample Extension of our Boundaries."[19]

Convinced that Vergennes intended to "embarrass and ultimately injure" the United States in peace negotiations with Britain, Adams sent Vergennes a curt reply: "With regard to my instructions, I presume your Excellency will not judge it proper, that I should communicate them, any further than to assure you as I do in the fullest manner, that they contain nothing inconsistent with the Letter or Spirit of the Treaties between his Majesty and The United States."[20]

The note infuriated Vergennes, but Adams shrugged and scoffed, "The Count de Vergennes had been so long in the habit of Intrigues to obtain the Instructions from foreign Courts to their Ambassadors, and probably paying for them very dear, that he had forgotten that the Practice was not lawful."[21] Although Vergennes wrote Congress demanding that Adams follow French government leadership in negotiations with England, Adams was determined to ignore the French and negotiate secretly with the British—independently of France.

Spain's entry into the war proved useless to the French—and the Americans, for that matter. Wind, fog, and storms combined with administrative incompetence to delay the departure of the Franco-Spanish armada for six weeks and strip the expedition of all elements of surprise. D'Estaing did not reach the English Channel until mid-August, his crews decimated by smallpox. With the September storm season upon him, he had little choice but sail to safe harbor and, as usual, abandon his mission. De Broglie's mighty invasion force, which had waited on shore for nearly two months, disbanded and returned to its bases.

Ironically, the only French success of the channel campaign came after John Paul Jones refitted six French derelicts, sailed for England, and attacked a fleet of thirty-nine British merchant vessels. Two British men-of-war escorting the fleet turned their sixty-six cannons on his ship and all but blasted her out of the water. As flames consumed his vessel, he defiantly rejected British demands to surrender with the shout: "I have not yet begun to fight."[22] As marksmen in the riggings strafed the enemy's decks, an American grenade set off a powder explosion on the English *Serapis*, toppled her mainmast, and forced her surrender. Jones transferred his 237-man crew from the inferno on his own ship and sailed the *Serapis* and the other British man-of-war to France.

The hapless Admiral d'Estaing, meanwhile, was still searching for victory—any victory—and sailed to the Caribbean with a fleet of thirty-five ships and 4,000 marines. Sailing out of the French islands of Guadeloupe and Martinique, d'Estaing captured the British islands of St. Vincent, Grenada, St. Kitts, Nevis, Tobago, and Saint Lucia and extended the French hold on the Antilles across almost all the Leeward and Windward islands. Emboldened by his triumphs, d'Estaing turned northward to open trade routes to U.S. ports at Savannah and Charleston. As they had in New York, however, his ships drew too much water to enter the Savannah River to within cannon range of British fortifications in the city. With 1,400 American troops ready to attack the city by land, d'Estaing led his marines upriver on small boats to attack by water, but without the protection of shipboard cannon fire, the French and Americans were no match for British defenders. The Redcoats slaughtered 800 French and American attackers and wounded most of the rest, including d'Estaing himself. The British lost only 150 men.

Despite the American commander's pleas to continue the fight, d'Estaing saw little prospect for victory, and with the hurricane season approaching, he led survivors back to their ships and sailed to safety in the French West Indies. As in Newport, his departure forced Americans to cede the field and left the British firmly in control of the South. Although he had demonstrated personal courage in battle, his four failures in America—at Philadelphia, New York, Newport, and Savannah—made him the target of a spate of satiric cartoons in the American and English press forever after.

Distressed by d'Estaing's fiascos, Lafayette convinced Vergennes that the Americans needed more men and money to defeat the British, but his estimate of how many men and how much money differed sharply from that of the foreign minister—as did his motives. Lafayette embraced the American dream—the dream of Washington—to create a strong, independent republic under a constitutional government. His ties to Washington had grown deeply emotional. He called the American commander "my adoptive father" and

Admiral Comte d'Estaing. The commander of the French in the Americas, d'Estaing inspired many cartoons in the British press that poked fun at his questionable naval skills after he lost four successive engagements in North American waters.

named his only son George-Washington Lafayette. Washington reciprocated his feelings, telling the French ambassador "I do not know a nobler, finer soul, and I love him as my own son."[23] Washington happily agreed to be godfather to Lafayette's son.

In contrast to Lafayette, Vergennes only supported the American Revolution to recapture New France without bankrupting Old France. Late in 1779, the French foreign minister seemed to yield to Lafayette's extravagant demands and agreed to send a fleet of French warships to America with an expeditionary force of 6,000 infantrymen. In addition, the French promised to send 15,000 muskets, clothing, and other materiel to the American Army and to open discussions with Franklin for new loans to the United States government. Although Lafayette asked to lead the expeditionary force, Vergennes wanted a commander of unquestioned loyalty to France who would not put American interests first in territorial disputes or hesitate to act decisively in a French cabal against Washington. Instead of Lafayette, therefore, the king appointed fifty-five-year-old Jean-Baptiste-Donatien de Vimeur, comte de Rochambeau. A major general for nineteen years, Rochambeau had fought in the Seven Years War and was a brigadier general before Lafayette was born. Vergennes did yield on one important point: to avoid misunderstandings between American and French forces, he agreed to place Rochambeau under Washington as second in command, although above all other American officers. He gave Rochambeau secret instructions "to permit no separation of French troops from one another and to assure their serving at all times in a single army corps under French generals."[24] Vergennes envisioned Washington falling from his horse, and Rochambeau assuming command of all military forces in America.

Vergennes's vision was hardly far-fetched. In early spring 1780, a 14,000-man English army overwhelmed Charleston, South Carolina, capturing 5,500 Americans and four ships. It was the worst American defeat of the war, and together with d'Estaing's failure at Savannah, cost the Americans the only ports from which to ship tobacco and rice—the two most important American commodities in the arms trade, each the equivalent of cash. The fall of Charleston gave the British Army control of both Carolinas, Georgia, New York, and Newport, Rhode Island, along with all coastal waters south of Cape Cod. American trade came to a halt; Congress declared the nation bankrupt and devalued the Continental dollar 97.5 percent—a staggering forty-to-one ratio.

Devaluation forced the army to cut rations to one-eighth normal provisions and provoked mutinies by New Jersey and Connecticut troops, who threatened to march to Philadelphia and hold Congress hostage. Although Washington suppressed the army mutinies by force, he could do little to assuage public anger over devaluation. The devaluation also provoked consternation in France, where United States debts had soared to nearly 25 million Spanish dollars—then the basic international hard currency. Vergennes declared the devaluation nothing less than outright theft. He sent orders to French ambassador Gérard in Philadelphia to protest to Congress.

"The devaluation," he wrote, "will have the harshest consequences for the French, who alone had the courage to trade with Americans and procure essential materials for them and who alone will now suffer the harshest effects of this measure. What will other

Comte de Rochambeau. The commander in chief of the French armies in North America arrived with too small a force to engage the British and prolonged the war by refusing to join with Washington's forces to attack New York.

nations now think of America's good faith after seeing how she tricked the nation that offered the most generous help in the midst of her distress."[25] At Vergennes's behest, Gérard warned Congress that continued French support might well hinge on American renunciation of costly westward expansion.

Gérard urged Congress to renounce claims to the "isolated and scattered" settlements of Americans along the Mississippi River, to which Spain and France had as much or more right than the United States. "I noted," he wrote to Vergennes, "that United States territorial rights did not extend beyond their borders as English colonies and that the allies of the United States would not remain at war a single day to add to that territory."[26] To Gérard's distress, Congress refused, declaring the Mississippi the western boundary of the United States and insisting that "the United States shall enjoy the free navigation of the river Mississippi into and from the sea . . . always."[27] Despondent over his diplomatic failure, Gérard sent Vergennes his resignation. Vergennes called the American declaration "madness" but made plans to find an emissary who could deal more effectively with the intemperate Americans. In the meantime, he would rely on General Rochambeau to further French interests in America.

Before Vergennes's letter reached America, John Adams fired his own answer to the French foreign minister: "The plan of Congress is not only wyse, but just," Adams declared, and, rather than complain, France should recognize her obligations to America for having weakened England enough for France to recapture military and economic parity.[28] Adams's letter so infuriated Vergennes that he declared Adams persona non grata at Versailles.

With his value in Paris limited again, Adams moved to Amsterdam to try to obtain a $10 million loan from Holland. Of all nations in the Western world, Holland had profited most from the American Revolution. While the war interrupted direct trade between England and her thirteen colonies, indirect trade—*via Holland*—had continued and, indeed, flourished. Dutch ships carried British goods between Britain and America via the Dutch Caribbean island of Saint Eustatius, which became one of the world's busiest ports with merchants from almost every European and Asian country on the island to trade.

On July 10, 1780, another French fleet sailed into Newport—without d'Estaing this time but with no greater prospects for victory. The French government failed to fulfill its pledges to Lafayette and sent a smaller than expected fleet that would not give the Americans naval or military superiority to attack New York or Charleston, South Carolina. None of the promised arms, ammunition, and clothing for the American Army were aboard. Instead of 6,000 troops, Rochambeau brought 5,000, of whom 2,000 were ill and unfit for service. Some 1,300 sailors were equally sick and unfit, leaving the small fleet unable to engage the British. Indeed, it appeared as if Vergennes had purposely sent too small a force to be of value. Rochambeau refused to engage the British without an additional division of French troops and enough ships to give the French clear superiority over the British in coastal waters. Until then, his army would stay put while British and American forces wore themselves out—as Vergennes had planned. Within days of the French arrival, twenty British ships of the line blockaded the waters off Newport and locked the French fleet in Narragansett Bay to prevent it from harassing British shipping.

With still another French military expedition deteriorating into a useless adventure, Washington began suspecting French motives for "helping" America. Sensing the incongruity of the world's oldest, most despotic monarchy supporting rebellion by commoners against a kindred monarchy, he warned Congress, "The generosity of our allies has a claim to our gratitude, but it is neither for the honor of America nor for the interest of the common cause to leave the work entirely to them."[29] He sent Lafayette to Newport as his personal representative to urge Rochambeau to send healthy troops to join Washington's army in attacking New York. Washington entreated Rochambeau to consider everything Lafayette might say "as coming from me," and Lafayette, in turn, told the French commander that "it is important for us to act."[30] Rochambeau was incensed at having to negotiate with an officer younger than his own son. He demanded a face-to-face meeting with Washington and refused further contact with Lafayette.

In September, Washington, Lafayette, and other members of Washington's staff rode to Hartford, Connecticut, to meet Rochambeau. They agreed the Americans would need an army of no fewer than 30,000 troops—10,000 of them French—to dislodge the British from New York and a powerful fleet of no less than thirty ships of the line. Sailing home to France for the last time, French ambassador Gérard carried their request to Versailles, where Vergennes concluded that Americans seemed too willing to let the French fight the War of Independence alone. "I have little confidence in the spirit of the United States," he declared when he learned that the heroic American major general Benedict Arnold had defected to the British.[31]

After receiving the Rochambeau-Washington request for more men and supplies, Vergennes reviewed his nation's finances and found them "truly alarming." He decided that France had "no other recourse but peace as promptly as possible."[32] When, therefore, Russia and Austria offered to mediate an end to the war, Vergennes accepted. Spain, too, favored peace. Though exhausted economically and militarily, England demanded French withdrawal from North

America as a condition for peace talks. Vergennes balked and, with Edmé Genet, devised a scheme to lure the United States into French vassalage regardless of the outcome of peace talks with England.

They sent Anne César, chevalier de la Luzerne, a suave veteran of the Seven Years War, to replace Gérard as French ambassador in America. He carried secret instructions to convince Congress to cede autonomy in foreign affairs to the French government and let Vergennes assume direction of American foreign policy.

In the six years since the First Continental Congress had convened, the makeup of that body had changed drastically; many Founding Fathers had gone to war; some had returned home to govern their states; and others, like Adams, Jay, and Franklin, were overseas as congressional emissaries. Without them, Congress had deteriorated into a pit of petty squabbles over regional or personal interests. Seven states had overlapping claims beyond the Appalachian Mountains in the Illinois and Ohio country and along the Great Lakes. Congressmen themselves were among the speculators who claimed large tracts in those areas. The Lee family in Virginia had staked out tens of thousands of acres in western territories claimed by Virginia, Massachusetts, and Connecticut.

La Luzerne familiarized himself with sectional and personal motives driving the action—and inaction—of each member of Congress. More than suave, he was seductive, irresistible, and skilled at convincing members that their individual interests were identical to those of the nation. He "opened his purse" to some, promised land grants to others, and frightened the rest with warnings that Washington and the army might seize control of government and establish a military dictatorship. In the end, he convinced them to abdicate control of foreign policy to France and allow him to sue for peace on their behalf. With 5,000 crack French troops on American soil, Congress could surrender to either the British or French but could no longer resist both. The American Army was exhausted and had lost its will to fight—withered by hunger, lack of clothing and arms, mass desertions, and mutiny. And Congress was bankrupt, with no prospects of raising money to pay and supply its troops.

"The truth is," Vergennes pointed out, "the United States must recognize that not a single European court [other than France] has

taken the slightest step or even hinted that it is considering recognizing the United States. . . . The truth is that the United States remains isolated; that they have only one friend, France, and that they
must depend on French forces for survival, not on any favors from
other European sovereigns. . . . I believe that Congress should be
somewhat modest in demanding conditions for peace."[33]

With Anglophobes still the majority, Congress meekly accepted
Vergennes's proposal and all but ceded sovereignty over the United
States to France. The French plot against America seemed close to
success.

Ecstatic over the congressional resolution, Vergennes pledged to
do all he could "to keep the 13 provinces in their present form. But
circumstances often allow the most powerful nations to dictate terms
to lesser powers. We cannot yet predict whether that will be the case
in America, but I can assure you that our firm intention is to do
everything in our power to avoid it and to achieve a peace settlement
without any sacrifice whatever. But, if sacrifice is necessary, it is best
to resign ourselves to it."[34] Vergennes said that if mediating powers
insisted, the United States might have to accept the territorial status
quo, leaving South Carolina and Georgia to the British, recognizing
Spanish sovereignty over the east bank of the Mississippi and the
Floridas, and ceding North American fishing rights. In effect, the
plan would give the United States partial independence as an economically dependent French protectorate, penned within its borders
by powerful European nations.

Because of Vergennes's intense dislike for John Adams and
Adams's unyielding stand for American independence free of French
influence, La Luzerne placed impressive sums in the hands of key
congressmen to dilute Adams's authority at the peace talks by sending John Jay and Thomas Jefferson to serve with Franklin. In addition, Congress agreed to make the American peace commissioners
subordinate to the French foreign ministry. On June 15, 1781, Congress issued these extraordinary "Instructions to the Commissioners
for Peace":

In any and all peace negotiations: . . . you are to make the most
candid and confidential communications upon all subjects to the

ministers of our generous ally, the King of France; to undertake
nothing in the negotiations for peace or truce without their knowledge or concurrence; and ultimately to govern yourselves by their
advice and opinion, endeavoring in your whole conduct to render
them sensible how much we rely upon his majesty's influence for
effectual aid in everything that may be necessary to the peace, security, and future prosperity of the United States of America.[35]

In effect, the American commissioners could neither sign a peace
accord without French approval nor refuse to sign if the French
signed. In a letter to Vergennes, the French envoy chortled at his
handiwork: "Never has one state so completely and imprudently put
itself at the mercy of another . . . excepting the question of independence, the negotiations were placed in the hands of the [French]
king . . ."

Critics cried out that "Congress had sold the United States
to France" and replaced a British king with a French one.[36] They
demanded a recount of votes on the Instructions, but met with rejection, and the Instructions went off to Paris. "At worst," said apologists, "they could only be considered as a sacrifice of our pride to our
interest."[37] Vergennes and the king rejoiced when they saw the Instructions and the certainty of restoring French influence in continental North America.

George Washington, however, had different ideas, as did Adams
and Jay, an ocean away in Paris. Aware that their French ally was as
perfidious as their British enemy, Adams and Jay agreed to negotiate
with Britain secretly, without the knowledge or influence of the
French government. Mirroring Adams's distrust of French motives
for encouraging American independence, Washington devised a secret military strategy to confuse the French as well as British—and
even his own army leaders. Benedict Arnold's defection and Lee's espionage had taught him to keep his own counsel and share plans
with no one.

"Upon a full consideration of our affairs in every point of view,"
he wrote to Lafayette, knowing his letter would be intercepted by
spies, "an attempt upon New York . . . [is] deemed preferable to a
southern operation." Washington had sent Lafayette to Virginia with

a token force of about 1,000 troops to halt a northward thrust by the British army under Lord Cornwallis. Although Washington had promised to send Lafayette reinforcements, he minimized the importance of the Virginia campaign and warned his French friend "not to hazard . . . a General Action unless you have grounds to do it on. No *rational* person will condemn you for *not fighting* with the odds against you. . . . But all will censure a rash step if it is not attended with success." [38]

Meanwhile, Washington coaxed Rochambeau to meet at Wethersfield, Connecticut, where he won the French general's approval for a joint attack on New York. Rochambeau's secret instructions from Vergennes had been to use a victory in New York as "the key to Canada's re-entry into the maternal bosom of France" [39] After securing New York, he was to march northward to the St. Lawrence River on the Canadian border to rendezvous with a French fleet and about 3,000 marines to reinforce his army's invasion of Canada.

Washington convinced Rochambeau that Lafayette's campaign in Virginia would keep British troops and ships too occupied in the South to reinforce New York's defenses, thus leaving the city vulnerable to successful assault by combined French and American armies—especially if the French provided naval support. Rochambeau revealed that Admiral François de Grasse's fleet of thirty warships and 3,000 marines was prepared to sail north from the Caribbean, and he agreed to lead his army from Rhode Island to join Washington's troops north of New York.

Washington returned to his camp and seemed to prepare for a full-scale assault on New York: his troops set up a city of tents atop the New Jersey Palisades, a wall of rock cliffs on the west side of the Hudson River, overlooking British fortifications in Manhattan. At their base, in full sight of the enemy across the river, trains of covered wagons and artillery rumbled back and forth, carrying supplies to the encampment. He raised a second, equally large encampment of tents in Elizabeth Town, New Jersey, across a narrow waterway from Staten Island, and sent supply wagons rolling in and out.

The wagons and tents were empty.

As Washington had foreseen, a British spy had intercepted his letter to Lafayette and delivered copies to British headquarters.

Washington had written the letter "to misguide & bewilder Sir Henry Clinton in regard to the real object by fictitious communications, as well by making deceptive provision of Ovens, Forage & boats in his neighborhood. . . . Nor were less pains taken to deceive our own Army."[40] As Washington explained later, "Success depended upon secrecy. For want of it, most enterprises . . . are generally defeated, however well planned and promising."[41]

As the counterfeit encampment rose atop the Palisades, the French Army arrived from Rhode Island and encamped fifty miles north of New York. Convinced he faced a two-pronged assault by combined allied armies, Clinton issued orders that would cost his nation an empire: he called his most heavily armed ships from the South to New York to shell the empty American tents across the Hudson and ordered Cornwallis to abandon the Virginia campaign and lead his troops to Chesapeake Bay near Portsmouth and board transports to come and help defend New York.

Washington, meanwhile, sent Brigadier General Anthony Wayne and his Pennsylvanians to reinforce Lafayette's Virginians. With fresh troops and supplies, Lafayette sent Cornwallis reeling toward Chesapeake Bay; by July 1, when Washington began his feigned attack on New York, Lafayette had steered Cornwallis onto the southernmost Virginia cape and pinned the British against the waters of Chesapeake Bay at Yorktown. In New York, Patriot troops seized the high ground at Kingsbridge across the Harlem River from northern Manhattan and opened fire on British outposts. As Clinton's troops rushed to repel the incursion, Washington dumbfounded Rochambeau by ordering the French Army to cross the Hudson River and join American troops in what seemed a retreat from New York. Leaving a handful of Patriot troops to continue the charade near the empty tents on the Palisades and Staten Island, Washington led the allied armies to Philadelphia, and by the time the British recognized the ruse, it was too late.

On August 30, the American and French armies reached Philadelphia—just as de Grasse's huge fleet spotted signals from Lafayette scouts on shore to turn into Chesapeake Bay. After blocking the entrance to British ships, de Grasse landed 3,000 marines at Jamestown and urged Lafayette to strike the final blow and claim victory for France. To the admiral's consternation, young Lafayette refused, saying that as a major general in the American Army, he was obliged to follow his commander's orders. Washington's specific orders, he said, had been only "to prevent his [Cornwallis] escape by land." He argued that the allied army would soon arrive from the north and double their forces to 18,000 men. Cornwallis would have no choice but surrender "to spare the lives of the soldiers, which a good general ought always to do."[42]

De Grasse tried flattery: "I want to contribute everything I can to further your glory," he told Lafayette. Lafayette reiterated that an immediate assault would constitute a "murderous attack [and] shed a great deal of blood only to satisfy a vain lust for glory. . . . [I] would not sacrifice the soldiers entrusted to me to personal ambition . . . by waiting, the reduction of the army of Cornwallis was secured at little cost."[43]

In addition to concern for his men, Lafayette believed that final victory belonged to Washington and the Continental Army. They had earned it, and he refused to usurp their glory. Washington was grateful: "I have received with infinite satisfaction, My Dear Marquis, the information of the Arrival of Count de Grasse. And have an additional pleasure in finding that your ideas on every occasion have been so consonant with my own, and that by your military disposition & prudent measures you have anticipated all my wishes. . . . I hope you will keep Lord Cornwallis safe, without Provisions or Forage until we arrive. Adieu."[44]

De Grasse was furious and threatened to leave Chesapeake Bay, arguing that the hurricane season had arrived and put his fleet at risk. As it happened, Clinton's fleet from New York had appeared at the mouth of the bay to prevent de Grasse's departure. De Grasse wheeled his big ships about and turned his heavy cannons on the British attackers. The two fleets jockeyed before moving out of the bay into open waters for more room to maneuver. The duel continued for three days, with each fleet parrying, thrusting, firing, and shifting course but gaining little advantage. Then eleven more French ships arrived from Newport. Vastly outnumbered, the British put about and fled to New York, leaving de Grasse in control of

Admiral Comte de Grasse. The arrival of de Grasse's huge French fleet blocked the British Army's water escape routes at Yorktown and ensured victory— and eventual independence—for the United States.

Chesapeake Bay just as the allied army reached Head of Elk at the northern end of the bay.

Although de Grasse sent transports to carry allied forces down the bay to Yorktown, he no sooner put them ashore before again announcing his intention of leaving for the Caribbean rather than remaining for a long siege. Washington was incensed. With d'Estaing's earlier failures in mind, he sent de Grasse a blunt warning: "Your excellency's departure from the Chesapeake, by affording an opening for the succor of York, which the enemy would instantly avail themselves of, would be, not only the disgrace and loss of renouncing an enterprise, upon which the fairest expectations of the allies have been founded, after the most expensive preparations and uncommon exertions and fatigues, but perhaps the disbanding of the whole army for want of provisions." At Washington's urging, Lafayette was able to coax the embarrassed admiral to reconsider. De Grasse agreed to leave two ships of the line and three frigates to blockade Cornwallis at the mouth of the York River while he led his thirty-five other ships to the entrance of Chesapeake Bay to repel a British attack or to sail out to sea in the event of a hurricane.[45]

On September 28, the allied army, about 9,000 American and 7,800 French troops, marched out of Williamsburg to lay siege to Yorktown. "The English army," Lafayette wrote, "found itself enclosed on every side—and no possible means of escape was left to Lord Cornwallis."[46]

It was a surprisingly short campaign. A storm of shells reduced the town to rubble and opened wide breaches in the outer fortifications. As darkness fell on October 14, American troops charged into the breaches, bayonets fixed, flinging themselves at British defenders with "an ardor" that sent Redcoats fleeing in terror.[47] On October 17, 1781, Cornwallis sent Washington a message under a flag of truce: "Sir,—I propose a cessation of hostilities for twenty-four hours, and that two officers may be appointed by each side . . . to settle the terms for the surrender of the posts at York and Gloucester."[48]

Two days later, Cornwallis, Washington, Rochambeau, and de Grasse signed articles of capitulation, but feigning illness, Cornwallis refused to lead his men to the surrender point—a defiant, personal refusal to recognize American independence and accept British defeat. He sent his adjutant, General Charles O'Hara, in his stead, with orders to surrender his sword to the commander of the French Army rather than participate in tacit recognition of American independence by surrendering to Washington. O'Hara handed his sword to Rochambeau, but the French general had the grace to reject it, insisting that Washington was sole commander in chief.[49]

Although Congress hailed the Yorktown victory, its excessive euphoria drew a stern warning from Washington that victory in a single battle—no matter how glorious—did not ensure victory in the war, let alone independence. He expressed "apprehension . . . lest the late important success, instead of exciting our exertions, as it ought to do, should produce such a relaxation in the prosecution of the war, as will prolong the calamities of it."[50]

Besides New York, Britain still controlled three vital port cities: Wilmington, North Carolina; Charleston, South Carolina; and Savannah, Georgia. Washington believed that with Cornwallis's army

Surrender at Yorktown. With Lafayette at his right (pointing), George Washington (to Lafayette's left) watches British general Charles O'Hara sign the surrender papers on behalf of his commander Lord Cornwallis.

demobilized, total victory was now possible, but only with an imme-diate assault on Charleston before the British could reinforce their positions. Assuming he could count on the French fleet, Washington ordered half his men to march to Charleston to reinforce General Nathanael Greene's militiamen, who had laid siege to the city but were unable to break through outer British fortifications. Washing-ton asked de Grasse to pause on his way to the West Indies to attack from the sea. To Washington's dismay de Grasse refused, saying he had no time and that, in any case, the danger of autumn hurricanes made navigation through the treacherous Carolina sandbars imprac-tical.

Once again, Washington grew irate. It was the second time in a few weeks that de Grasse had tried to withdraw support from the American Army. "No land force can act decisively unless it is accompanied by a maritime superiority," Washington declared. "A constant Naval superiority would terminate the War speedily—without it, I do not know that it will ever be terminated honourably."[1]

A year earlier, John Adams had issued a stern warning against excessive reliance on France, citing a British circular that declared "it has always been the deliberate intention and object of France . . . to encourage the continuation of the war in America in hopes of exhausting the strength and resources of [England] and of depressing the rising power of America."[2]

The de Grasse withdrawal from American waters left Washington little choice but to lead his men back to New York to guard the vital Hudson Valley. To the dismay of Tidewater plantation owners, they now found another foreign army—French instead of British—controlling vital waterways to international trade. Far from seeking to occupy Virginia, however, Rochambeau intended moving northward to reclaim Canada from the British, but without de Grasse to transport his troops, he had no choice but to stay in Yorktown and await further instructions from Vergennes.

6

Winners and Losers

THE AMERICAN VICTORY at Yorktown produced consternation in England and euphoria in France. French foreign minister Vergennes believed Yorktown had weakened England enough for France to invade Canada and reattach her to the motherland. The allies had put almost 8,000 British troops out of action at Yorktown, and 4,000 crack French regulars occupied the Virginia capes; French warships had seized control of Chesapeake Bay and the seas beyond.

Even more satisfying to Vergennes was the extravagant praise and gratitude American leaders were lavishing on the French military—and the trust Congress willingly conferred on French authorities. Congressional leaders heaped honors and encomiums on Lafayette, hailed him as "the Conqueror of Cornwallis," then willingly—indeed, eagerly—stepped into Vergennes's seductive web by appointing "Our Marquis" official emissary for American relations with France, England, and the rest of Europe. Congress ordered American secretary of foreign affairs Robert Livingston to instruct Franklin in Paris, Adams in The Hague, and John Jay in Madrid "to communicate and agree on everything with him [Lafayette]" and to notify French foreign minister Vergennes of Lafayette's new role in American foreign affairs. In effect, Congress placed the United States into French vassalage.

By then, however, Vergennes had lost one of the master planners in the plot against America. Edmé Genet had died in September. His death deprived him of the honor of announcing the Yorktown triumph to Vergennes and the king, and it left one of the most important and complex functions in the realm without an administrator. Fortunately, Genet had spared no effort in training his successor, and Vergennes waited less than a day to invite him to assume Edmé's enormous powers:

"My friendship and esteem for your late father," Vergennes wrote to Genet, "have provoked a sincere concern, Sir, for you and your family and the grief you must be suffering. In my anxiety to relieve your distress, I am pleased to tell you, Sir, that the King has been gracious enough to offer you the office held by your late father. I hope that this evidence of the King's grace will serve as some consolation to you and your family."[1]

No man in France was better equipped than Edmond Genet to assume his father's role as espionage chief—a role whose importance Vergennes recognized by changing his title from clerk-in-chief to assistant secretary for foreign affairs and elevating him to cabinet rank. Groomed from earliest childhood for the post, Genet, more than any palace personage not of noble blood, had the king's confidence and devotion. As a boy, Genet had played in the royal apartments, where his oldest sister, Madame Henriette Campan, was the queen's devoted companion and closest friend. His other two sisters had married highly placed court officials, and together, the Genets were privy to the court's most carefully guarded secrets. Genet entered his father's bureau as an apprentice translator at fifteen and won appointment the same year as interpreter to "Monsieur,"[2] Louis XVI's younger brother and future king Louis XVIII. Though largely ceremonial, young Genet's post afforded him easy social intercourse with the royal family, while his clerkship exposed him to the art and mechanics of politics, statecraft, diplomacy, and espionage—and put him in daily contact with swarms of spies and diplomats from nations around the world. When Genet turned sixteen, the king appointed him a lieutenant in the Corps of Dragoons—a post whose training masculinized the dandy mannerisms he had learned at court and almost took him to America with Rochambeau, until a shortage of transports forced his regiment to remain in France. In the year that followed, he learned English military and naval terms, studying with English prisoners of war before mustering out of the army and returning to Versailles. In 1780, Vergennes took a personal interest in the young man, then seventeen. He was more gifted even than his father in foreign languages and displayed startling good looks, exquisite taste in clothes, and a commanding military bearing and presence. After Genet completed a grand tour of Europe, Vergennes sent him to a German university to perfect his German before assigning him to the French embassy in Berlin. At the same time, he studied chemistry and mining at Berlin University.

Early in 1781, he transferred to a new, more demanding post at the French embassy in Vienna and the court of Queen Marie-Antoinette's family, but returned to Versailles six months later when his father became ill and died. Not yet nineteen, Genet took the reins of the vast espionage network his father had commanded for thirty years. One of his first tasks was to carry the news of Yorktown to Vergennes and the king.

In England, capture of Cornwallis's army crushed British hopes for victory in America. It crippled the nation's military and left the economically vital British Antilles vulnerable to French assault. To strengthen island defenses, the British evacuated Wilmington, North Carolina, in January 1782, and on February 27, the House of Commons voted against further prosecution of the war in the United States. The government fell, and by the end of March, a new government opened negotiations with American peace commissioners in Paris. In the meantime, British troops ceded more positions to Patriot forces in the United States and reinforced defenses in Canada and the Caribbean against possible French attack.

The strategy yielded immediate rewards. In April 1782, the British fleet surprised and all but destroyed the huge de Grasse fleet off the Îles des Saintes—two tiny islands off Guadeloupe. The encounter left 6,000 French sailors dead or wounded—and de Grasse a prisoner. The disaster stunned King Louis and his cabinet, who had unquestioningly supported Vergennes's costly expansionist policy. With the French Navy as emasculated as the British Army, France and Britain suddenly faced each other like two crippled giants, one without arms, the other without legs. Both suddenly recognized they had each lost the war in America and left America, the land they each had planned to conquer, as the only victor.

Under pressure from the French minister of finance to end the nation's financial hemorrhage, Vergennes reluctantly sent an emissary to England to discuss peace and ordered Rochambeau to transfer his army to Newport and Boston to await transport to the French Antilles. Ironically, talk of Anglo-French armistice strengthened the United States' bargaining position during the cautious early steps toward peace. With hostilities ended on American territory, continuation of the Anglo-French Caribbean conflict would weaken only the two great powers and make it more difficult, if not impossible, for either to subdue the United States—on the battlefield or at the peace table.

On April 12, the British sent an emissary to Paris to open talks with Franklin, the only American peace commissioner there at the time. The death of Jefferson's wife had forced him to remain in America to care for his children. Adams was still in The Hague and Jay in Madrid, each trying to win recognition of American independence by at least one nation other than France. Under instructions from Congress, Franklin invited Lafayette to the talks, only to find the marquis accompanied by Vergennes's private secretary. Negotiations dragged on aimlessly, with the British negotiator continually trying to lure the United States from the French sphere of influence with offers of reconciliation with Britain. The tactic incensed Lafayette. "I see that the expectation of peace is a joke," he exploded, "and that you only amuse us without any real intention of treating." In his report to the American secretary of foreign affairs, Lafayette declared, "A good army in America will do more to bring peace than one can imagine."[3]

Aging and ailing, Franklin felt uncomfortably alone in the vise between French and English negotiators and urged John Jay to abandoned his fruitless efforts to win Spanish recognition. "Here you are greatly wanted," Franklin pleaded. "I can neither make nor agree to propositions of peace without the assistance of my colleagues. . . . Spain has taken four years to consider whether she should treat with us or not. Give her forty, and let us in the meantime mind our own

Benjamin Franklin. The aging, ailing Benjamin Franklin opened peace talks with a British emissary in Paris in the spring of 1782 but found himself frustrated by British offers of reconciliation instead of independence.

business."[4] Jay agreed, but when he reached the peace table in Paris, he balked at French interference in the negotiations and complained to Foreign Affairs Secretary Livingston: America's commissioners, he wrote, "should be left at liberty to pursue the sentiments of their country. . . . I am persuaded . . . that this [French] court chooses to postpone an acknowledgment of our independence by Britain to the conclusion of a general-peace in order to keep us under their direction. . . ."[5]

Although Jay rejected Lafayette's scheme to send another French Army to America, the marquis had little difficulty rekindling fires of territorial ambition at the French foreign ministry. Despite pressures to end the war, Vergennes could not resist one last, powerful strike to recapture New France; Lafayette convinced him that a huge armada that combined the remnants of the French Navy with the powerful Spanish fleet would be enough to overwhelm exhausted British forces in North America. To win Spain's consent, Vergennes pledged to help Spain recapture English-held Gibraltar and Jamaica before sailing to America to dislodge the British from Charleston, New York, and Canada. The Spanish agreed, and the two Bourbon monarchies began assembling the greatest armada and invasion force in history—greater even than the Spanish Armada that had faced Sir Francis Drake in 1588. The armada of 1782 would boast sixty-six ships of the line (the earlier armada had forty) and transports for nearly 25,000 troops (the Spanish Armada carried 19,000).

Undeterred by d'Estaing's previous humiliations in American waters, Vergennes named him commander in chief of the French fleet, and d'Estaing, in turn, appointed Lafayette commander of land forces. In October 1782, Lafayette abandoned peace talks in Paris and went to Brest to assume his new role in what promised to be the decisive conflict for world dominance.

In late October, John Adams returned to Paris from Holland, where he had not only obtained Dutch recognition of American independence but also a $2 million loan from the Dutch government and negotiated a treaty of commerce and friendship. Jay immediately complained to him of Lafayette's role in the peace talks, insisting that the French "are not a moral people" and "don't play fair. The Marquis de La Fayette is clever, but he is a Frenchman."[6] Jay believed that the French were obligated by treaty to further Spanish interests as well as their own and, as such, were "endeavoring to deprive us of the fishery [fishing rights in the waters off Newfoundland and Nova Scotia], the western lands, and the navigation of the Mississippi. They would even bargain with the English to deprive us of them."[7]

Although Adams, like Jay, was personally fond of Lafayette, he, too, resented the marquis' presence in peace talks and wrote to President of Congress James Warren, a longtime political confederate from Boston. "That there have been dangerous [French] designs against our real independence if not against our Union and Confederation, is past doubt in my Mind—and we have cause to fear that such designs may be revived in various shapes." Referring to the de Broglie cabal, Adams asked, "If the Maréchal [de Broglie] had been Commander-in-Chief, as was proposed, what would have been the Situation of your Army & Country? In whose power should we have been?" Then Adams turned to his real concern:

> The Marquis de la Fayette is an amiable nobleman, & has great merit. I enjoy his friendship, & wish continuance of it. But I will conceal nothing from you. . . . The instruction of Congress to their foreign ministers to consult with him was very ill judged. It was lowering themselves & their servants. There is no American minister, who would not have been always ready & willing to consult with him; but to enjoin it & make it a duty was an Humiliation, that would astonish all the World, if it was known. Your ministers will never be respected, never have any influence, while you depress them in this manner. . . . Your ministers should confer directly with the Ministers of other powers; and if they chuse at any time to make use of a third person, they ought to chuse him. . . .
>
> He is connected with a family of great influence in France. He rises fast in the French army. He may be soon in the Ministry. This mongrel character of French Patriot & American Patriot cannot exist long—And if hereafter it should be seriously the politicks of the French Court to break our Union, imagination cannot conceive a more proper instrument for the purpose than the Marquis. . . .
>
> I know the Confederation of our States to be a brittle vessel. I know it will be an object of jealousy to France. Severe strokes will

be aimed at it, & if we are not upon our guard to ward them off, it will be broken.[8]

Lafayette's role in the peace talks became moot, however, when he left to take command of the French invasion army. Faced with a potentially seismic confrontation with the Franco-Spanish armada, British negotiators used Lafayette's departure to press aggressively for a separate peace with the United States. They appealed to the evident Francophobia of Adams and Jay: with Rochambeau's 4,000 troops still in New England, they argued, a successful invasion of New York by Lafayette's 25,000 troops would leave the French Army in control of the entire northeastern coast from New York to Boston. The English insisted that Vergennes was plotting "to divide America" and had even made secret overtures to England for such a division.[9]

Jay and Adams learned that Vergennes had sent his private secretary on a secret mission to London to propose an astonishing peace settlement ceding the Ohio territory and Illinois country to England, giving Canada to France, and giving Spain the entire Louisiana territory with exclusive navigation rights on the Mississippi. As Jay explained, "It was pretended he was gone into the country . . . [but] several precautions had been taken to keep his real destination a secret."[10] The British argument swayed Adams and Jay, who convinced Franklin to violate the treaty with France by negotiating with the British secretly and keep the French uninformed until successful conclusion of a peace agreement.

Infuriated by French perfidy, John Jay wrote to American secretary for foreign affairs Livingston:

> It is not their [the French] interest that such a treaty should be formed between us and Britain as would produce cordiality and mutual confidence. They will therefore endeavor to plant such seeds of jealousy and perpetually keep our eyes fixed on France for security. This consideration must induce them to wish to render Britain formidable in our neighborhood, and to leave us as few resources of wealth and power as possible
>
> It is their interest to keep some point or other in contest between us and Britain to keep us employed in the war, and dependent on them for supplies. . . . [11]

Jay warned Livingston that "if we lean on her [France's] love of liberty, her affection for America, or her disinterested magnanimity, we shall lean on a broken reed, that will sooner or later pierce our hands."[12] Thomas Jefferson agreed, having warned earlier in the year that Vergennes's "devotion to the principles of pure despotism renders him unaffectionate to our governments."[13]

Convinced that the French government was intent on preventing peace and reducing America to an impotent French protectorate, Jay, Adams, and Franklin decided to disobey congressional instructions and, without French participation or knowledge, secretly signed "provisional articles" of peace with England on November 30, 1782. Jay and Adams, especially, wanted to send a signal to France that the American states were independent and would not submit to French interference in their foreign affairs.

The Anglo-American articles of peace gave Americans all they had sought at Lexington seven years earlier—and far more. Britain recognized U.S. independence and ceded a vast territory that included the original thirteen colonies and all the lands stretching westward across the Great Lakes beyond Lake Superior and south along a line through the middle of the Mississippi River to the boundaries with Spanish Louisiana and Spanish Florida. Britain also granted the United States fishing rights off the coast of Newfoundland and Nova Scotia and navigation rights along the entire Mississippi.

> There shall be a firm and perpetual peace between His Britannic Majesty and the said States, and between the subjects of the one and the citizens of the other, wherefore all hostilities, both by sea and land, shall then immediately cease: All prisoners, on both sides shall be set at liberty; and His Britannic Majesty shall, with all convenient speed . . . withdraw all his armies garrisons and fleets from the said United States, and from every port, place and harbour within the same.[14]

In granting the Americans all they sought, England hoped to separate the United States from France and reestablish the rich commercial ties she had enjoyed before the war. As a sign of good faith,

the British evacuated Charleston before the end of the year and reduced the strength of their New York garrisons.

Vergennes was irate when he learned about the agreement—and
Spain was none too pleased. "I am at a loss, Sir," he wrote to
Franklin,

> to explain your conduct and that of your colleagues towards us. You
> have signed the preliminary articles without any communication
> between us, despite your instructions from Congress forbidding any
> action without the participation of the King. . . .
>
> You are wise and sensible, Sir, you know the rules of decorum;
> you have done your duty all your life. Do you think you did so with
> respect to the King? I will not carry these thoughts any farther, but
> will leave them to your own integrity.[15]

Recognizing that British concessions to the Americans "exceed
all that I could have thought possible," Vergennes temporarily abandoned hope for recovering New France, and on January 20, 1783,
France signed preliminary articles of peace with Britain. Spain followed suit immediately.[16] On February 4, Britain, France, and Spain
proclaimed a cessation of hostilities, and France and Spain disbanded
their huge armada. On April 15, Congress ratified the provisional articles of peace—but not without criticizing the commissioners for
having negotiated without consulting the French.[17]

On November 25, the British evacuated New York Island, and as
the last British troops left the docks, George Washington and New
York governor George Clinton rode into town and took the reins of
government. Early the next month, Washington bid farewell to his
officers at Fraunces Tavern in lower Manhattan before riding to An-
napolis, where Congress was in session. On December 23, he resigned his commission as commander in chief before Congress and
took his leave "of all the employments of public life."[18]

The loss of Britain's trade monopoly in the United States devastated the British economy and poisoned the political atmosphere. As
British statesman Edmund Burke lamented, the American Revolution
had cost England "thirteen provinces . . . 100,000 men, and seventy
millions of money" and reduced her "from the most flourishing empire

in the world to one of the most unenviable . . . on the face of the globe." The loss of the thirteen colonies, according to one historian, "permanently extinguished . . . the glory and greatness of Britain."[19]

Nor was the war any less devastating for France, the ostensible victor. Indeed, Princeton professor of politics Edward S. Corwin characterized the costs of French victory as "suicidal."[20] True, France had avenged her humiliation in the Seven Years War and helped humble her ancient enemy Britain; she had captured some of Britain's lucrative American trade and expelled the hated British commissioner from Dunkerque. But the six-year war in America had bankrupted the French treasury without achieving the primary goal of the twenty-year-old Choiseul-Vergennes policy: to recover the French empire in North America.

France spent more than 140 million livres on the war, hoping to recoup that sum and more from American trade. The results were quite the opposite. Americans preferred British goods to French goods, and most American merchants were too used to dealing in a language and a currency they understood. Although the value of French purchases of American goods reached 9 million livres a year, Americans never spent as much as 2 million livres a year on French products. By 1792, when the French Revolution disrupted trade between the two countries, France had accumulated a trade deficit with the United States of nearly 65.5 million livres, which combined with the 140 million spent on the American Revolution to collapse the French economy.

France paid a steep social as well as economic price for her participation in the American Revolution, according to Edmund Burke. Tens of thousands of French soldiers, sailors, and officers returned to France having witnessed individual liberties for the first time and bearing testimony to their benefits. As Burke put it:

> They imbibed a love of freedom nearly incompatible with royalty. It seemed a grand stroke of policy to reduce the power and humble the pride of a great and haughty rival . . . for as it was universally supposed that the loss of America would prove an uncurable, if not a mortal wound to England, so it was equally expected that the power of the Gallic throne would thereby be fixed on such a per-

manent foundation as never again to be shaken by any stroke of fortune.[21]

By fueling the flames of revolution in America, writes Professor Corwin, Vergennes lit "the funeral pyre" of the Bourbon monarchy and sparked 150 years of revolution, world war, and state-sponsored genocide that would extinguish hundreds of millions of lives.[22] Vergennes died in 1787 before he could see the effects of his political handiwork. His policies left the nation bankrupt, unable to feed its people. Even as he lay on his deathbed, politically ambitious rabble-rousers were whipping hungry mobs into a frenzy of rioting, plunder, and slaughter that plunged the nation into a decade of anarchy and genocide.

In the end, Americans were the only clear winners in the War of Independence—although their victory was less than the complete one Washington and other Founding Fathers had envisioned. The United States won political independence from Britain, and with it came commercial independence to trade with the world. English, French, Dutch, and other European ships sailed in and out of American ports, and American vessels traveled the globe, exchanging tobacco and other commodities for a variety of products that enriched American markets. In 1784, the first American ship reached Canton, China, and returned the following year with so profitable a cargo of tea and silks that merchants in Philadelphia, Providence, and Boston outfitted entire fleets designed solely for the lucrative China trade.

But political and commercial independence did not produce political or commercial stability—largely because the "United" States were not united—constitutionally or legally. The Articles of Confederation that linked the states during the war gave them each so much "sovereignty, freedom . . . power, jurisdiction" as to render the central government impotent, with no president or chief executive and a unicameral Congress whose measures were only recommendations, without the force of law. The United States faced anarchy at the end of the Revolution, with most states feuding viciously over boundaries and territorial claims. Eight states had armies; each printed its own currency and imposed duties or embargoes on goods from other

1783

North America after the
American Revolution.

states; some restricted immigration across state lines. With the ink
still drying on the peace treaty with Britain, Pennsylvania's militia
massacred settlers from Connecticut who had moved into the
Wyoming Valley of northwestern Pennsylvania. New York threatened to do the same to New Jersey farmers who dared compete in
New York City markets.

American emissaries abroad found it all but impossible to negotiate trade agreements and treaties: European nations, in turn, found it
too cumbersome to negotiate with each of the thirteen states—and
meaningless to negotiate a treaty with a Congress too impotent to
impose its will on member states. Indeed, so many states refused to
abide by the 1783 peace treaty that England refused to evacuate large
parts of the American frontier. When, in 1786, John Adams demanded that England abandon her military garrisons at Lake Champlain, Oswego, Niagara, Detroit, and other areas, England refused
until each state lived up to treaty obligations for English creditors to
collect prewar debts in America.

British military presence in the North and Northwest and Spanish presence along the Mississippi River and in the Floridas left the United States surrounded by enemies and subject to piecemeal erosion of sovereignty along its borders. Adding to the dangers were Indian tribes, whom Britain and Spain supplied with arms—and liquor—to massacre American settlers on the frontier.

As they had done at the beginning of the Revolution, America's leading citizens—Washington and the others—convened in Philadelphia, put aside regional rivalries, and in the summer of 1787 wrote a document that reunited them in common cause: a constitution to convert an impotent confederation into the world's first federated republic, with a central government empowered to pass binding legislation, raise and maintain an army and navy, tax its people, try and punish citizens, and determine national policy for foreign affairs, defense, and international commerce. For the first time, the United States would be able to send abroad ambassadors with power to represent the entire nation.

Even before the delegates met to deliberate, however, French agents were sowing seeds of dissent to prevent agreement on the Constitution. "The French ambassador," future foreign minister Talleyrand disclosed, "had instructions to block this enterprise. This same ally that had sacrificed so much to separate the American states from England, wanted to keep them disunited and separated from each other. [France] wanted to condemn them to a long and difficult infancy to keep them weak, without the means to govern or defend themselves effectively. The ambassador obeyed his instructions to the best of his ability by opposing passage of the Constitution during the convention [in Philadelphia] and in each state legislature during the subsequent ratification proceedings. Although his efforts failed to block passage, they did help sew seeds of antifederalism that would sap United States strength for generations."[23]

On the very day the First Congress of the United States convened in New York, the first French National Assembly met in Versailles to write a similar document—one that would convert an absolute monarchy into a constitutional monarchy and, presumably, solve French fiscal problems. Although oligarchs of the Cent Familles had come expecting to dominate the assembly, the influence of the American Revolution was too great to resist. The marquis de Lafayette proposed an American-style preamble—a Declaration of the Rights of Man written by Thomas Jefferson, then the American ambassador to France. Jefferson reiterated the principles of John Locke[24] that he had paraphrased in the American Declaration of Independence:

> All men are created free and equal.
> All men are born with certain inalienable rights, including life, liberty, property and the pursuit of happiness. . . .

Americans rejoiced over the document's resemblance to their own Declaration of Independence and the evident contagion of American ideals in Europe—especially in France, the nation that had been instrumental in liberating Americans from monarchic despotism. In France, however, the new constitution had different meanings to different classes of society. To French royalty and most of the nobility it was nothing less than heresy that blasphemed the king's divine right to absolute rule. The French king, after all, was "His Most Christian Majesty"—above "His Most Britannic Majesty of England" or "His Most Catholic Majesty of Spain." God had designated the *French king* His Most Christian Majesty—to rule the Christian world.

To ordinary French people who had lived for centuries under autocratic rule, the new constitution meant freedom from all self-restraint. Never having experienced self-rule, they interpreted liberty as license and stormed through Paris—at first to find food, then to vent their fury at authorities by besieging the hated Bastille prison. Although troops slaughtered the first attackers, the army suddenly broke ranks; soldiers recognized fathers, brothers, neighbors in the mob and turned against their officers, spun their cannons about, and aimed at the prison walls to blast a passage for the mob. On July 14, 1789, rioters seized the prison governor, dragged him to a lamppost, and to the cheers and jeers of thousands hung him by the wrists and disemboweled him.

"Then it is a full-blown riot?" asked the king when told of the violence.

"No, Sire," his aide replied. "It is a full-blown revolution."[25]

In the end, the National Assembly approved the Declaration of the Rights of Man and the king signed it, thus ending thirteen centuries of absolute monarchy in France. But it was too late. Starvation and unemployment had spread too widely; mob frenzy engulfed the nation; and rioters raged through cities, towns, villages, and countryside, looting and burning mansions, châteaux, manors, and any other structure that smacked of aristocratic plenty. No foreign armies would ever wreak as much destruction on French monuments and historic buildings as the French themselves.

American ambassador Thomas Jefferson called the French revolution "an illumination of the human mind . . . which shall assure to them [the French] a good degree of liberty."[26] He shrugged off outrages with his famous pronouncement: "The tree of liberty must be refreshed from time to time with the blood of patriots and tyrants." It was typical of Jefferson to ignore the blood of innocents who died at the hands of those who claimed to be their champions.[27]

The revolution left the royal family prisoners in their own palace and chased the king's brothers and most of the court to the safety of neighboring monarchies. Most of the Cent Familles followed in carriages laden with jewels, money, and family treasures. A few aristocrats remained in France, believing they could manipulate the revolution to their advantage but learned to regret their decisions. Louis Philippe Joseph, duc d'Orléans, the husband of Louis XIV's great-granddaughter, joined the revolutionary leadership and changed his name to Philippe Egalité—Philippe the Equal. After he voted with the revolutionaries to condemn his cousin the king to die on the guillotine, they turned on him and sent him to the same fate.

Within a year, two groups of revolutionaries were vying for control of French government: the radical, occasionally rational Girondins, provincials who focused on national political machinery, and the ultraradical, certifiably insane Jacobins, who controlled city streets and recruited agents across France to organize local revolutionary clubs. By 1792, they had formed more than a thousand Jacobin clubs, with thousands of members infiltrating every area of French life, inciting riots, and seizing control of local government. They honeycombed army and navy ranks and provoked massacres of officers of noble birth. Lafayette and other heroic military commanders fled to escape the butchery and left the armed services a rabble devoid of leadership.

On January 2, 1792, Girondin leader Jacques Pierre Brissot de Warville proclaimed the beginning of the "Era of Liberty," but, with no experience in government administration, he and his cronies proved incapable of restoring the nation's economy and agriculture. Before seizing power, Brissot had been a mediocre journalist and pamphleteer who envisioned himself a prophet. He founded a propaganda sheet that won him national prominence by accusing the king and royal family of treason. Originally a Jacobin, he collided with the equally ambitious madman Maximilien Robespierre, who refused to share power and expelled Brissot from the Jacobin Club of Paris. After dropping the aristocratic "de Warville" from his name, Brissot joined the opposition Girondins—a party of bourgeois merchants from the Gironde region of southwestern France, who welcomed revolution as much as the peasants. They favored a peaceful revolution, however, to replace absolute monarchy with constitutional monarchy. Girondin merchants carried their goods to market along roads that passed across vast royal estates and lands owned by the nobility with ancestral rights to collect exhorbitant tolls and duties that often emptied merchant wagons before they reached market. The Girondins favored a constitution that would guarantee their property rights against such legalized theft.

The practice of exacting tolls and duties also created chronic food shortages—especially during periods of drought. As food supplies in France shrank, hunger haunted the nation and goaded famished families into the streets to riot and loot. Brissot blamed king, nobility, and church; he confiscated their assets, outlawed the church, closed the Sorbonne and other universities, arrested the king and royal family, and shut down the royalist press. He ordered the arrest of more than 3,000 suspected enemies of the revolution, then opened the prison doors to let the mob vent its rage by massacring helpless suspects in their cells.

At the end of September 1792, the National Assembly voted itself out of existence; the National Convention, which replaced it, abolished royalty, declared France a republic like the United States, and voted to try the king for treason. It wrote a new constitution that proclaimed "the nation is sovereign," with citizens deriving rights from government. In effect, it retained the centralized statist government of the monarchy, with a coterie of revolutionary leaders replacing aristocrats in power. In sharp contrast, the American Constitution had dismantled centralized royal government and dispersed governing powers to individual states and communities; it proclaimed "We the People . . ." sovereign, with government deriving its rights from the citizenry. The differences between the French and American constitutions would forever engender bitter political frictions between the two nations.

With no one left in France to blame for starvation and anarchy, Brissot eyed rich crops and fat livestock in neighboring lands and sent hungry French mobs to topple other kings as they had toppled their own. "We will not be satisfied until Europe—all Europe—is aflame," he screamed. "France has been called to lead a gigantic revolution [and] worldwide uprising to liberate the oppressed peoples of the world. All Europe, as far as Moscow, will be Gallicized, communized and Jacobinized."[28]

Brissot revived the centuries-old French policy of self-enrichment from conquest and plunder by converting the nation's collective greed and hunger into a quasi-religious crusade that arrogated the right "to aid all peoples seeking to recover their liberty. . . ."[29] Before year's end, hundreds of thousands of famished French had joined the army and overrun Belgium. In the east, ragtag mobs of undisciplined French "Brissotins" and Jacobins charged like madmen into Prussian lines at Valmy, about forty miles west of Verdun. Unlike their well-fed, uniformed enemies, French armies became a mixture of professional soldiers, ill-clothed irregulars, and untrained peasants and workers—all of them ravenous for food, drink, and plunder. Howling hysterically *"Vive la Nation!"* they leapfrogged over fallen comrades into the steady hail of musket balls and bayonet thrusts. Ignoring death, they materialized from every direction; local peasants with picks charged into the fury from every farmhouse and village door. Rather than risk slaughter for a king and cause not their own, Prussian mercenaries pulled back from the insanity to natural defenses behind the Rhine River; within a month French hordes had overrun the entire Rhineland. As they piled victory upon victory, thousands more hungry, unemployed peasants joined the army to profit from plunder. In the north, the French Army in Belgium prepared to invade Holland. In the south and southeast, French forces swept through Savoy, seizing the capital city of Chambéry and the Mediterranean port of Nice. As they poised to invade Italy from the north, a French fleet sailed toward Naples to conquer southern Italy, the Vatican, and the rest of the Mediterranean world.

To the delight of Brissot and his Girondin government, profits of foreign plunder poured into the French treasury, where it inevitably seeped into their own pockets and made them the new Cent Familles. As they had done in France, French revolutionaries seized assets of royals, aristocrats, and churches in every conquered land, melted gold and silver relics into bullion, and sold lands at auction. "Vanity," chortled Brissot, "is my primary motive; desire for riches is my second."[30]

Far from bankrupting France, as the American Revolutionary War had done, the French wars of revolution resolved the nation's immediate fiscal and social crises. Foreign plunder replenished the French treasury and rebuilt the nation's military and naval strength. The wars also restored domestic peace by sending the French rabble that had razed French towns to burn and pillage foreign towns. The plunder did little to revive French agriculture, however, or ease famine. Drought had decimated southern crops, and peasants who had tilled northern lands had gone to distant battlefields and left fields unsown and barren. Nor were there crops to salvage in conquered territory after armies had finished trampling them. Brissot recognized he would have to look elsewhere.

In his lifelong lust for wealth, Brissot had visited America in 1788 for an investor syndicate headed by exiled Swiss banker Etienne Clavière. Brissot spent months buying shares in land development projects and other speculative ventures. He returned as a self-styled authority on American affairs, and in April 1792, when the Girondins seized the reins of French government, Brissot poured over Foreign Ministry documents relating to American relations. The Choiseul-Vergennes plot against America all but leaped off the pages as a certain way to restore the wealth and glory of France. By absorbing the Americas into the French sphere of influence as Vergennes had sought to do, Brissot would convert the United States into a source of foodstuffs to end famine in France. America would also feed raw materials to French manufacturers for conversion into finished goods for the American market. United States secretary of state Thomas Jefferson had himself proposed "mutual naturalization" of French and American merchants to allow them to buy and sell duty-free in both countries as if they were citizens of each.

Brissot knew Americans were deeply sympathetic to the French Revolution; many echoed Jefferson's call for closer economic and political ties to France. Beyond American boundaries, the French in Louisiana had chafed under Spanish rule for twenty years and had pleaded in vain with Rochambeau to march from Yorktown in 1781 to reunite them to France. South America also sought delivery from Spanish rule. Indeed, the champion of Venezuelan independence, Francisco de Miranda, had fought in the American Revolution and had then come to Paris and joined the Girondins to win their help in fighting for Spanish American independence.

With so many eyes in the New World turned toward France, Brissot believed Americans would welcome an aggressive revolutionary as ambassador to the United States and help him replant the tricolor in North America.

Edmond Genet had languished in St. Petersburg as French chargé d'affaires since 1789, earning little notice for reports from so distant a capital. Although he had inherited the directorship of his father's espionage bureau at Versailles in 1781, he was not up to the task. During two years of secret Anglo-American peace negotiations in Paris, he failed to keep participants under surveillance, and the peace treaty they signed caught him—and, of course, Vergennes and the government—entirely by surprise. Astonished by Genet's oversight, Vergennes looked for a successor but died before he found one, and the next foreign minister closed Genet's bureau as part of a broad government spending cutback. Queen Marie-Antoinette's intervention won Genet his post in St. Petersburg.

Raised and groomed for the diplomatic corps, Genet was above all a civil servant, loyal always to the state, no matter the government—royal, republican, or revolutionary. With the advent of republican government, he proposed reforms to appoint diplomats by merit, instead of allowing rich aristocrats to purchase appointments. When French revolutionary armies went to war, Genet sent his gold medal from the king of Sweden to Brissot to sell and use the proceeds to arm volunteers. And when the National Assembly abolished the title Monsieur in favor of *Citoyen*—"Citizen" instead of "Mister"—he responded accordingly and incurred the wrath of Catherine the Great when he called her "Citizenness." Like most monarchs, she despised the French Revolution and promptly ordered Genet expelled from Russia as a *demagogue enragé*.[31]

The Girondins welcomed him back to Paris as the only French diplomat "who had dared act like a free man."[32] They promoted him to adjutant general in the army and agreed that his loyalty to revolutionary principles and command of English made him the logical candidate as envoy to the United States.

As Brissot reformulated the French plot against America, he conceived the idea of sending the king and royal family—then in prison facing death—into exile in America as a gesture of friendship. Thomas Paine had pleaded that "France has today but one friend: the American Republic. Do not give the United States the sorrow . . . of witnessing the death upon the scaffold of a man who has aided my American brethren in breaking the fetters of English despotism."[33] Brissot knew that Americans revered Louis XVI for his support in the American Revolution and would certainly not look favorably on his death. As the new ambassador to America, Genet could restore good relations with America by escorting the royal family there and announcing that France was granting duty-free status to all American goods.

On January 21, 1793, the French Convention ignored Paine and sent the king to the guillotine for "conspiring with foreigners . . . to deprive the nation of its liberty."[34] Ten days later, France declared war on England. The execution stunned Europe and ruptured French alliances based on family ties. The French king was cousin to Spanish king Charles IV, and the imprisoned French queen, Marie-Antoinette, was the sister of Austrian emperor Leopold II. Both Spain and Austria declared war against France. Prussia and four other European monarchies also joined the struggle to repel French incursions and prevent

Execution of King Louis XVI. The executioner displays the head of King Louis XVI on the place de la Révolution (now place de la Concorde) on January 21, 1793. The beheading of the king outraged many Americans, who held the king in highest esteem for having supported the American Revolution with men, money, and arms.

the spread of revolution. While Europe's armies counterattacked, Britain's powerful fleet blockaded French ports and cut the flow of military and food supplies and foodstuffs from the French West Indies and the United States.

Besieged on all sides and facing famine from a yearlong drought, the French called on their American ally to attack British and Spanish colonies in North America, force Britain to fight on a second front, and relax its blockade of France. The strategy was offensive as well as defensive. French military and naval forces in the French West Indies planned to sail to the American mainland, link up with American troops, and invade British Canada and Spanish-held Florida and Louisiana. Ultimately, Franco-American forces would overrun the entire hemisphere and seize the Spanish gold and silver mines of Mexico and Peru.

In the West, the Spanish responded by shutting the Mississippi

River to all navigation by Americans. The Spanish had long tolerated but never officially sanctioned its use by American frontier farmers and trappers, who had no other viable route to carry furs and produce to market besides the all-but-impossible trek across the Appalachian Mountains. Steeped in the belief that all men had a natural right to access waterways, regardless of who owned the lands along its banks, they were ready to war against Spain to ensure that right, and they turned to Revolutionary War hero George Rogers Clark to organize a militia. A hero to westerners, Clark had captured St. Louis and the Illinois country from the British during the Revolutionary War, but had subsequently fallen on hard times and, deeply in debt, had turned to drink. Desperate to right himself and return to glory, he wrote to the French government in the autumn of 1792 for financial and military support in seizing the Mississippi River valley and New Orleans from the Spanish. Brissot determined to use Clark's militia to help recover Louisiana for France and prepared to ask the United States government for support in attacking Spain in the Americas while the French battled Spain in Europe. Under the Franco-American Treaty of 1778, France had sent troops, ships, and money to help Americans win independence from Britain. Now she called for repayment in kind. "France," the French assured Americans, "is not conducting a war against nations, but a defense of peoples against unjust aggression by kings."[35]

News of the king's execution, however, horrified many Americans and tempered their enthusiasm for the French Revolution. "Ninety-nine of our citizens out of a hundred have dropped a tear to his memory," wrote Benjamin Rush, the prominent Philadelphia physician and signer of the Declaration of Independence.[36] A clergyman friend of Jefferson agreed: "The melancholy news of the beheading . . . is regretted most sincerely by all thinking people. The French lose much of their influence upon the hearts of Americans by this event."[37]

Coming as it did after months of barbarity and bloodshed, the execution convinced President Washington that the French Revolution had little in common with America's uprising against the English. With France at war with both Spain and England, the president and his cabinet met to reassess American foreign policy and determine whether America's treaty with France required engaging in a suicidal war with England. The war was already devastating the American economy. England's blockade of French ports had not only interrupted Franco-American trade, the British had seized three hundred American ships and impressed hundreds of American seamen. Treasury Secretary Alexander Hamilton argued that rather than war with Britain, the United States should seek a trade agreement that would end the depredations. A lawyer by profession, Hamilton pointed out that the Franco-American treaty was a defensive alliance, whose military obligations applied only when a third nation attacked one of the signatories: "France being on the offensive in the present war, and our alliance with her being defensive only, it follows that the . . . condition of our guarantee cannot take place; and that the United States are to refuse a performance of that guarantee if demanded." [38]

Of all members of his cabinet, Washington respected Hamilton the most. Hamilton had served as one of his closest aides during the Revolution and had displayed exceptional heroism leading a Patriot battalion that breached British defenses at Yorktown. In addition to his strict reading of treaty terms, Hamilton offered Washington another reason for refusing to aid France: the United States had signed the treaty with Louis XVI, not the Girondins who had killed the king and seized power illegally. Hamilton insisted that under the laws of nations, the French king *was* the state—*l'état c'est moi*—and the French royal family in exile had already proclaimed Louis's son the new king of France. Hamilton urged Washington to ignore the treaty until the new king returned to the throne and not to receive the new ambassador from France until then.

Secretary of State Jefferson, on the other hand, argued that nations, not governments, make treaties, and they remain bound by treaty obligations regardless of the government in power. He insisted that American failure to observe Franco-American treaties would undermine the nation's honor and "gratify the combination of kings with the spectacle of the two only republics on earth destroying each other." [39] He charged Hamilton with siding with "the confederacy of princes against human liberty . . . under pretense of avoiding war. [40]

"Nothing," Jefferson declared, "should be spared, on our part to

Secretary of the Treasury
Alexander Hamilton.
A hero at Yorktown, he
was President George
Washington's most trusted
cabinet member, having
served as his personal aide
throughout the
Revolutionary War.

attach this country [France] to us. It is the only one on which we can
rely for support, under any event." Jefferson called France America's
"true mother country . . . since she has assured to them their liberty
and independence"[41] Embraced by French revolutionaries, the Virginian had been an enthusiastic witness to the storming of Bastille
prison on July 14, 1789, when Parisians dragged the prison governor
to a lamppost for hanging and evisceration.

"The liberty of the whole earth," Jefferson exulted, "depends on
the success of the French Revolution." He defended the most savage
excesses: "I would have seen half the earth devastated rather than it
[the French Revolution] should have failed."[42] Jefferson urged the
president to accept the new French ambassador's credentials, insisting that acceptance did not imply approval of his government's policies. An ambassador, said Jefferson, serves only as a conduit for
communication between the two governments, and he urged a warm
welcome for Genet.

In the absence of constitutional guidance, the president decided on a middle course that incorporated what he deemed the best elements of the Hamilton and Jefferson arguments. In doing so, Washington set a precedent that every administration would follow to this day. He agreed that treaties bound nations together regardless of changes in government, and he left the 1778 treaties with France in place. But he agreed with Hamilton that France had engaged in an offensive, not defensive, war and that the treaties did not apply to the current conflict. He also agreed with Hamilton in the wisdom of seeking rapprochement with England. With the nation all but defenseless—no navy and a tiny army pinned down fighting Indians in the West—the president could not risk war. In an instant, the powerful British Navy could blockade American ports and shut coastal trade, while the British military in Canada could combine with Spanish forces in Florida and Louisiana to sweep across the nation and divide it up between them. He appointed Chief Justice John Jay to go to England to negotiate.

To avoid entangling the nation in war, Washington wanted to issue a proclamation of United States neutrality, with a warning to Americans that "to involve ourselves in the contests of European nations . . . [is] unwise in the extreme" and would put the nation's fragile economy and very existence at risk.[43]

Washington's suggestion, however, did nothing but provoke another heated debate among his cabinet members, who were trying to work out a new form of government in a new nation without precedent in world history. They had but the Constitution as their guide. Magnificent in principle, it was nonetheless vague and failed to resolve a vast range of practical questions facing men who had to govern. The word *neutrality* did not appear in the Constitution. Jefferson argued that the Constitution clearly assigned Congress the power to declare war and that since "a declaration of neutrality [was] a declaration that there should be no war," it fell within the purview of congressional, not presidential, powers. With Congress in recess and the world's two most powerful nations poised for war with the United States, the president insisted on acting to preserve peace.

In the end, he and his cabinet worked out a compromise proclamation that omitted the word *neutrality* while forbidding Americans "to take part in any hostilities on the seas" or carrying "any of those articles deemed contraband by the modern usage of nations." It also enjoined them "from all acts and proceedings inconsistent with the duties of a friendly nation toward those at war. . . ."[44]

As Washington and his cabinet resolved the neutrality issue, however, the new French ambassador, Edmond Genet, was landing in Charleston, South Carolina, to begin his mission as the French Republic's first minister plenipotentiary to the United States. He had left France in February 1793 on the thirtieth anniversary—to the day—of the treaty with England that had stripped France of her North American territories, and he was determined to force America to join France at war to recover those territories. He carried two sets of instructions. His official instructions were to seek only passive American cooperation under the Franco-American Treaties of 1778 for mutual defense. The treaty gave each nation the right to bring captured ships and cargoes into the other's ports for refitting and auction. Genet was also to renegotiate United States war debts to allow him to purchase badly needed American foodstuffs to ship back to France.

His secret instructions, however, ordered him to raise an army in the United States to invade and reconquer Louisiana, Florida, and Canada and to launch a fleet of privateers to prey on British shipping.[45] If President Washington's government refused to cooperate, he was to exploit pro-French ferment to foment revolution, topple the government, and convert the United States into a French puppet state.

"Americans," Genet's instructions assured him, "are like children. They are especially childish in politics, indeed very much like spoiled children—always rather difficult to manage. . . . The man who succeeds in managing them will be able to exercise that mastery for a long time." His instructions stated that, in contrast to President Washington, Congress had long been "disposed to embrace a plan of conquest" to wrest Florida and Canada from Spanish and British control. "Citizen Genet must assure them that the [French] Republic will send a formidable fleet to their shores, and land forces that will absorb the [American] army into their own. Your mission is, therefore, to assist in every way the extension of the Kingdom of Liberty [France] . . . the emancipation of Spanish America . . . the deliverance of our ancient

brothers of Louisiana from the tyrannical yoke of Spain . . . the addition of the beautiful star of Canada to the American constellation . . .
and prepare the uprising of the Spanish colonies [in South Amer-
ica]." [46]

In addition to territorial conquest, he was to offer Congress a new
treaty "in which the two nations should amalgamate their commercial and political interests and establish an intimate concert, which
would promote the extension of the Empire of liberty . . . [and] mutual naturalization of French and American citizens." His instructions assured him he would find a steadfast ally in Secretary of State
Thomas Jefferson, who had first suggested mutual naturalization
when he was American ambassador to France in 1785. The French
believed he would welcome union of the United States and France. [47]

7

The Appetite of Despotism

WHILE MASS BUTCHERY in France dampened the fervor of some Americans for the French Revolution, it excited bloodlust in others. Ironically, thousands who had refused to enlist—or had deserted—during the American Revolution rioted for the right to fight for France against England, Spain, and other European monarchies. Even clergymen joined the chorus, citing the prophet Daniel in Sunday lessons and sermons:

> Blessed be the name of God forever and ever;
> For wisdom and might are his and he changeth the times and seasons.
> He removeth Kings.[1]

Pro-French newspapers blamed the French nobility themselves for their plight beneath guillotine blades. The French Revolution, wrote one editorialist, was "a lesson to oppressors" that served the cause of all mankind.[2] Boston celebrated the bloodshed with an enormous "Civic Feast" that shut down the city for two parades that converged on a park where the public gorged on barbecued ox. Two balloons flew above Faneuil Hall bearing the words LIBERTY and EQUALITY while bands blared the terrifyingly bloody hymns of the French Revolution that celebrated mass slaughter of aristocrats on the gallows:[3]

Oui, ça ira, ça ira, ça ira;
Les aristos à la lanterne;
Oui, ça ira, ça ira, ça ira;
Les aristocrats on les pendra.[4]

After ragtag mobs of French revolutionaries defeated the vaunted Prussian Army at Valmy, pro-French newspapers in America likened the victory to Lexington. "I believe from my soul," John Adams scoffed, "there have been more cannons fired here in the celebration of French victories than the French fired in achieving them. I think I have counted twenty-two grand civic festivals, fifty-one of an inferior order, and one hundred ninety-three public dinners."[5]

News of the French king's execution added to the joy of the Francophile press, spawning humorous headlines such as "Louis Capet Has Lost His Caput" in Philadelphia's *National Gazette*.[6] Another Philadelphia newspaper advocated "permanent placement of a guillotine in the State House Yard."[7]

While John Adams and other Francophobes expressed horror at the "bloody French mobs," Jeffersonian Republicans snapped back, "The Sacred Cause of Liberty Is at Stake" in the French Revolution.[8] Francophile apologists hailed the outlawing of the Catholic Church in France and conversion of the French "from idolatry and the Popish priests who have been always striving to keep the people in ignorance."[9] Later, the *New-York Journal* would cheer the Pope's capture by French troops as the overthrow of the "Anti-Christ."[10] And across the nation, Francophilic hysteria engulfed daily life. Americans called each other "Citizen" and "Citess" (for women) and shot angry stares and even threats at those who failed to use them. Monarchist forms of address such as "Mister," "Sir," or "Madam" were "an offense to republican ears." The title "Reverend" was "not only anti-republican but blasphemous."[11] The editor of the *Boston Gazette* instructed readers that "every friend to the Rights of Man in America will constantly feel an *attachment* for their French *brethren* and not suffer the *partial* interests of a few Aristocrats (or rather Tories, whose souls are absorb'd in the funds) to influence our conduct with respect to them. Let it be remembered that . . . [France] is contending the cause both of EUROPE and AMERICA, and GOD grant [her] success."[12]

When, therefore, Genet landed in Charleston, South Carolina, as the French Republic's first ambassador to the United States, bold newspaper headlines reflected the thunderous welcome of pier-side crowds. Charleston was ready to march to war under the French tricolor. Instead of sailing on a conventional ship to Philadelphia to present his credentials to the chief of state—the normal course for arriving diplomats—Genet scoffed at diplomatic protocol and commandeered a warship to Charleston, South Carolina, where, his instructions asserted, "we are pretty well assured of their good disposition." In fact, Francophilia and Anglophobia were raging in the South—along with rage against the Washington administration, which had won congressional passage of a bill for the federal government to assume Revolutionary War debts of the states. With federal assumption came a new federal tax to spread war costs equitably across the nation by forcing southern states that had spent little on the war to absorb some debts of northern states that had spent more. The tax left some Carolinians as angry at the federal government as they had been against England when the Stamp Act went into effect twenty years earlier. Adding to anger over federal taxes was the federal government's refusal to protect frontier settlements against Spanish and Indian attacks along the Florida and Louisiana borders. Many leading citizens, including South Carolina governor William Moultrie, had staked claims to large tracts that Indian attacks rendered worthless. When France and Spain went to war, they prayed France would invade Florida and expel the Spanish.

Charleston, therefore, not only embraced Genet's arrival, Governor Moultrie gave Genet all the assistance within his power. Americans, Moultrie declared, owed France at least as much help as the French had given during the American War of Independence. "The cause of France is our own," he told a local newspaper. "Treaties solemnly made . . . ought to be inviolably adhered to." [13]

Waving the French banner of worldwide revolution for the rights of man, Genet replied that survival of liberty in America depended on French victory in Europe—that if Britain crushed the French Revolution, she would crush the United States. Aware that Washington had sent Chief Justice John Jay to negotiate a rapprochement

with Britain, Genet assailed the president and his Federalist supporters as monarchists seeking to restore ties to England.

"In the United States," Genet cried out, "men still exist who can
say, 'Here a ferocious Englishman slaughtered my father; there my
wife tore her bleeding daughter from the hands of an unbridled Englishman,' [and] those same men can say, 'Here a brave Frenchman
died fighting for American liberty; here French naval and military
power humbled the might of Britain."[14]

He said the United States owed the French "fraternal assistance"
under the Franco-American Treaties of 1778, which bound America
to give French privateers free entry into American ports and exclude
those of French enemies. To strengthen ties between the United
States and France, he proposed "a true family compact" between the
two nations—"a national pact in which the two peoples will amalgamate their commercial and political interest and establish an intimate concert, to promote the extension of the Empire of liberty [and]
guarantee the sovereignty of all peoples."[15]

The crowd roared its approval, and after the French among them
erupted into choruses of "La Marseillaise," Charlestonians adopted
Genet's cause as their own. Night after night, Charleston's leading
citizens embraced him at banquets, public receptions, and concerts.
Governor Moultrie, a hero of the Revolutionary War, wined and
dined him at his mansion. General Charles Cotesworth Pinckney,
another war hero, whom the British had captured, and John Rutledge, the wartime governor who signed the Declaration of Independence and Constitution, welcomed him to endless entertainments
and sponsored committees that turned the city into a cauldron of
sedition.

With support from Charleston's wealthiest, most powerful citizens, Genet spent ten days implementing his scheme for French conquest, spinning webs of intrigue while attending a succession of
processions and banquets. Moultrie helped him commission four
privateers, the *Republican, Anti-George, Sans-Culotte*,[16] and—of
course—*Citizen Genet*. The promise of plunder lured hundreds of
American volunteer seamen, despite the risk of death if captured by
the British. Moultrie "had the forts . . . put in a state of defense,"[17]
and the four privateers set out to sea with Genet's own frigate, *l'Em-*

buscade, to attack British shipping off the American coast. In the ensuing days, they captured scores of British vessels, which they brought into ports up and down the American coast for French consuls to sell or refit with cannons to expand Genet's fleet of privateers. To Charleston's delight, Genet was doing what Washington had refused to do—sending American ships to war against Britain.

Building on a firm base in Charleston, Genet began raising an army—to drag America into the French war and help restore French sovereignty over New France. "I am arming Canadians to throw off the yoke of England," he wrote to the French foreign minister. "I am arming the Kentuckians, and I am preparing an expedition by sea to support the descent on New Orleans." [18]

With 250 blank military and naval commissions for qualified officers to lead the assaults, Genet and French consul Michel Ange Mangourit recruited hundreds of French and American volunteers in Charleston. The French were to go to Canada to provoke anti-British uprisings by French Canadians in Quebec and Montreal. For the campaigns on the southern and western frontiers, Genet promised Indian fighter Elijah Clarke $10,000 and a commission as a French major general to lead American militiamen into Spanish Florida. He ordered Mangourit, a fervent Jacobin, to recruit two divisions of Carolinians and Georgians—2,500 men each—to serve under Clarke. After more than a decade of savage Indian and Spanish raids, southern frontiersmen went "recruiting-mad for the French service." [19] He also held a French major general's commission for George Rogers Clark to lead the Mississippi valley and New Orleans campaign against the Spanish. He sent French agents to New Orleans to incite insurrection by local French Creoles who had chafed under Spanish rule since France ceded the area to Spain in 1763. They had appealed repeatedly for French government help. [20]

By April 18, Genet's plans were complete. "I have prepared the revolution of New Orleans and Canada," he wrote to the French foreign minister in Paris. "I have destroyed the maritime commerce of the English in these waters . . . I have provisioned our islands and our fleets." [21] He needed only to rally the American people, he wrote, to force the Washington administration to support him with additional troops, weapons, and funds.

Edmond Charles Genet. The French Republic's first minister plenipotentiary to the United States, Genet arrived in the spring of 1793, fully intending to export the French Revolution to North America and reattach Canada and Louisiana to France.

With his frigates and privateers marauding British ships along the coast, Genet left Charleston for Philadelphia in a coach and four. Moultrie sent messengers ahead "to announce me to the people" along the route and personally escorted him to Camden, South Carolina, where the heroic Baron de Kalb had fallen in the American Revolution. Genet's own agents preceded him from town to town to announce his coming and assured tumultuous welcomes with barrels of free rum. Church bells tolled his approach, cannons boomed, French flags flapped in the wind, and thirsty crowds slathered and splashed in free-flowing rum, roaring "hip-hip-hoorahs" for France and growling at neutrality and anything else they could think of to damn. In most communities, town fathers took up (and often pocketed) collections to buy food for France. His journey grew into what he called "a succession of civic festivals." In almost every town, he found himself "clasped in the arms of a multitude that rushed out to meet me" to express "the fraternal sentiments of the American people for the French people."[22]

Wherever possible, he fed French agents enough funds to orga-nize "Democratic Societies" to inflame passions for war with Britain and promote Franco-American ties. Revolutionary France had orga-nized similar groups—Jacobin clubs—as an inexpensive system of foreign conquest—a system that Nazis and Communists would, by their own admission, copy in the twentieth century. Instead of drain-ing the national treasury for armies to battle for every inch of foreign territory, a handful of agents organized the disaffected to rebel, over-throw their own governments, and, after raising the banner of in-ternational brotherhood, welcome French occupying authorities to convert their nations into French puppet states. Before Genet left Charleston, the Democratic Club he organized there enrolled its members in the original Jacobin Club in Paris.

By the time Genet reached Richmond, Virginia, his activities had plunged the American capital into crisis, creating bitter divi-sions in the cabinet and Congress. Washington was furious, fearing that Genet's activities would provoke Britain into declaring war on the United States. Jefferson tried to calm the president, contending that Genet's military schemes would give the United States sover-eignty over Florida, while a French flag over Louisiana would ensure American navigation rights to the Mississippi—rights that the Span-ish had steadfastly refused to grant. Treasury Secretary Alexander Hamilton supported Washington.

The press added to the acrimony. The Jeffersonian *New-York Journal* claimed the nation's honor depended on Washington's adher-ence to the treaty with France. It called for an immediate declaration of war against America's former oppressor, Britain. The Hamiltonian press thundered its reply: "The friendship of France, instead of being a blessing, is to be dreaded by the United States as the most danger-ous mischief. Her *enmity* alone can save us from ruin . . . the French government professes to be pursuing *liberty* while it is extending its territories."[23]

On April 22, President Washington responded to Genet's activi-ties by signing the "Neutrality Proclamation," forbidding foreigners to outfit privateers on American territory. Americans were quick to take sides. Freed from British ties for only a decade, most remained bitterly divided in their allegiances. Some retained deep emotional and familial connections to the former motherland; others harbored smoldering hatreds that flared up in riotous street demonstrations. Apart from Americans, more than 50,000 Irish immigrants needed not so much as a thimble of rum to spill out of taverns to rail against British persecution in Ireland—or assault passersby whose clothes were a cut too English. Adding to the anti-British fervor were 30,000 Frenchmen—a mix of former officers and soldiers from the American Revolution and refugees from Acadia, Canada, whom the British had brutally ripped from their homes and shipped penniless to alien shores.

Newspapers did everything to incite both sides—and sell newspapers by doing so. Although some praised the wisdom of the president's proclamation, most called for war on one side or the other. Pro-British newspapers condemned the savagery, anarchy, and godlessness of French revolutionaries and warned Americans against propaganda that France was fighting for liberty: "The French," wrote New York editor Noah Webster, "are contending for plunder and empire."[24] But pro-French newspapers displayed equal wrath against the British for refusing to evacuate troops from America's western frontier in accordance with the peace treaty of 1783. Editorialists accused the British of planning to reclaim their former American colonies.

Genet's fleet of privateers, however, rendered the debate over neutrality all but moot, sailing, as they did, in and out of American harbors with impunity. As if to taunt the American president and expose his impotence, l'Embuscade sailed into Philadelphia on May 2 with several British merchant vessels in tow—one of them captured in American territorial waters in Delaware Bay. British ambassador George Hammond was irate and threatened war with the United States for violating its neutrality pledges. Attorney General Edmund Randolph agreed that the seizure was illegal, and on Washington's orders, Secretary of State Jefferson demanded that the French return the English vessel and its crew and cargo to the owners. Two days later, the French complied.

"It has been an extremely fortunate circumstance," Hammond wrote to British foreign secretary Lord Grenville, "that almost immediately after the appearance of this declaration of neutrality, events should have arisen that brought the sincerity of it to a practical test."[25]

Genet approached Philadelphia in mid-May convinced that "the ardent and sublime love of the good country people . . . for the principles of France" had spawned "a very distinct party" in opposition to the president and neutrality. "His political enemies are especially numerous in the rural districts." [26]

Although a procession of five hundred carriages of ardent Francophiles waited to escort his coach from Chester into Philadelphia, Genet wanted to display his populist colors by abandoning his aristocratic carriage and riding a public coach into the capital unnoticed along a different road. When he finally reached Philadelphia on May 16,[27] *l'Embuscade* was waiting in the harbor to fire its forty-four guns and set the bells of Philadelphia churches pealing. Thousands rushed into the streets to cheer and march—and discard all pretenses of neutrality or loyalty to the president. "The bosoms of many hundreds of freemen beat high with affectionate transport," Genet exulted, "their souls caught in the celestial fire of struggling liberty." [28]

An estimated 5,000 welcomers rallied outside his hotel window that evening and "sent their sentiments of attachment" to France echoing across the city. One hundred of Philadelphia's leading citizens feted Genet at a lavish banquet. Pennsylvania governor Thomas Mifflin, the former merchant who had profited from troop deprivations at Valley Forge, began the many toasts: "The Republics of France and America," Mifflin called out and raised his glass to heaven. "May they be forever united in the cause of liberty." [29] As the flags of France and the United States fluttered atop the hotel, guests intoned fifteen more toasts, the last culminating with choruses of cheers as Genet donned the cockaded red liberty cap of the French Revolution and led the audience in singing "God Save the Rights of Man" (to the melody of "God Save the King") and "La Marseillaise."

Demonstrations raged through the night and grew even more tumultuous the next day—and the next and the next. John Adams shuddered when he recalled "the terrorism excited by Genet in 1793, when 10,000 people in the streets of Philadelphia, day after day, threatened to drag Washington out of his house and effect a revolution in the government or compel it to declare war in favor of the French Revolution and against England." The rioting grew to such violent levels that Adams ordered "chests of arms from the war office" to protect his house.[30]

Genet pounced like the devil himself to stir further disorder—as his instructions had urged:

> In order to make your representations more effective, [you are] to direct opinion by means of anonymous publications. The Boston and Baltimore gazettes will be the best ones to use . . . to turn aside suspicion of authorship from you; but the more you contrive to influence public opinion, the more . . . [it] must be kept secret so as not to arouse alarm. . . . Your mission requires of you a great deal of astute activity, but to be effective it must be secret.[31]

Accordingly, Genet spewed anti-British venom in pseudonymously signed articles and letters to the press in major cities and inevitably closed with assurances that France "repels every idea of aggrandizement" and wants only "to assist" oppressed people in ridding their lands of despots. Newspapers across the nation reprinted his articles.[32]

"Minds were electrified," Genet chortled. "All the gazettes of the continent were filled with articles, each stronger than the others in favor of our cause. . . ." One gazette, he said, printed a cartoon depicting George Washington's head impelled into a waiting basket by the stroke of the guillotine blade.[33]

Noah Webster's *New York Spectator* countered Genet's propaganda with stern warnings that "the French government professes to be pursuing liberty while it is extending its territories . . . it pretends great friendship for nations which it intends to conquer. In the face of formal declarations . . . the French government has annexed the little, helpless republic of Geneva. Holland is enslaved . . . its money gone, its trade ruined. Venice has been annihilated—divided and sold! So much for the promised respect which France was to pay to the independence of other nations."[34]

Genet's propaganda, however, gained a tight hold on public sentiment in Philadelphia, where his network of agents filled the air with anti-British rhetoric—in taverns, on street corners—stirring hatred everywhere, encouraging depredations against suspected Tories and their properties. Under his name, the club sent letters to French agents across the United States and formed a vast, intricate web of affiliated groups through which Genet could influence popular thinking and government policy. A hallmark of club activity was condemnation of Washington's neutrality proclamation. In Philadelphia, Charleston, New York, and elsewhere, propaganda mills promoted French interests and stirred discontent with American government policies. A word from Genet flooded the press with inflammatory articles he wrote under pseudonyms praising France, denouncing England, or assailing Washington and neutrality. A snap of his fingers sent orators to street corners to shout for "all good republican citizens to provide themselves as speedily as possible with such implements of war as may be necessary for their defence."[35]

Across the nation, Genet's agents called for overthrow of Washington's government to save democracy: "He who is an enemy of the French Revolution," they harangued the crowds, "ought not to be intrusted [sic] with the guidance of any part of the machine of government." A club in Portland, Maine, called "the cause of France . . . our own," while Virginia club members cried out, "Let us unite with France and stand or fall together."[36] In Philadelphia, leading "Republican Americans" flocked to Genet's banner.

With Washington helpless to control the terrorism, Genet sensed the time was right to confront the American president with his credentials as French ambassador—and an ultimatum to unite with France in war with Britain. Genet believed he would enter the presidential mansion not just as French envoy but as de facto leader of a powerful continet-wide military and naval force: his privateers were decimating British offshore shipping; the French fleet was ready to sail from the West Indies to attack Nova Scotia; armed bands stood poised about the country to invade Canada, Florida, and the Louisiana Territory. Genet believed Washington would have no choice but to sanction American participation in the war and place his nation's military under the French flag—or step down as president in favor of Jefferson.

Or . . . perhaps Genet himself.

By then, Genet's arrogance and ambitions knew no bounds, entwined as they were with restoration of French glory and encouraged by roadside crowds of fanatic Francophiles. "All the old spirit of 1776 is rekindling," Jefferson wrote to his nephew. "A French frigate took a British prize off the capes of Delaware the other day and sent her up here. Upon her coming into sight, thousands and thousands of the yeomanry of the city crowded & covered the wharves. Never before was such a crowd seen here and when the British colors were seen reversed & the French flag flying above, they burst into peals of exultation."[37]

Anglophiles tried dismissing the impact of Genet's arrival, insisting that "not a tenth part of the city" had been present at the demonstrations for Genet. "A crowd will always draw a crowd, whatever the purpose," scoffed Treasury Secretary Hamilton, who called comparisons between the French and American revolutions absurd. "Would to heaven we could discern in the mirror of French affairs the same humanity . . . the same order, the same dignity, the same solemnity which distinguished the [American] cause. . . . When I contemplate the horrid . . . massacres . . . when I perceive passion, tumult and violence usurping reason and cool deliberation. . . . I acknowledge that I am glad to believe their is no real resemblance between what was the cause of America and what is the cause of France."[38]

A few days after his arrival in Philadelphia, Genet met with Jefferson and seduced the secretary of state with assurances of French love and respect for the United States. He told Jefferson he had no intention of luring America into a war she could not afford and said he hoped Americans would "cherish your own peace and prosperity. . . . Our republic, founded like yours . . . on equality, ought to be your true ally . . . we ought in some sort to form one people."[39] Genet did not even mention American obligations under the treaties of 1778 and asked only for advance payment of United States Revolutionary War debts to France. He pledged to spend the monies in the United States on foodstuffs to combat starvation in France, and he proposed that France and the United States draw up a new "family compact." He tried enlisting Jefferson in the local Philadelphia Democratic Club by promising the secretary of state its support for his elevation to the presidency. Jefferson declined joining an organization critical of the government he served, but Genet's generosity moved the secretary of state to pen these words—famous for their naïveté—to his

Thomas Jefferson. An ardent supporter of the French Revolution, the secretary of state attempted to establish intimate commercial, military, and political ties between the United States and France.

friend Virginia congressman James Madison: "He [Genet] offers everything & asks nothing." Declaring Genet a friend of the nation, he assured Madison, "It is impossible for anything to be more affectionate, more magnanimous, than the purport of his mission."[40]

Rejoicing with visions of establishing a firm, long-lasting alliance—and brotherhood—with France, Jefferson escorted Genet to President Washington's house to present his credentials. The president reacted with unmistakable iciness. Although Genet bowed obsequiously, he harbored nothing but scorn for the American hero, whom he described as "almost criminal . . . [with] an aristocratic or monarchical tendency." With public adulation affecting his perception, he was convinced that "a very distinct party has risen against Washington."[41]

Genet took advantage of Philadelphia's pro-French ardor by converting eight more American ships into French privateers. The promise of plunder from English and Spanish ships brought throngs of rowdy American seamen flocking to dockside to sail under the

French flag. After Britain threatened to declare war on the United States over the French attacks, Washington sought to end Genet's activities with a set of "Rules Governing Belligerents," which prohibited foreign nations from arming privateers and recruiting American volunteers in United States territory. The president instructed Jefferson to notify Genet that his grants of military commissions infringed on United States sovereignty and that he was to remove his ships from American waters.

By then, however, the secretary of state was so deeply involved with Genet, he feared the Frenchman might reveal their connection. According to Genet, the secretary of State had already "initiated" him in "the foibles and secrets of your Cabinet [and] political divisions of your country." Jefferson even told Genet he believed the president "was controlled by the English and the aristocrats" and that he, Jefferson, was "the only one in the Cabinet who still took an interest in France."[42]

Torn between loyalty to France and his obligation to serve the president, Jefferson was in an untenable position that approached disloyalty to the nation. He offered his resignation, but the president insisted that he remain in the cabinet, and Jefferson reluctantly transmitted the presidential order for Genet to remove his privateers from United States waters and end sales of booty in American ports. Jefferson explained that President Washington was exerting "the *right* of every nation to prohibit acts of sovereignty from being exercised by any other nation within its limits . . . [and] that the granting of military commissions within the United States by any other authority than their own is an infringement of their sovereignty."[43]

Genet exploded with rage, charging President Washington with supporting "the king of England and other kings, his accomplices, to destroy . . . French republicans and liberty. . . . No one," he shouted, "has the right to shackle our operations. . . . The French republicans, sir, know the duties which nations owe to one another. They know how to distinguish their enemies and their friends."[44]

Genet's outburst stunned Jefferson. "He took up the subject in a very high tone and went into an immense field of declamation and complaint," Jefferson noted later. "I found it necessary to let him go on, and in fact could not do otherwise; for the few efforts which

I made to take some part in the conversation were quite in-effectual."[45]

Genet went on to mock the president's orders, proclaiming that his ships would continue to "seize every occasion" to attack British shipping. By then, Genet and his consuls had outfitted almost a hundred privateers, which, in the absence of an American navy, sailed in and out of American ports at will in open violation of American law. They had captured more than eighty British mer-chant ships—many in American territorial waters. Almost every day saw French consuls selling captured ships and cargoes at pier side while American customs officials looked on helplessly. In each port, Genet ordered Jacobin clubs to offer free rum on the quays to ensure riotous welcomes for every privateer. To the cheers of thousands, one French privateer sailed into Boston with a banner flying from its masthead listing eleven prominent Bostonians as "aristocrats" and "enemies of France."[46]

With no navy to patrol coastal waters and the tiny remnants of the American Army pinned down fighting Indians in Ohio, Wash-ington was helpless to enforce his own rules. A jubilant Genet sa-vored his triumph. In brazen defiance of Washington, Genet took out boldfaced newspaper advertisements calling on "Friends of France"[47] to ignore Washington's neutrality proclamation and enlist in the French service to fight the British:

> Does not patriotism call upon us to assist France? As Sons of Free-dom, would it not become our character to lend some assistance to a nation combating to secure their liberty. Two thousand of our Rifle Men and hardy woodsmen would be a great acquisition to the French Army and a terrible scourge to their enemies. Let a sub-scription be set on foot, an adequate sum would soon be raised to give sufficient encouragement to that number.[48]

A few days later, the Philadelphia *National Gazette* reported:

> The information lately published . . . to raise a party of American volunteers to be sent to France to assist the patriotic party was highly pleasing to all staunch Americans. The time seems to have arrived when these volunteers are to be called forth . . . a corps to

consist chiefly of riflemen. They are to rendezvous in Providence
. . . for Havre de Grace.[49]

Within two weeks of the Jefferson-Genet meeting, the president
bypassed Jefferson and asked Attorney General Edmund Randolph to
order the arrest of American seamen when they stepped ashore after
serving on French privateers. Authorities arrested two American seamen on the *Citizen Genet,* a privateer the modest Frenchman had
outfitted and renamed in Charleston. Genet wrote an angry letter of
protest to Jefferson: "The crime of which they are accused, which my
mind cannot conceive and my pen reluctantly records, is serving
France, defending with her children the common and glorious cause
of liberty."[50]

Charged with conspiring to attack the property and citizens of
nations at peace with the United States, one of the men went to trial
before the Federal Circuit Court of Philadelphia, with Genet paying
for his defense. Although judges ordered a jury verdict of guilty,
Genet bribed jurors to ensure the opposite. Cheering members of the
Jacobin Democratic Society led the sailor from the courthouse back
to his ship to reenlist before attending a celebratory dinner that
Genet sponsored that evening to celebrate the young man's triumph
over the federal government. The seaman's insolence further exposed the president's impotence—despite having won reelection to a
second term by the same unanimous vote that had carried him to office four years earlier in 1789.

As a further insult to the president, Genet ordered a British ship
his privateers had captured, *The Little Sarah,* refitted and armed—
under the president's nose in Philadelphia. Acting under the president's instructions, the governor of Pennsylvania ordered the ship
detained. Genet sent an angry complaint to the French foreign minister in Paris that President Washington "interferes with my progress
in a thousand ways, and obliges me secretly to urge the convocation
of Congress, the majority of which . . . will be decidedly in my favor."
Genet told Pennsylvania commonwealth secretary Alexander J. Dallas that he would appeal President Washington's decisions to "the
real sovereigns of the United States—the people."[51] He thereupon
defied the American government, ordered *The Little Sarah* renamed

Petite Démocrate, and sent her out to sea to attack British shipping. Although the governor considered firing on the vessel to prevent her leaving port, Jefferson warned it would be an act of war against France and that a powerful French fleet was approaching from Saint Domingue (the French portion of Santo Domingo, now Haiti). Jefferson realized America could no more afford war with France than with England. But the *Petite Démocrate* drew the United States ever closer to war with so many attacks on British vessels that the British retaliated by seizing American cargo ships and impressing or imprisoning American crewmen. Despite Washington's efforts to keep America neutral, war with Britain seemed inevitable unless he stopped Genet.

After the *Petite Démocrate* had left, Genet took the first steps to attack Louisiana. He had received another letter from George Rogers Clark reiterating his plea for French help. Genet's instructions were clear:

> Kentuckians have long seethed with a legitimate desire to enjoy free navigation of the Mississippi—a natural right that you can help them acquire without compromising the Congress. The [French] executive council, therefore, authorizes Citizen Genet to form and maintain a network of agents in Kentucky as well as Louisiana and to supply them with whatever funds they deem necessary to execute the plans . . . to invade Spanish America, open the Mississippi to free navigation by Kentuckians and deliver our former brothers in Louisiana from the yoke of [Spanish] tyranny.[52]

Clark reported that widespread anger of Kentucky frontiersmen toward the Spanish had simplified the task of recruiting a western army. Soldiers, he said, had expressed willingness to accept captured lands as pay for the expedition, and after he had offered 1,000-acre land grants to prospective enlistees, more than 2,000 Kentuckians had volunteered, with 4,000 more signing "intents." Clark said his men would be ready to march once he received appropriate commissions for his officers, along with money for boats, guns, and ammunitions.

In accordance with his instructions, Genet enlisted André

Michaux, a renowned French botanist and Girondin loyalist, to travel to Kentucky and, under the pretense of searching for new specimens, deliver funds for Clark's expedition. He gave Michaux a commission making Clark a French major general and commander of the Legion of Revolution and Independence of the Mississippi. Michaux also carried Genet's instructions for coordinating the Louisiana offensive with the French fleet when it arrived to besiege New Orleans.

Genet's government had given him only 60,000 livres to cover his own salary and expenses but assured him that Jefferson would fund military expeditions by paying U.S. war debts to France in advance instead of annually. Genet laid out his plans for the Florida and Louisiana expeditions before the secretary of state, along with formal requests for American financial and military aid. He also asked Jefferson to waive the neutrality proclamation and allow him to continue to refit privateers, recruit American seamen, and sell captured prizes in American ports. Jefferson took notes at the meeting:

> He called on me and read . . . an address to the inhab. of Louisiana, & another to those of Canada. It appears that besides encouraging those inhabitants to insurrections, he speaks of two generals at Kentucky, who have proposed to him to go & take New Orleans if he will furnish the exp. about £3,000 sterl. He . . . proposes that officers shall be commissd. by himself in Kentucky & Louisiana, that they shall rendezvous out *of the territories of the U.S.* in Louisiana . . . and getting what Indns. they could, to undertake the expedn against N. Orleans, and then Louisiana to be established as an independent state . . .[53]

In a near-treasonous action that he hid from the president, Jefferson gave Michaux a warm letter of introduction to Governor Isaac Shelby of Kentucky, implying approval of the Clark expedition against the Spanish. With Jefferson's quasi-diplomatic imprimatur in hand, Michaux left for Kentucky in mid-July. Jefferson then passed along Genet's requests for arms, cannons, and money to the appropriate cabinet members. Secretary of War Henry Knox, a fierce Washington loyalist, replied angrily that he would not lend Genet so much as a pistol. Treasury Secretary Hamilton reacted similarly to Genet's request to draw down funds from American Revolutionary War debts.

Jefferson explained the refusals to Genet in softer tones. He said advance debt repayment would exhaust the American government's cash reserves and, in any event, was not required under terms of the loans. He said the tiny American Army could ill afford to spare the few cannons it owned. Jefferson said that while the United States "did not care what insurrections should be excited in Louisiana," he warned that "enticing officers and soldiers from Kentucky to go against Spain was really putting a halter about their necks, for they would assuredly be hung if they committed hostilities against a nation at peace with the United States."[54]

Jefferson's sudden turnabout infuriated Genet, who charged the secretary of state with having previously espoused the French cause to further his political ambitions—"solely to win those tender objects of your desires . . . the great and lucrative posts of the Federal Government. . . ."[55]

Feeling abandoned by Jefferson, the Frenchman carried out his threat and began appealing to the American people to rise against the Washington government. He expanded the number of "Democratic Societies" to nearly forty and changed their stated mission from promoting Franco-American friendship to promoting revolution, union with France, and war against Britain. He ordered them to infect the nation with pro-French war fever. The results terrified supporters of Washington and neutrality. Like Jacobins in France, society members infiltrated the American press and local political establishments, and at a signal from Genet, they could fill the streets with shrieking mobs and frighten newspaper readers with menacing headlines.

"The freedom of this country," claimed New York's *Columbian Gazetteer*, "is not secure until that of France is placed beyond the reach of accident."[56] The *Baltimore Daily Repository* warned that if Europe's monarchs defeated France, "the craving appetite of despotism will be satisfied with nothing less than American vassalage in some form or another." Philadelphia's *General Advertiser* insisted that "the salvation of America depends on our alliance with France."[57]

Genet waxed ecstatic in his report to the Foreign Ministry in

Paris: "Composed of the patriots of '76 [and] the most respectable citizens," he explained, "the Democratic Societies have formed as if by
magic from one end of the continent to the other, and set down as a
foundation for their association these powerful words, Liberty, Equality, Rights of Man, Country, France, Republic. . . . The [American]
people voluntarily constituted themselves France's advocate."[58]

The final element in Genet's strategy for cowing the Washington
administration fell into place with the arrival of the French fleet in
Philadelphia from the Antilles. Genet ordered gangways lowered and
sent French seamen to join his Jacobins marauding across the city.
The British consul sent a frightening report to London: "The town is
one continuous scene of riot. The French seamen range the streets by
night and by day, armed with cutlasses and commit the most daring
outrages. . . . President Washington is unable to enforce any measures in opposition." Genet seemed ready to "raise the tricolor and
proclaim himself proconsul."[59]

8

"Down with Washington!"

WITH NO NAVY to repel the French, Washington and his cabinet recognized French warships for what they were—an occupying force that Genet could use to dictate policy. Washington called an emergency session of the cabinet, and, frustrated by his own impotence, he exploded with anger. Was Genet to be allowed to "set the acts of this Government at defiance *with impunity?*" the president demanded. "What must the world think of such conduct, and of the Government . . . submitting to it?"[1]

Genet's ineluctable ascent to power reached a peak on August 1, 1793, when he arrogantly bypassed diplomatic protocol by ignoring Secretary of State Jefferson and treating directly with President Washington as an equal—an unheard-of act by an ambassador toward a head of state. Genet sent Washington an ultimatum "in the name of France," demanding that the president call Congress into special session to choose between neutrality and war. Convinced that the adoring street mobs would overthrow the president and "persuaded that the sovereignty of the United States resides essentially in the people and in its representation in the Congress," Genet warned Washington that if he refused to declare war on Britain the Frenchman would "appeal to the people . . . [the] decisions of the President."[2] Genet reported to the French foreign minister that the American government "does not like our principles . . . [but] I can at least console myself . . . [that] I have acquired the esteem and the

good wishes of all Republican Americans by tightening the bonds of
fraternity between them and ourselves." He predicted that the "good,
generous, grateful people [will] rally from all sides to support the
envoy of the French nation [and] demonstrate to him with cries of
joy . . . that the democrats of America realize perfectly that their fate
is ultimately bound with ours. . . ."[3]

With Genet's influence evolving into an ominously powerful political movement, Washington lashed out angrily, calling Genet's political activities an "imminent danger" to the Constitution and
declared, "We are an independent nation. We will not be dictated to
by the politics of any nation under Heaven."[4] Washington accused
the Democratic Societies of planning "nothing short of the subver-
sion of the Government of these States, even at the expense of
plunging this country in the horrors of a disastrous war."[5]

As Genet's mobs held the city in thrall, the Frenchman crossed
the line of rational, not to mention diplomatic, behavior by barging
into a presidential reception and demanding an immediate interview
with the president. To avoid public scandal, the president led the in-
truder to a private study, where Genet urged the president "to put
himself in my place and consider that by his proclamation of neutrality . . . he had annulled the most sacred treaties, taken from the
French people, at the time when it had the greatest need of it in
order to defend its colonies, an alliance which it looked upon as a
possession dearly bought; he would agree that unless I were a traitor I
could not act otherwise. . . ."[6]

Genet's confrontation with the president went so far beyond the
pale of diplomatic protocol that Washington took no formal notes of
the conversation. Genet alone commented that "the President listened to everything and said to me simply that it was of very slight
importance to him whether his administration was talked about. We
went out, he accompanied me as far as the stairs, took my hand and
shook it." The next day, Genet approached Jefferson and "used every
method to find out if the President had spoken to you of my efforts,
but you were impenetrable." As Jefferson expressed his "astonishment" that Genet had dared approach the president directly, Washington himself strode into the secretary of state's office. Genet stood
and, as he described it, "looked from one to the other of you to see if

I might read in your eyes an invitation to remain . . . but a very imperative sign from you forced me to retire."[7]

Unnerved by accusations in Hamiltonian newspapers that he was in the pay of the French government, Jefferson again offered Washington his resignation. This time the president accepted but insisted Jefferson remain until the end of the year. His influence in the cabinet, however, diminished steadily, and he began trying to disassociate himself from Genet. "I am doing everything in my power," he wrote to James Monroe, "to moderate his impetuosity . . . and to destroy the dangerous opinion that excites him that the people of the United States will disavow the acts of their Government, and that he has an appeal from the Executive to Congress and from both to the people."[8]

With Jefferson's resignation in sight, the president himself took more control of foreign affairs. At a cabinet meeting the next day, Washington said he would ask the French government to recall Genet. He then asked for opinions on whether the Democratic Societies presented enough of a menace to warrant a ban on their activities. Hamilton called them Jacobins, paid by Genet and the French government to undermine the American government. Secretary of War Henry Knox concurred and read an article from a society pamphlet attacking Washington's "aristocratic or monarchical tendency"—words Jefferson recognized as Genet's. Jefferson described the president's reaction:

> The Presdt. was much inflamed, got into one of those passions when he cannot command himself, ran on much on the personal abuse which had been bestowed on him, defied any man on earth to produce one single act of his since he had been in govmt which has not been done on the purest motives, that . . . *by god* he had rather be in his grave than to be made *emperor of the world* and yet they were charging him with wanting to be a King.[9]

Abandoning all hope for cooperation from the American government, Genet ordered the fleet to sail to New York for repairs and resupply before dividing into three squadrons for the assaults on Canada, Florida, and Louisiana. Before he arrived, however, the British frigate *Boston* sailed into New York waters from Halifax to combat French depredations on British cargo vessels. When he saw the French fleet in New York Bay, the captain of the *Boston* disguised his ship as a French frigate—*La Concorde*. He then raised the French tricolor and signaled an invitation to the captain and officers of *l'Embuscade* to dine and share a rare brandy. The French captain all but leaped into a dinghy with his men, who rowed across the bay and delivered themselves into British hands—and irons.

As New York's Tories doubled over in laughter, Jacobin clubbers and Francophiles rioted in the streets, demanding revenge for the "vile" English trick. Within days, the British captain obliged with a formal challenge to his captives to a one-on-one naval duel between the British and French frigates—a challenge he posted on the door of the Tontine Coffee House for all to see. After the French captain accepted, the English released him to prepare for contest, which they agreed to hold on August 1 off the coast of Long Branch, New Jersey. As word of the impending duel spread, life in New York and nearby communities came to a standstill; the entire population, thousands upon thousands, fought their way onto every imaginable means of transport—carriages, large and small boats, horses, donkeys, anything—to take them to the Jersey shore to watch the historic combat. Many waged their life savings on the outcome. As crowds thickened, periodic arguments and fights sent tents tumbling and small boats overturning; rioting threatened to engulf the beaches until the echo of shots over the water drew the crowd's eyes toward the two combatants.

With the signal to begin, the cannons of the two ships launched a fearsome two-hour barrage that filled the air with spectacular displays of smoke and fire; hailstorms of cannonballs, nails, broken glass, and other shrapnel damaged both ships and littered their decks with dead and injured sailors. After the British captain fell—fatally, as it turned out—the *Boston* abandoned the battle and sailed away, with *l'Embuscade* in pursuit. Five hours later, *l'Embuscade* returned in triumph and led the fleet of fifteen French warships into New York Harbor and a roar of welcoming cannon blasts, pealing church bells, and raucous cheers. Huge banners streamed from her mastheads: "Enemies of equality: Reform or Tremble!" read the banner on the foremast. "Freemen, Behold! We are your friends and brothers!" flew from the mainmast. "We are armed for the defence of the Rights of Man!" waved from the mizzen.[10] More than 5,000 French sailors and marines spilled over the rails to join the city's Jacobins and Francophiles in an endless orgy of drunkenness and violence that all but leveled the waterfront's tumbledown warehouses. Within days, Tories and their families joined a long train of carriages fleeing the city tumult and the constant, unnerving chant, *Oui, ça ira, ça ira, ça ira—dum, da-da dum, da-da dum, da-da-dum—oui, ça ira, ça ira . . .*

A week later, on August 7, Genet arrived in New York in his adjutant general's uniform and, to the cheers of thousands, prepared to mobilize Americans to unseat the president. The hysterical mobs did nothing to dissuade him. Chanting "Genet to power!" and "Down with Washington!"[11] the huge throng serenaded him with French revolutionary airs while cannons and church bells repeated their explosive welcomes. The crowd swept him away on an endless series of unruly parades through Manhattan's narrow streets, barking their frenzied calls for revolution in counterpoint to the incessant thunderclaps of church bells. Adoring women leaned from their windows, cheered his every step, and pledged to follow the handsome young Frenchman into battle.

"Americans are ready to mingle their most precious blood with yours," one editorialist assured Genet.[12] Cartoons of guillotined American leaders adorned newspapers. One showed Vice President John Adams embracing "a stinking prostitute"—drawn to resemble Washington. Another showed Chief Justice John Jay leading royalist plotters in seating "King Washington" on the American throne. And still another showed Genet tearing the crown off the president's head.[13]

"The whole of America has risen to acknowledge me," Genet cried out jubilantly.[14] At thirty years of age, he was ready to raise the French flag, reclaim New France, and restore his nation's glory, which Britain had stained so irreverently at his birth. At a dinner hosted by New York's ardently Republican governor, George Clinton, that evening, Francophiles hailed the "great and godlike work" of France in ensuring the "triumph of Liberty," and, in a message resonant with irony, Genet replied that "the cause of France is the cause of mankind. . . . Whatever fate awaits her, you are ultimately to share." All but swooning at his words was the governor's daughter Cornelia, whose father had broken with tradition and given her as thorough an education as he would have a son. A fervent republican like her father, she had canonized butchers of the French Revolution as heroes and fell instantly in love with Genet.[15]

The next morning, August 15, Genet issued drafts totaling $100,000 to local shipbuilders to repair and refit the fleet for its mission. As church bells pealed once more, he climbed aboard his flagship, dressed in full military regalia, to issue orders to the fleet to divide into three squadrons for assaults on Halifax, Canada; St. Augustine, Florida; and New Orleans, Louisiana. On the quays below, crowds formed to serenade him:

> Liberty! Liberty! Be thy name adored forever;
> Tyrants beware! Your tott'ring thrones must fall;
> Our int'rest links the free together,
> And Freedom's sons are Frenchmen all.[16]

By midday, however, the chant diminished; one by one, the church bells ceased ringing, and as the atmosphere about the ship turned silent, Genet looked over the rail. The waterfront was deserted; the air still and silent. He disembarked and walked toward his home. A servant awaited, his bag packed to leave. Genet demanded to know why. The answer struck like a dagger:

Yellow fever!

"The coolest and the firmest minds," John Adams recalled later, "have given their opinions to me, that nothing but the yellow fever . . . could have saved the United States from a fatal revolution of government."[17] Had the epidemic arrived a month later, Genet's armies would have invaded Florida and Louisiana; he himself would have aroused his Jacobin legions in New York, Boston, and Philadelphia to march against Washington.

On August 15, however, the terrible, swift disease sent New Yorkers and Philadelphians—Jacobins and non-Jacobins alike—fleeing by the thousands to the perceived safety of the countryside. Life came to a standstill in both cities; the entire government shut down in Philadelphia. Most blamed the French fleet for bringing the contagion—and Genet for bringing the French fleet. Before autumn rime arrived to kill the offending mosquitoes, a series of other, unexpected events combined to prevent Genet from reviving the conspiracy.

Exhausted and traumatized by slave uprisings in Santo Domingo, French sailors in New York mutinied when they learned Genet planned to send them to war instead of home to France. Genet pleaded, shouted patriotic slogans, spoke of loyalty to the nation, the republic, the revolution—all for nought. The mutineers were resolute. When he ordered a group of officers to disarm the mutineers, they joined the rebels and marched to Genet's house and burned it down before sailing home to France.

To add to Genet's indignities, he ran out of funds and, having failed to obtain advance payment from Hamilton on American debts to France, was unable to pay his frontier armies. Also unpaid were outstanding bills for military supplies from merchants in Boston, New York, Philadelphia, Charleston, and elsewhere. The drafts for $100,000 he had issued to New York shipbuilders to refit the fleet were worthless.

As newspapers reported his insolvency, Alexander Hamilton exposed Genet's threat to appeal the president's decisions to the people. Front-page newspaper articles declared that "Genet, the French Minister, had said he would appeal to the People certain decisions of the President." Using the pen name "No Jacobin," Hamilton bitterly attacked Genet, decrying "the very disrespectful treatment we have experienced from the agents of France, who have acted towards us from the beginning more like a dependent colony than an independent nation."[18] Even staunch Francophiles turned on Genet for plotting "to bring down the federal government and . . . incite insurrection, riot, and treason, if necessary."[19] A letter that found its way to many newspapers blatantly accused Genet "of hatching some as yet obscure plot against America. . . ."[20]

Stunned by attacks in newspapers that had once heralded his virtues, Genet wrote an angry letter to the president demanding that he disparage the "dark calumnies" and issue "an explicit declaration that I have never intimated to you an intention of appealing to the people. . . ."[21] If his earlier behavior had only crossed the lines of diplomatic propriety, his letter erased those lines entirely. Genet's old friend the secretary of state replied coldly: "I am desired to observe to you that it is not the established course for the diplomatic characters residing here to have any direct correspondence with him [the President]. The Secretary of State is the organ through which their communications should pass. The President does not conceive it to be within the line of propriety or duty for him to bear evidence against a declaration which, whether made to him or others, is perhaps immaterial; he therefore declines interfering in the case."[22] Few Americans—indeed, few Republicans—were willing to support even so appealing a foreigner as Genet against the heroic father of their country, whom they revered and had twice elected unanimously to lead their nation.

At a cabinet meeting on August 1, President Washington's patience with Genet came to an end, and he carried out his threat to demand Genet's recall. To avoid conflict with France, Secretary of State Jefferson's carefully worded letter drew "a clear line between him [Genet] & his nation, express[in]g our fr[ien]dship to the latter but insist[in]g on the recall. . . ." Jefferson explained his request in blunt terms: "When the government forbids their citizens to arm and engage in war, he undertakes to arm and engage them. When they forbid vessels to be fitted in ports . . . he commissions them to fight and cruise. When they forbid an unceded jurisdiction to be exercised within their territory by foreign agents, he undertakes to uphold that exercise and to avow it openly."[23] Fearful that Genet might retaliate by inciting a Jacobin rebellion, the cabinet postponed notifying him of the recall until a month after they had sent it to Paris—too late for him to commandeer a ship to intercept it. Jefferson did not give Genet a copy of the recall request until mid-September. Clearly taken aback but not humbled—never humbled!—Genet nonetheless realized that the departure of the fleet and the dispersal of Jacobin mobs had left him powerless to respond with arms. He therefore sent Jefferson an audacious letter renewing his threat to appeal to the American people:

> Persuaded that the sovereignty of the United States resides essentially in the people and its representation in the Congress, persuaded that the executive power is the only one which has been

confided to the President . . . persuaded that this magistrate [the president] has not the right to decide questions the discussion of which the Constitution reserves particularly to the Congress; persuaded that he has not the power to bend existing treaties to circumstances and to change their sense. . . . I will suffer no precedent against the rights of the French people while there remains in me one breath of life. . . . It is in the name of the French people that I am sent to their brethren—to free and sovereign men; it is then for the representatives of the American people and not for a single man to exhibit against me an accusation if I have merited it.[24]

Had Jefferson been more mean-spirited and less fervently Francophile, the letter might well have cost Genet his life. As it was, Jefferson simply disregarded the note. Embarrassed by his once-close ties to the Frenchman, Jefferson distanced himself by accusing Genet of having conducted himself as if he were "co-sovereign." In a letter to his confidant James Madison, by then the Republican leader in Congress, Jefferson denounced Genet for having

thrown down the gauntlet to the President . . . and risking that disgust which I had so much wished to be avoided. I believe it will be true wisdom in the Republican party . . . to abandon Genet entirely with expressions of strong friendship and adherence to his nation. . . . In this way we shall keep the people on our side. . . . I have been myself under a cruel dilemma with him. I adhered to him as long as I could . . . [but] finding at length that the man was absolutely incorrigible . . . I saw the necessity of quitting a wreck which would but sink all who should cling to it. . . .[25]

With Madison's approval, Jefferson sent Genet a curt reply that Republican congressmen would not consider his appeal. Not only did Jefferson and Madison abandon Genet, even South Carolina governor Moultrie, Genet's earliest champion in America, wrote the Frenchman that his insults to the president had offended and alienated all the friends that France had once claimed in America.

Neither Genet nor the Washington administration had yet learned that the venomous Robespierre and his bloodthirsty Jacobins had seized power in France and sent Brissot and the Girondins to the guillotine. Although Robespierre lusted for foreign conquest as much as any of his predecessor French rulers, he faced the immediate task of feeding his nation. French farms remained barren, neglected by anarchic peasants and desiccated by heaven's drought. The United States was France's lone remaining ally and only source of food. Recognizing the need for American help, Robespierre grew incensed by Genet's reports and concluded that his ambassador had "employed the most extraordinary means to irritate the American Government against us. . . ."[26] When Robespierre received Jefferson's request for Genet's recall, he sent the American the "strongest assurances [that he] unequivocally disapproved" of Genet's conduct and pledged to expedite his recall "without delay."[27]

No longer intimidated by Genet's Jacobins, Washington revoked the accreditation of the French vice-consul in Boston for ordering an armed patrol to free a French privateer from the custody of American authorities. Jefferson sent a letter to all other French consuls threatening the same fate if they failed to comply with American laws.

Genet continued peppering the press with angry articles questioning presidential authority and threatening to appeal to Congress, but when Congress reconvened in December, it referred all his documents to Jefferson without a reading. Jefferson, in turn, returned the correspondence to Genet with a curt warning to stop meddling in American government affairs. Henceforth, the American government would have nothing to do with him and await his replacement for any further diplomatic intercourse with France.

Many historians dismiss Genet's conduct as attributable to mistaken beliefs that the French and American systems of governments were identical. Genet's "French background," according to the distinguished historian Henry Ammon, "led him to regard public sentiment as the determining element in the political process"—that the people were sovereign and the president, or executive, an impotent functionary relegated to fulfilling the dictates of the people as expressed either in the streets or through their assembly in Congress. Indeed, the French constitution of 1793 canonized the people's right of insurrection "when the government violated the rights of the people" or otherwise failed to achieve "the common good." This belief, say some historians, led Genet to misunderstand "the rhetoric of pub-

Maximilien Robespierre. The psychopathic left-wing extremist, who seized power over revolutionary France, tried to restore harmonious commercial relations with the United States to restore the flow of American foodstuffs to famine-stricken France.

lic demonstrations" as "the voice of the people." Indeed, even his diplomatic credentials supported this view: they were addressed to the Congress of the United States instead of the president.[28]

Professor Alexander DeConde supports Professor Ammon's view, asserting that Genet could not help but be swayed by street demonstrations: "He saw about him evidence . . . that public support for him and the alliance [with France] was greater than for the Federalist administration. . . . Who might not have been turned by the public demonstrations, the mass adulations, and the evidence on every hand that he was the lion of the hour and that public favor was his for the asking?"[29]

Other historians take a psychological approach to explain—or excuse—Genet's irrational conduct in America. They cite Jefferson's appraisal of the Frenchman after the two had fallen out. In a letter to Madison, Jefferson called Genet "hot headed, all imagination, no judgment, passionate, disrespectful & even indecent towards the P[resident] in his written as well as verbal communications, talking

of appeals to Congress, from them to the people, urging the most un-
reasonable & groundless propositions, & in the most dictatorial style,
& c, & c, & c."[30]

In contrast, documents in the archives of the French Ministry of
Foreign Affairs in Paris invariably show Genet to have been both rational and exceptionally knowledgeable about the American political system. Indeed, he appears to have had no less an understanding
of American government than Jefferson; he had studied the workings
of the American and many other political systems for more than fifteen years under the tutelage of the most experienced diplomats in
the Western world. He and his father had been intimates of Franklin,
Adams, Jefferson, and other American emissaries in Versailles; they
had left him with no illusions about America's system of government
before the American Revolution, during the Confederation, and
after enactment of the Constitution. Genet was an experienced
diplomat who spent hours—days—listening to Jefferson explain the
American system of government, the separate *but equal* powers of the
president, Congress, and Supreme Court and the role of each. Although Professor DeConde asserts that American street mobs swayed
Genet, it was Genet himself who organized those mobs; it seems unlikely that a man who organizes and converts a mob to his beliefs
could be swayed by that mob to adopt beliefs he harbored in the first
place. Professor DeConde modifies his assertions by noting subsequently that "Genet was not a wild-eyed revolutionary; he was a cul-
tured, educated, intelligent young man . . . and often created his own
difficulties"[31]

Far from irrational or ignorant about American politics, Genet
was, quite simply, a cold, calculating, and experienced agent of the
French government, brilliantly trained for more than a decade in
diplomacy and espionage and fanatically dedicated to implementing
his nation's historic policy of territorial conquest and world domina-
tion. Genet followed his government's instructions to the letter,
using mercurial behavior as a calculated tool to terrorize Americans
to do the bidding of France. Professor DeConde concedes that
"Genet was not the fool he often has been depicted. Almost any
minister from France would have run into difficulty in 1793 if he had
come with Genet's instructions."[32] Even Genet's arch rival in

Philadelphia, British ambassador George Hammond, agreed that "however intemperate, reprehensible, and unwarrantable his conduct may have been he has not essentially exceeded the spirit of his instructions."[33]

On December 31, 1793, Jefferson resigned from office and returned to his Virginia plantation. To Washington's deep relief, a new French ambassador, Jean Antoine Joseph Fauchet, arrived in Philadelphia about a month later. After presenting the president with his credentials, he gave the new secretary of state, Edmund Randolph, a French government warrant for the arrest and execution of Citizen Edmond Charles Genet. A guillotine aboard ship stood ready to carry out the sentence. Vice President Adams, who despised Genet, could not help recoiling at the cruel fate the Frenchman now faced: "Poor Genet, I fear, is undone," Adams wrote to his wife, Abigail. "Bad as his conduct has been, I cannot but pity him. What will become of him, I know not."[34]

9

Toasts to Sedition

ON MARCH 6, 1794, newspapers across America published Joseph Fauchet's proclamation revoking French military commissions to American citizens and forbidding French citizens from violating American neutrality. Although the French minister's proclamation ended the crisis over neutrality, it provoked as much embarrassment for President Washington as it did satisfaction. In one stroke of the pen, Fauchet did in a day what the president's threats and decrees had been unable to do in a year. In canceling the frontier expeditions, Fauchet had demeaned the president as much as Genet had in organizing them. In each case, a French emissary had exposed presidential impotence and proved more powerful than the president.

In the months that followed, Genet's expeditionary forces gradually disbanded, but the frontier remained a tinderbox, with settlers armed and ready to regroup for war against Spain. Although their numbers shrank dramatically when Genet ran out of cash to feed and arm them, their hatred of the Spanish for depriving them of Mississippi River navigation rights only increased—as did resentment against the United States government for its unwillingness to confront Spain to secure those rights. Not only were frontiersmen ready to march into Spanish territory, they were willing to secede from the United States and either establish an independent state or unite with France.

Fauchet's "conciliatory plan of reversing the errors of his predecessor"[1] almost lulled the Washington administration into complacently reembracing the nation's French ally. "The manners of Mr. Fauchet, and of Mr. Genet," Washington purred at first, "appear to have been cast in very different moulds. The former has been temperate, and placid in all his movements . . . the latter was the reverse in all respects. The declaration made by the former [Fauchet], of the friendly dispositions of his Nation towards this Country and of his own inclinations to carry them into effect are strong and apparently sincere."[2]

The thirty-three-year-old Fauchet spoke no English when he landed in Philadelphia, and his consequent reserve at diplomatic functions—in contrast to Genet's exuberance—won favor among Federalists as well as Republicans. Behind Fauchet's mask of reserve, however, was the face of a rabid Jacobin. Like Robespierre, Fauchet was a lawyer who had been brutally active in the French Revolution, earning enough notice to win appointment to lead the vital task of salvaging French relations with the United States.

Robespierre sent three other "diplomats" to help Fauchet. One was the ghoulish former head of the Paris Police Department, who carried orders to arrest and execute Genet. Two of the other commissioners spoke English and had considerable knowledge of the United States and its people. They immediately joined the Philadelphia Democratic Society and helped Fauchet reorganize it and the other societies into a more efficient espionage network of about forty clubs in key areas of the United States. "Fauchet has wrapped himself round with intrigue from the first moment of his career in the United States," Alexander Hamilton charged. "At the festivals of these [Democratic] clubs," Hamilton noted, "he is always a guest, always swallowing toasts full of sedition and hostility to the [American] government . . . he knew and approved a conspiracy which was destined to overthrow the administration of our government. . . ."[3] Even some Francophiles expressed concern about Fauchet and his aides: "The political character of these gentlemen," James Madison warned Jefferson, "give some uneasiness to the Republican party."[4]

But most Jeffersonians remained blithely unaware of espionage agents in their midst and saw the clubs as political vehicles for their hero's run at the presidency. They used the clubs to enlist merchants who wanted to build trade with France, while the agents among them continued the seditious work Genet had started. They were particularly active in the trans-Appalachian region, where they encouraged secessionism with promises of Mississippi River navigation rights once they raised the French flag over Louisiana.

If Fauchet and his agents left James Madison uneasy, they terrified Genet—and with good reason. Fauchet had presented Secretary of State Edmund Randolph with the warrant for "Citizen" Genet's arrest, "to bring him back to France aboard one of the ships in port and force him to account for his conduct towards an ally whose friendship and esteem are so dear to the French government."[5] Genet pleaded with Randolph for help, all but sobbing that the former Paris police chief waited below deck on Fauchet's ship sharpening the blade to sever Genet's neck. A former Virginia governor who had been Washington's attorney general before he succeeded Jefferson, Randolph showed the warrant to the president. After a moment's thought, the president said, "We ought not to wish his punishment," and granted the Frenchman political asylum.

Fearing that Fauchet's agents would kidnap him, Genet wore disguises and hired an armed guard to protect him day and night. He finally sneaked out of Philadelphia one night, unnoticed by the very Jacobin agents he had recruited to spread turmoil in the American capital. He found his way to a secluded hideaway on a friend's farm in Bristol, Connecticut, where he temporarily disappeared from public view, although his name constantly appeared in the nation's press, and he was reviled by Republicans and Federalists alike for his seditious activities.

With Genet nowhere to be found, Fauchet turned to his diplomatic responsibilities, asking first for advance payment of American war debts and pledging to use the funds to buy American food for the starving French people. Washington remained adamant against changing methods of debt repayment from annual installments. Unlike Genet, Fauchet wasted no time in angry debate. Instead, he used what money and credit he could raise to charter cargo ships and fill them with foodstuffs. In mid-April, he sent 130 ships from Chesapeake Bay loaded with nearly 25 million tons of flour to relieve the famine in France. On June 1, as the convoy approached the British blockade near France, the French Navy sailed out to engage them and drew enough British warships away from their positions in the blockade to open a clear passage to the French coast. Although the battle crippled the French war fleet, it allowed the convoy to reach the port of Brest and relieve the famine—without losing a single ship.

While Fauchet focused on feeding France, the other French "commissioners" fed the fires of secessionist sentiment on the trans-Appalachian frontier. Although France and Spain remained at war, they had stopped firing at each other and were secretly negotiating to resume their alliance and restore Louisiana to France. The Franco-Spanish rapprochement was a result of Chief Justice John Jay's mission to London to negotiate American rapprochement with England. Apart from English depredations on American trade with France, Britain had, for ten years, refused to withdraw from frontier military garrisons or give Americans access to the western fur trade until the United States compensated Tories for property losses during the revolution.

A resolution of these problems would threaten both French and Spanish interests by unleashing unimpeded American migration westward across the Ohio, Illinois, and Missouri rivers and the northern reaches of the Mississippi River. Frontiersmen would have no reason to secede, and France would have no reason to send her troops to America. Once settled throughout the Northwest, Americans would inevitably sweep southward to New Orleans and Texas—perhaps even to the gold and silver treasures of Mexico. Immediate Spanish retrocession of Louisiana to France, on the other hand, would permit the French Army to occupy the territory and buffer Spanish possessions in the West and Southwest from American expansion and deter Anglo-American aggression. It would also rid Spain of a troublesome French population in New Orleans that had chafed—and often rebelled—under Spanish rule for three decades.

Late in the summer of 1794, Treasury Secretary Hamilton unwittingly helped the French scheme to provoke secession of western frontiersman. British depredations on American shipping had cut American government tax revenues and left the treasury near bankruptcy. Hamilton desperately searched for new sources of revenue and sent agents west to enforce for the first time a two-year-old excise tax on distilled liquors. For years, western farmers had converted corn and rye into whiskies, which were easier than grain to transport across the Appalachians to eastern markets. In addition, a jug of whiskey had become universal currency for isolated frontiersmen, who depended on barter and had little use for paper money. The excise tax, therefore, represented both confiscation of revenues and rank interference with day-to-day commerce. French agents in Democratic Societies had no trouble channeling farmer fury into outright rebellion.

For the first time, Washington openly denounced the clubs: he called the Whiskey Rebellion "the first *formidable* fruit of the Democratic Societies; brought forth . . . primarily to sow the seeds of jealousy and distrust among people of the government. . . ."[6] He attacked the clubs as "the most diabolical attempt to destroy the best fabric of human government and happiness that has ever been presented for the acceptance of mankind." Washington blamed Genet for having "brought the eggs of these venomous reptiles to our shores. . . ."[7]

After the president assailed Genet, the Frenchman emerged from his rural hideaway to march at the head of the July 4 parade in New York City. He strode arm in arm with Republican governor George Clinton and the governor's daughter Cornelia, a rabid Republican who shared Genet's fiery, revolutionary fantasies. Along the parade route, members of New York's Democratic Societies cheered his unexpected reappearance. After he escaped the shipboard guillotine the previous winter, Genet had recognized the impossibility of returning to France, and he had asked for and won Cornelia Clinton's hand. A handsome dowry from her father bought him a 325-acre property near Jamaica, Long Island, and under the governor's protection, he settled uncomfortably into the life of a gentleman farmer. But he resumed writing insanely angry newspaper articles denouncing the American government and inadvertently furthering Fauchet's plans to promote western secession. Fauchet made no further attempts to arrest Genet.[8]

Not long after Independence Day, Washington issued a proclamation ordering western insurrectionists to lay down their arms and return to their homes. When they refused, he ordered Revolutionary War hero Henry Lee and Alexander Hamilton to crush the rebellion by leading 13,000 militiamen into the Monongahela Valley—the site of Washington's first military action four decades earlier. Randolph opposed sending American troops against Americans and turned to the French ambassador for help in suppressing activities of western Democratic Societies—with bribes if necessary.

"Thus, with some thousands of dollars," Fauchet wrote to the Foreign Ministry in Paris, "the [French] Republic would have decided on civil war or on peace! Thus the consciences of the pretended patriots of America have already their scale of prices!"[9]

Randolph's plea to Fauchet came too late, however. Hamilton's militiamen had already left Harrisburg and crossed the Alleghenies. To their surprise, the rebels had all but vanished. Hamilton and his huge army returned with but twenty insurrectionists, whom they marched down Market Street in Philadelphia and dumped into prison, where they languished for months until their release. Only two were convicted of treason, and Washington pardoned both.

Washington's public denunciation of Democratic Societies awakened Americans to the dangers of foreign interference in the nation's internal affairs, and their awareness devolved into abject fear when news arrived that Robespierre's butchery had raised the weekly toll of French guillotines from 100 executions to nearly 1,500. Although the revulsion that followed did not destroy Democratic Societies in America, it weakened their influence in the Northeast—especially after clergymen joined the Federalist press in attacking societies as "sowers of sedition infiltrating the country to divide and weaken it." Reverend David Osgood, of Medford, Massachusetts, warned that French sponsors of Democratic Societies were "execrable monsters" who had "butchered two million people, men, women, and children, including twenty-four thousand men of the cloth! As mothers pleaded for their children, their outstretched hands were chopped off."[10]

In midsummer, Robespierre's excesses grew intolerable for even his most loyal French supporters. After accusing his own Jacobin associates of plotting against him, he demanded immediate arrest and execution of the entire Convention—every member—and seemed ready to execute everyone in France. By then, the number of widows and orphans had reached staggering proportions; they and tens of thousands of ordinary citizens who had gone into hiding to escape Robespierre's guillotine blades suddenly emerged en masse and marched to the convention hall roaring. *"À bas Robespierre!"* Convention delegates summoned up the courage to order his arrest, along with his terrorist confederates. The following day, the guillotine blade sent his head tumbling into a blood-soaked basket, followed by those of his nineteen closest political allies, including his brother. While a mob watched in hushed disbelief, seventy-one Robespierristes met the same fate the following day in a bloody finale to "The Terror" and Jacobin rule in France.

Toward the end of the year, the Spanish all but quashed French prospects for returning to America by reopening the Mississippi River and granting Americans the right to deposit imports and exports in New Orleans duty free while awaiting transshipment. The agreement also fixed America's western and southern boundaries with Spain and all but ended the immediate threat that westerners would need French help to take Louisiana by force and secede from the United States.

The fall of the Jacobins also ended Fauchet's mission to the United States. He did not leave without a flourish, though—indeed, several flourishes. In the winter of 1795, Chief Justice John Jay returned from England with the Anglo-American treaty he had negotiated. It was a treaty Washington knew would please no one, but, as Jay related, it was the best a nation as weak as the United States could obtain from so powerful a nation as Britain. The British agreed to abandon military posts in the Northwest Territories and grant the United States most-favored-nation trading status, but the treaty left so many other Anglo-American problems unresolved that Washington decided not to disclose its terms until the Senate could consider it in special, secret session. As the debate began, Fauchet bought a copy with a few well-placed bribes and sent it to the French Foreign Ministry in Paris. France responded by attacking America's ocean-going commerce, and Fauchet appealed in newspapers to Congress and the public to reject the Jay Treaty. The president ordered Secretary of State Randolph to rebuke the French emissary for breaching "the sovereignty of the United States." Randolph's letter warned that "it will ever be denied as a right of a foreign minister, that he should endeavor, by an address to the people, oral or written, to forestall a pending measure, or to defeat one that has been decided."[11]

Before Fauchet could respond, his successor arrived, and Fauchet left for Newport, Rhode Island, to sail back to France. As he traveled overland, a British frigate captured the coastal sloop that carried his personal effects from Philadelphia. Among his private papers, the British found—and released to the press—a copy of a Fauchet letter to the French foreign minister reporting that Secretary of State Randolph had solicited bribes to disclose terms of the Jay Treaty in advance of Senate ratification. "Mr. Randolph came to see me," Fauchet wrote, "with a countenance expressive of much anxiety, and made to me the overtures of which I have given you an account in my No. 6. . . ."[12]

The letter staggered Washington, who had known and trusted Randolph for years and considered him a close personal friend and counsel in the cabinet. Both of them were Virginians; Randolph had been governor of Virginia. A wealthy plantation owner like Washington, he had been Washington's aide-de-camp in Boston in 1775. The president all but broke down in tears. First Arnold, then Lee, now Randolph . . . it was all too much. Greene had been right . . . "so many spies in our midst."[13]

Concluding that Randolph had pocketed thousands of dollars solicited from Fauchet, Washington showed Randolph the letter and asked for "such explanations as you choose."[14] Randolph denied having asked for or received money from Fauchet, but Washington had lost all faith in his friend, and Randolph resigned.[15]

Newspapers called the letter final proof of treachery by the French government, by the Democratic Societies, and by American Francophiles who had supported Fauchet's conspiracy "to separate the western country from the Atlantic States." Although Fauchet issued a statement absolving Randolph, most Americans "read it with disgust—clearly, the French Govt. by their ministers here have had much to do in our parties ag[ains]t govt. for three years, or since Genet's time."[16]

Ratification of the Jay Treaty and the revelation of Randolph's treachery left the Franco-American Treaty of 1778 in shreds. In the course of 1795, French warships captured and sold more than three hundred American ships and their cargoes, without compensating owners, and they committed untold atrocities against captured American seamen—either executing them at sea or tossing them into chains in the Bordeaux prison.

Fauchet's successor tried to heal the rift at first but only inflamed the American government's growing antipathy toward France. Pierre August Adet was in his early thirties—a chemist by education and destined to become a physician like his father when the French Revolution shut down the nation's universities. Adet escaped violence by burying himself in the faceless civil service bureaucracy and working his way up in the bureau of colonial affairs and, eventually, the diplomatic service. Although Washington administration officials described him as "mild tempered," "well educated," and "no Jacobin," Adet lost no time in reviving all the old issues that Genet and Fauchet had raised—advance repayment of American Revolutionary War debts to France, exclusion of French privateers from American ports, and so forth. It was a tiresome plaint.

Although the Senate had not yet ratified the Jay Treaty, Adet knew from the copy Fauchet had obtained that the treaty would admit British privateers into American ports while continuing the ban on French privateers. In truth, the treaty not only violated the Franco-American Treaties of 1778, it effectively made the United States an enemy of France. When the Senate finally ratified the treaty and Washington signed it, Adet publicly assailed both the Senate and the president: "The President has just signed the dishonor of his old age and the shame of the United States; he has ratified the Treaty of Commerce and Amity with Great Britain . . . and pledged [his] blind submission to the supreme will of [King] George."[17] Like Genet and Fauchet before him, Adet decided to appeal the president's decision—and, in this case, the Senate's as well—to the people. He bribed a senator to give him a finished copy and passed it to the pro-French *Aurora* to publish. As Adet had hoped, America's Republicans and Francophiles arose as one, raging that the Jay Treaty "insidiously aims to dissolve all connections between the United States and France, and to substitute a monarchic for a republican ally."[18] Even Thomas Jefferson entered the fray, with a near-treasonous letter to his friend Philip Mazzei, an Italian doctor-turned-wine merchant who had bought a farm adjacent to Jefferson's Monticello.

> In place of that noble love of liberty & republican government which carried us triumphantly thro' the war, an anglican, monarchical & aristocratical party has sprung up, whose avowed object is to draw over us . . . the forms of the British government. . . . Against us are the Executive, the Judiciary . . . all the officers of the government, all who want to be officers, all timid men who prefer calm despotism to the boisterous sea of liberty, British merchants & Americans trading on British capital, speculators & holders in the banks & public funds, a contrivance for the purposes of corruption & and for assimilating us in all things, to the rotten as well as the sound parts of the British model.[19]

Jefferson vilified the man who had entrusted him with the conduct of the nation's foreign affairs: "It would give you a fever," Jefferson wrote to Mazzei, "were I to name to you the apostates who have gone over to these heresies, men who were Samsons in the field and Solomons in the councils, but who have had their heads shorn by the harlot England."[20]

When the Jay Treaty took effect early in 1796, the French government declared the United States in violation of "the alliance which binds the two peoples"[21] and repudiated the historic Franco-American treaties of 1778 that led to American independence.

French foreign minister Charles Delacroix sent Adet new instructions to eschew subterfuge and "use all the means in his power in the United States to bring about a successful revolution and Washington's replacement."[22] Delacroix told Adet to mobilize Americans against the Jay Treaty and Washington's policy of neutrality. "There is not an instant to lose in attaching the [American] nation to France in the war against England and Spain; the conquest of Canada and Louisiana must be made this very winter; fleets of privateers, sustained by our warships must go and destroy the commerce of our mutual enemies."[23]

On September 19, 1796, President Washington announced he would retire at the end of his second term and not seek reelection. The political struggle over the Jay Treaty had exhausted him, and the barrage of personal attacks—the first in his presidency—had wounded him deeply. Although he had decided to retire almost six months earlier, he had kept his decision secret to limit the time for electioneering that he feared might divide the nation and provoke insurrection or civil war. The "President's Farewell Address" to the nation appeared in the *American Daily Advertiser* in Philadelphia and began with Washington's invocation:

> That your Union and brotherly affection may be perpetual; that the free Constitution, which is the work of your hands, may be sacredly maintained; that its administration in every department may be stamped with wisdom and virtue; that . . . the happiness of the people of these states, under the auspices of liberty, may be made complete. . . .[24]

Washington went on to defend his policy of neutrality and issued this stern warning:

> Against the insidious wiles of foreign influence, I conjure you to believe me, fellow citizens, the jealousy of a free people ought to be *constantly* awake. . . . Even our commercial policy should hold an equal and impartial hand. . . . 'Tis folly in one nation to look for disinterested favors from another. . . . There can be no greater error than to expect or calculate upon real favors from nation to nation.[25]

With Washington's voluntary withdrawal from office, Adet altered his strategy. Instead of inciting revolution in the streets, he would ensure election of a pro-French president—Jefferson—with a barrage of pseudonymous warnings to the press that only Jefferson's election could prevent war with France. Assured of French government support, Republicans and their Francophile allies began an aggressive campaign that divided the nation. Although they were Republicans and Federalists on the ballots, each side called the other the French or British Party.

Late in October, Adet intensified his warnings in the press of imminent war with France. On October 27, he issued an appeal to Americans to renew their friendship with France by annulling the

Jay Treaty and reinstating the Franco-American Treaty of Amity and Commerce of 1778. A week later, he sent newspapers the so-called cockade proclamation, which called on French citizens and Friends of France to wear the red, white, and blue French cockade—"the symbol of liberty, which is the fruit of eight years toils and privations, and of five years victories."[26] Failure by French citizens to wear the cockade, he warned, would cost them the services of French consuls and protection of the French flag. Across the nation, Democratic Societies sent members into the streets to pin cockades on passersby— sometimes by force. French flags appeared in windows everywhere, along with signs calling for union with France. Pennsylvania's Quakers grew so fearful of war with France they unanimously voted for Jefferson and his Republicans.

"French influence never appeared so open and unmasked," South Carolina congressman William Loughton Smith wrote to Hamilton, who had left government to practice law in New York. "French flags, french cockades were displayed by the Jefferson party and there is no doubt that French money was spred. . . . In short there never was so barefaced and disgraceful an interference of a foreign power in any free country."[27]

Although Washington assailed Adet's "meddling in American politics," he had no way of stopping the Frenchman, and on November 15, Adet issued his final, most menacing warning to the secretary of state: he called "the treaty of commerce concluded with Great Britain equivalent to a treaty of alliance" and said it had so offended the French government that it had sent him orders "to suspend, from this moment, his ministerial functions with the Federal Government"—in effect breaking diplomatic relations with the United States. But, in an astonishing addendum, he appealed to the people—as Genet had threatened to do—with a declaration that

> the American people are not to regard the suspension of his ministerial functions as a rupture between France and the United States, but as a mark of discontent, which is to last until the Government of the United States returns to sentiments, and to measures, more conformable to the interests of the alliance, and the sworn friendship between the two nations . . . this alliance has always been dear

to Frenchmen; they have done everything to tighten its bands. The Government of the United States, on the contrary, has sought to break them. . . . Let your Government return to itself, and you will still find in Frenchmen faithful friends and generous allies.[28]

As Adet announced his recall from America, the French government accused President Washington of having ruptured Franco-American relations. French foreign minister Delacroix not only refused to receive America's new ambassador to France, Charles Cotesworth Pinckney, he ordered Pinckney expelled as an undesirable foreigner. Pinckney took refuge in Holland, where John Quincy Adams, the vice president's son, was ambassador. "There is a great ignorance," Adams responded, "of the character and sentiments of the American people in France among those who imagine that any manoeuvre of theirs could turn an election against the President of the United States."[29]

As Adams predicted, Adet's appeals produced an effect exactly opposite to the one he intended. Secretary of State Timothy Pickering expressed his indignation and refused to reply to Adet. Federalist newspapers across the north demonized Adet and warned that a Jefferson presidency would be "fatal to our independence, now that the interference of a foreign nation in our affairs is no longer disguised."[30] The *Connecticut Courant* called Adet's press campaign an attempt to "wean us from the government and administrators of our own choice and make us willing to be governed by such as France shall think best for us—beginning with Jefferson." New York newspaper editor Noah Webster demanded to know "how long the *delicacy* of our government will suffer every species of indignity from the agents of the French nation in this country?"[31] Writing in the *American Minerva,* Webster subsequently warned that

> an open enemy is less dangerous than an *insidious friend.* . . . Interest is the pole star of their conduct; such it has proved in every stage of their connections with us. Have they not told us themselves, that they will not regard their treaties if they afterwards discover them to be disadvantageous? Americans have more to fear from the French than from the English. The French . . . are determined *to have* a ruling influence, and control over the councils of

our nation, and over the good people of the United States. . . . *the first words our children should see in the primer, after;* WORSHIP *thy* CREATOR, *ought to be* NO FOREIGN INFLUENCE.[32]

Republicans were almost as offended by Adet's meddling in the American election as Federalists. One Republican railed that Adet's meddling had destroyed Jefferson's chances for election and that electors would "sooner be shot than vote for him." Another lamented that Adet had "irretrievably diminished the good will felt for his Government and the people of France by most people here."[33] Jefferson, too, recognized the adverse effects of Adet's campaign, and he remained in seclusion at Monticello, as far as possible from the political turbulence his candidacy had provoked. By the end of the year, Adet began questioning Jefferson's loyalty to France: "I do not know if . . . we shall always find in him a man wholly devoted to our interests. Mr. Jefferson likes us because he detests England; he seeks to draw near to us because he fears us less than Great Britain; but he might change his opinion of us tomorrow, if tomorrow Great Britain should cease to inspire his fears. . . . Jefferson is American, and, as such, he cannot be sincerely our friend. An American is the born enemy of all the European peoples."[34]

When Congress reconvened in December, Washington assailed French depredations against American shipping and called the atrocities against American seamen "outrageous beyond conception."[35] Adams agreed, declaring that "in their trances and delirium . . . they think to terrify America." Republicans countered that the British had seized fifty ships for every one seized by the French, but Noah Webster had the final word, pointing out that no agent of the British government had "dared to foment sedition in our peaceful land" by turning the American people against their own government, as Genet, Fauchet, and Adet had done. "Such bold insults are practiced only by our *generous allies* [the French]. It is right; it is necessary that the insidious designs of such *sly, intriguing,* but *ambitious* and *domineering allies,* should be unmasked. They are more dangerous than armies of foes."[36]

In the final days of the Washington administration, French leaders intensified their undeclared war on America, ordering seizure and

confiscation of all American ships and the arrest of American seamen on British or other enemy ships as pirates, subject to immediate
execution. By decimating America's ocean commerce, France hoped
to starve America into rebellion against the Adams candidacy. For
Vice President Adams and the Federalist-controlled Senate, there
seemed but one way to respond: war.

On February 8, 1797, John Adams won election as second president of the United States. Jefferson captured the second most electoral votes and, under election rules then in place, acceded to the
vice presidency. Had Adet not intruded himself in the campaign, the
results might have been reversed. Before leaving office, Washington
again reported to Congress the unceasing French attacks on American shipping and cruelties inflicted on captured American seamen.
When he left office and public life, the alliance he had embraced to
win American independence had ended; America and her French
ally were essentially at war.

10

The War with France

THE BLOODY END of Robespierre's Jacobins did not overturn what the French still call their First Republic. After approving a new constitution that deceitfully reaffirmed the Rights of Man, French rulers sent troops to annex tiny Belgium and then ordered the army to massacre starving Parisians demonstrating in the streets for bread.

The Convention looked for leadership to Paul Barras, a sly aristocrat-turned-Jacobin who had emerged from the fringes of Jacobin leadership by organizing the coup d'état that sent his mentor, Robespierre, to the blade. Barras took command of the Paris National Guard, then seized control of key government ministries and promoted young Colonel Napoléon Bonaparte to general. A former officer himself, Barras had worked with Bonaparte in the campaign to expel the British from Toulon in December 1793. When Barras snatched the reins of the Convention the following year, he and Bonaparte formed a symbiotic relationship that assured Barras military support for political power and Bonaparte political support for military power. To consummate their union, Barras conferred his mistress, Joséphine de Beauharnais, on Bonaparte and "gave the bride away" at the wedding.

After toppling Robespierre, Barras and his political friends dissolved the Convention and its unruly commoners and surrounded themselves with military leaders, clerics, and a coterie of nobles who had survived the revolution. Together, they devised a new "republican" government that was only slightly less chaotic than anarchy, with a five-man executive commission, or Directory, and a bicameral legislature—a lower house, or Council of Five Hundred, and an upper house, the Council of Elders, with members at least forty years old. The two councils elected the five directors, replacing one each year for a term of five years.

"We plan to end political factionalism and ensure national harmony," the Barras Directory pledged when it took office, "by restoring public morals, industry, commerce, the arts and sciences and public credit and by replacing revolutionary chaos with social order."[1] From the moment they took office, the directors did just the opposite and took full advantage of the disorder to enrich themselves.

With the British still blockading French ports and the French treasury almost empty, inflation and starvation provoked a plague of insurrections. In Paris, the poor rose in rebellion after Jacobin leader François Noël Babeuf, the "father of French communism,"[2] issued his inflammatory Manifesto of Equality:

"No more private property," he declared. "The earth belongs to no one; its fruits belong to every one. Let us end the disgusting distinctions between rich and poor, great and small, masters and servants, governors and governed. There is but one sun, one air for all to breathe."[3] The Manifesto incited rebellion across France, as famished peasants joined ill-clad and equally deprived soldiers in rioting. To counter anarchy, merchants, bankers, and clerics formed the Friends of Law and Order and supported a royalist counterrevolution.

Faced with civil war, Barras turned to Napoléon, who ordered troops to crush the peasant revolt, execute Babeuf, and put down the royalist counterrevolution. After the Friends of Law and Order fled to exile, Barras rewarded Napoléon with command of the mutinous French Army of the Interior. Bonaparte assuaged their anger and hunger with promises of rich pastures across French borders:

> You have no shoes, uniforms or shirts and almost no bread. Our stores are empty while those of our enemies are overflowing. I will lead you into the most fertile plains in the world. Rich provinces

and great cities will be in your power. There you will find honor, glory and wealth. It is up to you to conquer. You want to conquer. You can conquer. Let us march! *Marchons!*[4]

In lightning strikes that overwhelmed western Europe, his armies overran and plundered Holland, the Rhineland, Switzerland, Italy, Venice, Dalmatia, and the Ionian Islands. To forestall the onslaught, Russia, Austria, and Spain sued for peace in the spring of 1797, when Bonaparte's armies were about sixty miles from Vienna. He was unstoppable, unpredictable, never fighting a battle the same way twice. Europe's finest military minds were unable to understand, let alone resist or counter, his brilliant battlefield strategy. After overrunning northern Italy, French troops seized the Vatican and the Papal States, captured Pope Pius VI, stripped him of temporal powers, and, as Philip IV's armies had done in 1309, waylaid him and the papal court to France, where he died a year later.

Napoléon's conquests restored the French national economy with hundreds of millions of francs in reparations from conquered lands—more than 60 million francs from northern Italy alone, along with 10 million more in gold, silver, and jewels. "You can now count on 6 to 8 millions in gold or silver ingots or jewels," he wrote to Barras in triumph, "which are now at your disposal in Genoa."[5] The Pope paid an additional 30 million francs—and ceded Bologna, Ferrara, and the Romagna. With relatively little great native art in France, Napoléon stripped Italy of its finest paintings and sculptures and converted the Louvre in Paris into what is still the world's greatest repository of stolen art. To disguise the theft, he ordered artists' names Gallicized: to this day, Bernini remains Bernin; Tintoretto, Tintorette; Michelangelo, Michelange, and so on—in the Louvre, as well as French history and art texts and reference works.

Bonaparte's brilliant military tactics and conquests raised him to heroic stature in France. The French compared him to Charlemagne, Saint Louis, Louis XIV, and Roman emperor "Jules Caesar." In September 1797, Barras called the Corsican hero back to Paris to break a political deadlock in legislative councils. Backed by Bonaparte's bayonets, Barras eliminated 2 directors, expelled 198 members of the 2 councils, and sent 18 others to prison in French Guiana. With the noisiest dissenters out of earshot, Barras anointed himself "king of the republic," appointed Napoléon commander in chief of French armies, and named Charles Maurice de Talleyrand-Périgord foreign minister.

A friend of Barras from Jacobin Club days, Talleyrand was part of a small but steady stream of aristocrat émigrés returning from exile to reclaim ancestral lands and their roles in national leadership. During the Terror, Talleyrand spent two years in exile in the United States and laid claim to considerable knowledge of North American affairs. Like Barras, Talleyrand was the consummate hedonist, never allowing loyalty or morality stand in the way of insatiable financial, political, aesthetic, and sexual appetites. An injury to his foot as a youngster left him with an ugly limp to complement his grotesque face. His external deformities corroded his inner being—infusing him with greed and scorn for humanity. Although he was unfit for military duty, his aristocratic origins opened the doors of the church, and his seductive voice, brilliant wit, and winning conversational and political skills won him, at thirty-four, a prestigious bishopric that made him chief spokesman for the entire French clergy. He reaped a fortune in gifts, commissions, and bribes; a bevy of mistresses; and, in 1789, a seat in the Jacobin Club when it was still a salon for aristocrat intellectuals. With Robespierre's rise to power, Talleyrand displayed chameleonic instincts by discarding his clerical robes, renouncing the Catholic Church, and swearing allegiance to secularism, state, and revolution. Sent to England as special emissary, he paid one too many visits to the lavish London quarters of his friend the duc d'Orléans, pretender to the French throne.

When Talleyrand returned to France, Jacobins accused him of royalist collaboration, and he fled to America, where he strode into the presidential mansion in Philadelphia expecting a reception worthy of his aristocratic lineage. President Washington refused to see him on grounds that reception of exiled aristocrats was tantamount to public rebuff of the existing French revolutionary regime. Talleyrand never forgave Washington, and he twisted the President's rejection into a hatred for all things American. "If I have to stay here another year," he wrote to his friend French novelist Madame de Staël, "I shall die."[6] He despised everything American—even the women, whom he described as "adorable at fifteen, faded at twenty-three, old at thirty-five, decrepit at forty or forty-five, losing their shape, their teeth and their hair."[7] Talleyrand complained that the United States had denied him opportunities, and he castigated Americans for making gold "the American God." He nonetheless left the United States a devout convert to that god, having accumulated a small fortune from speculations on land, commodities, banking, and outright usury. For the rest of his life, he would base virtually every political decision on the amount of gold he could extract from those needing his favors.

After the Directory came to power, a strong recommendation from Madame de Staël to Barras won Talleyrand appointment as foreign minister. Barras, no less than his predecessors in power, believed in the mystical "natural right" of France to give the law to the world. To recover that right, he turned to Choiseul's scheme for recovering the French colonial empire of the 1750s, before the Seven Years War. With western Europe in thrall, only Britain blocked French return to glory and world dominance, and Britain seemed ready to fall.

As Napoléon's armies ravaged continental Europe, the French Navy wreaked havoc on Anglo-American trade in the Caribbean and on the Atlantic. By late 1797, when Napoléon returned to Paris, French depredations on American and British shipping had pushed both nations to the brink of financial collapse: the French had seized 340 American ships—more than half the American merchant fleet—with cargoes valued at more than $55 million. Hundreds of America seamen languished in prison chains in Brest, Bordeaux, and the French West Indies. Insurance rates on Caribbean-bound ships increased fivefold in two years, from 6 percent to 35 percent of cargo values, and priced American exports out of world markets. Meanwhile, the Bank of England defaulted on English government bonds; 50,000 British seamen mutinied over lack of pay; and Britain seemed defenseless against French invasion of Canada, Ireland, and even the English homeland. Rebels had taken up arms in Ireland, and Talleyrand assured Barras, "The intelligence I have from Canada indicates a strong desire of Canadians to reunite with the [French] motherland."[8]

In the fall of 1797, Napoléon massed an army at Boulogne in northern France—l'Armée de l'Angleterre—to invade Britain, but

Charles Maurice de Talleyrand Périgord. The French foreign minister under the Directory and Napoléon I, Talleyrand demanded a bribe of $250,000 as the price for opening peace negotiations with United States peace commissioners in Paris.

after surveying Channel waters, he deemed the project all but impossible without a much larger naval force to occupy the entire Channel and prevent destruction of troop ships before they could reach England. "To carry out a descent on England without mastery of the sea would be the boldest and most difficult operation ever undertaken," Napoléon declared.[9]

Instead of risking a costly and potentially bloody assault on England, Napoléon and Barras decided to isolate her from her sources of colonial wealth. A small force, Napoléon said, could ensure Irish independence and create a barrier island to England's westward trade routes to North America, while the conquest of Malta and Egypt would cut England's Mediterranean routes to India. "In order truly to destroy England, we must occupy Egypt," he insisted.[10] Barras and Talleyrand agreed with Napoléon's plan—for many reasons. It would minimize French costs in money and lives while weakening England enough to permit French reconquest of much of her former empire. At the same time, it would distance Napoléon from the center of power in France, where his immense popularity might threaten their control of government.

Disdaining command of the small Irish expedition, Napoléon set off for Toulon to organize the great expedition to the East, where he envisioned rivaling the conquests of the Khans. "Europe is a bunch of mole hills," he scoffed. "The only great empires to conquer are those of the Orient . . . that is where greatness is to be found."[11] Barras, meanwhile, sent 1,000 French troops to support the Irish rebellion and ordered Talleyrand to lay the groundwork for recovering New France, by negotiating Spanish retrocession of Louisiana and Florida to France.

For Spain, Louisiana had become an economic and political burden, costing more to maintain than it produced in revenues. Apart from disgruntled French Creoles who sought reunion with their motherland, hordes of aggressive American immigrants were pouring across the Appalachians and inserting themselves, their language, religion, and political beliefs throughout Louisiana. Unwilling to integrate into Spanish life, Americans and their claims of "natural rights" to lands they tilled represented a threat to Spanish authority and monopoly of resources. "The effect of political equality," Talleyrand warned, "invites every citizen, regardless of class, to acquire wealth that rightfully belongs to the aristocracy and monarchy."[12]

With her army spread across Latin America, Spain had too few troops to block American expansionism. To protect her western territories, with their wealth in gold and silver ores, Spain accepted Talleyrand's proposal to retrocede Louisiana and allow the French army to build "a wall of brass forever impenetrable" to what he called "the American menace."[13] Encased by the French Army in the west and the French Navy on the east, America's expansion would come to an abrupt halt and leave the new nation dependent on France for her economic and military survival.

In the United States, Secretary of State Pickering accused France of renewing "the ancient plan of her Monarch of circumscribing and encircling what now constitutes the Atlantic States."[14] Both President Adams and the Federalist-controlled Senate were prepared to declare war to prevent that eventuality. Only the Republican-controlled House of Representatives opposed a declaration of war because they believed it would provoke a French invasion. President Adams replied that America had no choice: France, he said, "has already gone to war with us. . . . She is at war with us, but we are not at war with her."[15] Republicans demanded that Adams at least send a mission to France to try to heal ruptured Franco-American relations—much as John Jay had secured rapprochement with England in 1794.

In an unusual turnabout, Federalists sided with Republicans—if only to silence accusations of Federalist warmongering—and Adams appointed a three-man bipartisan commission to go to France to seek peace: Federalists Charles Cotesworth Pinckney of South Carolina and John Marshall of Virginia, and Republican Elbridge Gerry of Massachusetts.

Talleyrand, however, had no intention of negotiating with the United States until they renounced the Jay Treaty with England—an eventuality he believed unlikely. "Everywhere I traveled in America," he recalled, "I did not find a single Englishman who did not feel like an American and not a single Frenchman who did not feel like a stranger. . . . All American habits are English, thus tying the American merchant to England—not only by the nature of his transactions and the lines of credit established over the years, but by irresistible law of the marketplace imposed by consumer demand."[16]

On October 8, 1797, Talleyrand agreed to see the three American peace commissioners at his home but told them he would not receive them officially or open negotiations until he obtained instructions from the Directory. Ten days later, a Swiss financier, Jean Conrad Hottinguer, showed up after dark at the Left Bank quarters of the Americans and told them President Adams had insulted Barras in a speech assailing French attacks on American ships. To begin negotiations, said Hottinguer, Barras would require an official apology—along with "sweeteners"—douceurs—for the Directors, Talleyrand, and other officials. Such "gratifications," the banker asserted, were "customary distributions in diplomatic affairs in Europe."[17] In disbelief, Pinckney demanded the request in writing, and two days later—again, at night—Hottinguer showed up with a second banker, "Monsieur Bellamy." Swiss-born but living then in Hamburg, Bellamy claimed intimate friendship with Talleyrand. He explained that the foreign minister considered himself a friend of the United States, but that the Directors felt insulted by John Adams and required a "spontaneous gesture of friendship or gift"[18] to placate them enough to receive the American envoys. Bellamy estimated that 120 million francs—about $250,000—might suffice. In addition, the American government would have to show its good faith with a loan of $12.8 million.

Stunned by the demands, the American commissioners told Bellamy they would have to inform President Adams. Bellamy was indignant. He reminded the Americans that the Directors had the right to expect the same fealty and remuneration as "the ancient kings of France. You must understand," he all but shouted, "without money, you will not be received. You must pay money—a great deal of money."[19]

After Pinckney and Marshall showed the agents to the door, Hottinguer reported to Talleyrand—only to return a week later to warn the Americans to "think of the power and violence of France. Buy some time; give them the gifts and loans and buy some time! If you don't, I fear that the Directory will declare war on America."

The commissioners replied that war would be no worse than the depredations the French were already committing against American shipping. "We are unable to defend our commerce on the seas, but we will defend our shores," Pinckney cried out.

Hottingeur feigned anger: "It is not a question of war, but money. The Directors are waiting for an offer of money."

"We have already answered that demand," Pinckney shot back.

"No, you have not," Hottinguer insisted. "What is your answer?"

"It is no! Not even six pence!" Pinckney shouted.[20]

Hottinguer sighed but kept his calm. He spent two more hours pleading, cajoling, threatening: a bribe would be of great advantage to the Americans; old allies should not bicker over money; the commissioners were risking war and endangering their nation by refusing to pay so small a sum—perhaps, given the anger of the Directors, even putting themselves in personal danger in Paris. Again Hottinguer failed to budge the Americans, and Talleyrand sent a third emissary—Lucien Hauteval—to see them. Talleyrand could not understand the American position; European emissaries had given him millions for the privilege of negotiating with France; he said French consuls in America had routinely bribed American officials for favors. Hauteval, however, had as little success as his predecessors with the strange threesome from America.

Knowing Gerry was an ardent Republican, Talleyrand sought to weaken commission unanimity by inviting the New Englander for an informal one-on-one meeting. He warned Gerry that the Directory might attack the United States within a week if the commission did not respond to its demands. Gerry had no sooner delivered the warning to his colleagues when Hauteval arrived for an answer. The Americans asked whether payment of the bribe would end French attacks on American shipping; when told no—that the attacks would end only after the signing of a new treaty—they demanded to meet with Talleyrand. Talleyrand ignored the demand, and Marshall wrote to Secretary of State Pickering:

> Our situation is more complicated and difficult than you can possibly imagine. They repeat their demands for money again and again. We despair of succeeding in our mission. An American citizen, Mr. Putnam was thrown into prison, charged with fraud against the French, but this was simply a pretext designed to instill fear in Americans generally. We have not yet been received officially and the seizure of our ships continues. Frequent, intense efforts have been made to persuade us to negotiate with people who have no official status, whose goal is to obtain money. But we have continually refused to have any diplomatic contacts with such people, including some with close personal contacts in the foreign ministry.[21]

Talleyrand's efforts to extort bribes from the American commissioners knew no bounds. When Hottinguer, Bellamy, and Hauteval failed, he sent Tom Paine, Connecticut artist John Trumbull, and other Jacobin Americans to see the commissioners—to no avail. As weeks elapsed, the commissioners grew anxious about the mounting costs of their Paris stay. "Every day there is something new and magnificent to see," Marshall wrote to his wife. "At night, there are astonishing spectacles that enchant the soul."[22]

To economize, the commissioners sought less costly quarters.

"Friends" steered them to a hotel owned by Voltaire's niece—a delightful thirty-two-year-old widow whom the great philosopher had adopted as his daughter and subsequently his mistress. Madame de Villette charmed the commissioners as much as she had her uncle, with magnificent suppers and front-row seats at theater and other entertainments. The commissioners luxuriated in their new quarters, which, though inexpensive, were more lavish than their previous lodgings and offered a sweeping view of the magnificent gardens of Marie de Medici's palace.

"Why will you not lend us money?" Madame de Villette blurted out one evening in a seductive whisper that stunned Marshall. "If you would only give us the money, we could arrange everything satisfactorily. We gladly loaned you money during your revolution."[23] Astounded by the sudden shift in conversation, Pinckney and Marshall realized that she, too, was a Talleyrand agent, and that without knowing it, they had rented lodgings subsidized by the French Foreign Ministry to lure them into the arms of a seductress. Pinckney stood and announced he would return to America. Madame de Villette warned that if he ended his mission, France had a powerful political party in America ready to seize power from the Adams administration by force if necessary.

Bellamy reappeared the following day to mediate. For many years, he said, Beaumarchais and his company, Hortalez & Cie, had been trying to collect £145,000 for Revolutionary War supplies he had sold to the Virginia militia. Bellamy proposed that the United States mingle the money for Talleyrand and the Directors with the funds Virginia owed Beaumarchais, and the French playwright would then pay the "sweeteners" without disclosing American government involvement.

Marshall and Pinckney all but threw Bellamy out the door. The next day, Talleyrand sent Beaumarchais to plead the case personally. "France is powerful enough to give the law to the world," he warned—powerful enough to defeat England and isolate the United States in the world. When the Americans again rejected paying bribes, the playwright used his acting skills to beg them, even shedding tears to describe the cruel fate that awaited him if he failed in his mission to obtain the payments.

In April 1798, Marshall and Pinckney abandoned their mission. "There is not the least hope of an accommodation with this government," Pinckney wrote in disgust. "We sue in vain to be heard."[24] Gerry quarreled bitterly with the two Federalists and said he would remain as a private citizen and continue to negotiate a new treaty. "To prevent war," he declared, "I will stay."[25] Gerry was convinced that he could achieve peace by personally apologizing to the Directory for the president's anti-French statements. Outraged by Gerry's disloyalty, Pinckney and Marshall showed Gerry to the door and never spoke to him again. Although Pinckney's daughter contracted a fever and delayed his departure until August, Marshall boarded an American ship in Bordeaux on April 24 and "bid an eternal adieu to Europe & to its crimes."[26]

Talleyrand was delighted. He had succeeded in dividing the commission, and, he believed, he would be able to prolong negotiations with Gerry long enough to permit the "French Party" in America—Jefferson's Republicans—to seize power. When more than a hundred French legislators protested Talleyrand's alienation of the United States, the Directors sent soldiers with bayonets to the legislative halls to annul their votes and force the council to vote unanimous support for Talleyrand's policies.

Like so many French foreign ministers before and since, Talleyrand completely misjudged the temper of the American people. The so-called French Party in America had indeed agitated for rapprochement with France, but even the staunchest Republican congressmen grew uneasy at the end of 1797, when they failed to receive any report from the commissioners in Paris. In March 1798, the first dispatches finally arrived—mostly in cipher that would take days, even weeks, to decode. The president was able to glean enough information from a few letters to be outraged by the "unexampled arrogance" of Talleyrand and the French Directory. He sent a message to Congress with the essence of what he understood and asked for funds to rebuild American coastal defenses, arm merchant ships, build a navy, and prepare for war. Vice President Jefferson called the president's message "insane"; other Republicans charged the president with concealing all but the negative aspects of the dispatches. By then, Talleyrand had issued his own interpretation of the breakdown of peace talks. He called the Americans "picky men, shy and stubborn" who had "twisted the meaning of honest conversations" and "neglected the opportunity of meetings in society and nowhere presented themselves to the minister."[27] Republicans demanded to see the full, deciphered text of all the dispatches. Most Federalists agreed—if only to silence the Republicans.

On April 3, President Adams sent the deciphered messages to Congress but disguised the names of Talleyrand's agents—Beaumarchais, Hottinguer, Bellamy, and Hauteval—as W, X, Y, and Z—to protect them from retaliation. As Federalists had hoped, the XYZ dispatches, as they were called, silenced the French Party in Congress and across America. As Secretary of State Pickering put it, "The Democrats in neither House of Congress make much opposition; and out of doors the French Devotees are rapidly quitting the worship of their idol." Vice President Jefferson predicted that "to wipe off the imputation of being French partisans" some Republicans would "go over to the war measures so furiously pushed by the other party."[28]

The always acerbic first lady, Abigail Adams, gloated that "the olive Branch tendered to our Gallic Allies . . . has been rejected with scorn . . . public opinion is changing here very fast, and the people begin to see who have been their firm unshaken friends, steady to their interests and defenders of their Rights and Liberties."[29]

Former secretary of war Henry Knox, who had commanded the Continental Army artillery in the Revolutionary War, waxed ecstatic over the evident Adams triumph against American Jacobinism: "The President Shines like a God in the Declaration of his Sentiments. They must electrify all the good people of the US—but all are not good. We must have some short but sharp internal conflicts."[30]

Knox was prescient in all respects. The XYZ dispatches provoked a frenzy of war fever and violent anti-French demonstrations. Mobs attacked the home of Benjamin Franklin Bache, the fanatically pro-French editor of the Jeffersonian *Aurora*. Across the nation, town meetings, merchant associations, and militia companies sent petitions of support to the president. More than a thousand young men in Philadelphia marched to the president's house to volunteer to fight against France; President Adams came out to address them, dressed incongruously in full-dress military uniform complete with sword. After Abigail greeted one group with a flowerlike device of radiating bows of black ribbon, Federalists converted it into a black cockade that became their symbol of opposition to the French tricolor cockade. "Every [black] cockade will be another Declaration of Independence," wrote the editor of the Columbian Centinnel in Boston.[31] Within days, Abigail Adams's black cockade sprouted on the hats and lapels of the president, his cabinet members, and every "good American"—man, woman, and child—across the land. Fights broke out on street corners, in shops, sometimes between old friends at church over the color of cockcades they wore. Clergymen preached the dangers of French atheism and, worse, French popery. In New Haven, Connecticut, Yale president Timothy Dwight, a fervent Congregationalist clergyman, fretted openly that if the French invaded America, "We may see our wives and daughters the victims of legal prostitution; soberly dishonoured; speciously polluted. . . ."[32] In Cambridge, Massachusetts, Harvard College canceled the French oration at graduation exercises; and in the State House yard in Philadelphia, wearers of black cockades ripped tricolor cockades off the clothes of Republicans and set off a riot that needed a troop of cavalry to break it up.

Across the nation, Federalist newspapers called for expulsion of French and Irish aliens for plotting with Jacobins and Republicans to overthrow the government. Many of the 40,000 Irish immigrants in America were indeed former revolutionaries who had fled English suppression, but the 30,000 French immigrants included royalist émigrés who detested revolution. Federalist newspapers depicted them all in the same color and frightened thousands into fleeing onto crowded ships back to Europe to escape the wrath of nativist lynch mobs. In May, the United States government rejected the credentials of the new French ambassador, and together with all French consuls in America, he returned to France and left the United States devoid of French diplomatic representation. Rumors followed their departure that Napoléon's armies were on their way to the United States.

Americans had good reason for such fears. Napoléon was conquering the world. Not satisfied with swallowing half of Europe,

Bonaparte had set off for the Levant in mid-May with the largest force to cross the Mediterranean since the Crusades—four hundred transports with more than 35,000 elite troops, escorted by thirteen battleships of the line and more than forty frigates and corsairs. On June 12, Napoléon captured Malta, and after confiscating the bullion and treasures of the ancient Knights of St. John, he sailed for Alexandria.

"Soldiers!" he proclaimed. "You are going to undertake a conquest whose effects on civilization and the commerce of the world will be incalculable. You will strike the greatest and most painful stroke against England until you can deal her final deathblow."[33] On July 2, Alexandria capitulated. Leaving 6,000 men to hold the great port city, Bonaparte marched southward with 25,000 troops, and after slaughtering an 18,000-man defending army at the Pyramids, he seized Cairo on July 24, at a cost of only 30 French lives. As Bonaparte moved eastward to Suez, another French army landed in Ireland to support the Irish rebellion. A week later, at the end of August, successive victories against the British troops at Balayna and Cartlebar emboldened the Irish to proclaim independence and leave England surrounded by enemies.

Henry Knox warned President Adams that the French would soon sail for America—most likely the South, to provoke a slave rebellion of "ten thousand blacks." Knox had read that French agents were secretly arming slaves in the Carolinas and Virginia in anticipation of French landings. "Take care, take care, you sleepy southern fools," warned a Federalist newspaper. "Your negroes will probably be your masters this day twelve month."[34] George Washington agreed, responding from his retirement home in Mount Vernon that "if the French should be so mad as openly and formidably to invade these United States, in expectation of subjugating the Government, laying them under contribution, or in hopes of dissolving the Union, I conceive there can hardly be two opinions respecting their Plan, and their operations will commence in the Southern quarter."[35]

Although Federalists united behind President Adams in demanding a declaration of war against France, enough House Republicans held their ground to prevent it. Public pressures forced them to yield on defensive measures, however. The army had only 3,500 troops and no new cannons, small arms, or ammunition; coastal forts had deteriorated into useless piles of rubble; and the navy's only three frigates were still under construction.

Congress quickly remedied the situation. In April 1798 it created a Department of the Navy and authorized acquisition of twelve ships with up to twenty guns each. In May it authorized procurement of cannons, arms, and ammunition, an increase in regular army strength. It ordered the navy to "seize, take and bring into port" French privateers and other raiders in or near American waters, and it imposed an embargo on all commerce with France and her dependencies and banned all French ships from American ports. Congress also passed a law allowing American merchant ships to arm and defend themselves against French attackers and to seize French ships and contribute them to the navy for 6 percent government bonds. In July, Congress established the Marine Corps, authorized construction or purchase of twenty-four additional navy ships, and ordered the navy "to protect the commerce of the United States" on the seven seas and seize French warships anywhere in the world.

War preparations doubled government spending from $5.8 million in 1796 to $11.5 million in 1799. Congress authorized the president to borrow $2 million at up to 6 percent and another $5 million at market rates of 8 percent. In addition, Congress raised another $2 million by enacting a direct property tax on houses and slaves. Housing taxes ranged from a flat 40 cents on houses with a value of $200 to 30 cents per hundred dollars of valuation on houses worth $500 or more. Slave owners paid a tax of 50 cents for every slave between the ages of twelve and fifty.

John Marshall returned to America in the summer of 1798 and put to rest any doubts that the French had been responsible for subverting American peace efforts. Adams responded angrily in a message to Congress after Marshall's arrival: "I will never send another minister to France without assurances that he will be received, respected and honored as the representative of a great, free, powerful, and independent nation."[36]

Congress authorized the president to expand the army to 10,000 men and, if needed, to call 80,000 state militiamen to active duty. Two weeks later, the president named—and the Senate confirmed—

George Washington as commander in chief of the armed forces. The former president immediately named Alexander Hamilton as inspector general and second in command. Aware of French ambitions in Florida and Louisiana, Hamilton began planning to attack the two territories, which he called "essential to the permanency of the Union. . . . If we are to engage in war, our game will be to attack where we can."[37]

Hamilton won support from the Federalist press. "A war with Spain is absolutely necessary to the salvation of this country if a war with France takes place or if the Spaniards have ceded Louisiana to France," wrote William Cobbett, the English-born editor of the Federalist *Porcupine's Gazette*. "They must both be driven into the Gulf of Mexico, or we shall never sleep in peace. . . . Besides, a war with Spain would be so convenient!"[38]

By midsummer, the Federalist press inflamed rampant nativism to mass paranoia by again urging expulsion of French and Irish aliens. England had already done so, and according to one Federalist congressman, "Unless we follow their example, we shall not, like them, escape the scourge which awaits us."[39] Congressman Harrison Gray Otis of Massachusetts agreed, and after standing in Congress to denounce Jeffersonian Democratic Societies, he asked, "Do we not know that the French . . . organized bands of aliens as well as their own citizens in other countries, to bring about their own nefarious purposes . . . ? By these means they have overrun all the republics in the world but our own." Gray warned that "French apostles of sedition" were using "the same means . . . against this country."[40]

On June 18, 1798, Congress passed the first of four Alien and Sedition Acts to rid the nation of French and Irish influence and limit freedoms of speech and press by government opposition groups. To prevent immigrants from voting (most French and Irish voted Republican), the Naturalization Act extended the period of residency for naturalization from five to twelve years and forced aliens to register with and report regularly to immigration authorities. A week later, Congress passed the Act Concerning Aliens, which gave the president power to arrest and deport without trial any aliens deemed "dangerous to the peace and safety of the United States." The Act Respecting Alien Enemies of July 6 detailed presidential powers for arresting, detaining, and deporting aliens in case of war. Although the government had no manpower to enforce the Alien Acts, their enactment frightened thousands of French and Irish into fleeing the country—despite the built-in expiration date at the end of the presidential term in 1800.

In a symbolic broadside at France, Congress passed the most oppressive of the four laws—the Act for the Punishment of Certain Crimes—on July 14, the French national holiday commemorating the storming of the Bastille. Known as the Sedition Act, or Gag Law, the original bill labeled France and the French people "hostile" to the United States and imposed the death penalty on anyone convicted of aiding them. Faced with overwhelming opposition by members of their own party, Federalist sponsors modified the punishment, imposing only fines and imprisonment on anyone who opposed or interfered with application or enforcement of American laws—or conspired to do so. The publication of any "false or malicious writing directed against the President or Congress" was declared a misdemeanor. Like the Alien Acts, the Sedition Act proved more an effective threat than an actively enforced measure.

Despite its warlike measures, Congress steadfastly refused to declare war against France until France herself declared war. "Congress," complained Federalist senator Rufus King of New York, "have left the country neither in peace nor in war! & france [sic] is too skilful not to profit from this ambiguity of situation." The attorney general put it differently: "There exists not only an *actual* maritime war between France and the United States, but a maritime war *authorized* by both nations."[41] South Carolina's Pinckney, back from the XYZ confrontations in Paris, concluded, "If we would have peace with France, it must be obtained, not by negotiation, but by the sword."[42]

While America waited for shipyards to build and launch a navy, English prime minister William Pitt sent secret proposals to President Adams for an alliance against France and Spain, with Britain providing the fleet and America the troops to free the Americas from French and Spanish rule. Francisco de Miranda had been to London and convinced Pitt that Latin Americans were prepared to rebel against Spain and welcome a liberating army of Americans. Hamilton favored the alliance. To "detach South America from Spain," he said, would block "the channel through which the riches of Mexico and Peru are conveyed to France." He attached one condition: that "all on this side of the Mississippi must be ours."[43]

President Adams, however, rejected the plan. Americans, he said, were not ready to reestablish military ties to their former oppressor, let alone return to a state of naval dependence on Britain. Adams believed it imperative that the United States establish its own powerful, independent fleet to protect American shores and maritime commerce. As for aiding Latin American rebels, the unexpected butchery of the French Revolution, he said, dissuaded him from "engaging myself and my country in most hazardous and expensive blood experiments to excite similar horrors in South America."[44]

Nonetheless, Adams recognized the urgency of ending French depredations, and he agreed to a temporary, unwritten naval accord with Britain—a quasi-alliance for a quasi-war. Until American production facilities came online, the United States would borrow British arms and ammunition for American merchant ships and privateers, and British warships would escort convoys of American merchant ships.

"We draw the Government of the United States closer to Great Britain," crowed the British emissary to the United States, "and give consistency to measures which tend to widen their breach with France."[45]

The Anglo-American entente sent tremors through the French foreign ministry in Paris. Unless France acted immediately, the British Navy would prevent French troops from reaching America and leave Hamilton's planned invasion of Florida and Louisiana unimpeded.

Construction and refitting of American warships proceeded faster than anticipated. By the end of June, the first two frigates—the *United States* and the *Constellation*—were plowing through American coastal waters, and early the next month, the *Delaware*, a converted sloop with sixteen guns, captured the first French prize of the quasi-war off southern New Jersey—a twelve-gun schooner that a shipyard refitted and sent back to sea to strengthen the United States Navy. By the end of October, the navy had launched a third frigate, the *Constitution*, and armed more than a thousand merchant ships. Together, they cleared American coastal waters of French marauders and freed the British fleet to chase French ships from the rest of the North Atlantic.

With offshore shipping protected from French assault, the U.S. Navy sailed to the Caribbean to wage offensive warfare against France for the first time. President Adams ordered the navy to "sweep the West India seas" of French ships and seize French seamen as hostages for the thousands of American seamen languishing in French prisons. Congress supported the president with legislation "to cause the most rigorous retaliation to be executed on . . . citizens of the French Republic."[46] At the beginning of 1799, the French had captured more than eight hundred American vessels, but by the end of the year, the surprising American Navy had retaliated by seizing eighty-four French vessels. Four American squadrons of five ships each had gained control of Caribbean waters, with Captain Thomas Truxton's squadron taking so many French vessels that Washington called him the equal of a "regiment in the field."[47] On February 9, 1799, Truxton's *Constellation* scored the first major American victory in the quasi-war by engaging and capturing the French Navy's big frigate *Insurgente* off the island of Nevis. Astonished to find himself in American hands, the French captain protested, "Our two nations are at peace." Bridling at the ambiguity of what he called a half war with France, Truxton penned his reaction in the ship's log: "The french Captain tells me, I Have caused a War with France, if so I am glad of it, for I detest Things done by Halves."[48]

America's naval successes stunned Talleyrand and the Directors, who, like the British at Lexington, had scorned Americans as a nation of ragtag commoners—farmers and woodsmen incapable of building and operating a modern navy that could withstand the might of professional French forces. The farmers and woodsmen, however, were pushing France to the brink of economic and military catastrophe. The embargo on French goods had closed rich American markets to important revenue-producing products such as wines, brandies, ribbons, silks, linens, and porcelain, while British ships prevented French transports from carrying essential goods from the French Antilles back to France. French fortunes were declining dramatically on other fronts as well. Napoléon's boundless ambitions for conquest had led him to misjudge the strength and resourcefulness of his enemies.

On August 1, 1798, a week after Napoléon had entered Cairo, Admiral Horatio Nelson's British fleet surprised and annihilated the French fleet of 55 warships and 280 transports at Aboukir Bay, near Alexandria. The French Army was trapped in Egypt. Hoping to establish an overland route to France via the Levant and Constantinople, Napoléon left half his army in Cairo and led 13,000 troops across the Sinai Peninsula to Palestine, where they captured Gaza and Jaffa and laid siege to Acre. After five unsuccessful assaults, plague killed half the men and forced the rest to slink back to Cairo.

Convinced that Barras and the Directors had betrayed him to the English to prevent his accession to power, Napoléon made secret arrangements to sail back to France with a handful of trusted aides on two frigates that had survived the Nelson assault. He sailed off in the dead of night, leaving only a hastily scrawled note to announce his clandestine departure to his second in command, General Jean Baptiste Kléber. The note shocked Kléber, who accused the Corsican of "desertion. . . . There is no doubt: Bonaparte has sacrificed this country [Egypt]," Kléber wrote, "and he has fled in order to escape the catastrophe of surrender."[49] Within a year, invading English troops would force the ill-fated French expeditionary force that Napoléon deserted to lay down its arms and surrender.

In Ireland, the French suffered a similar humiliation when a British fleet trapped and captured nine French warships and transport vessels in Donegal Bay. Cut off from escape by sea, the French invaders cawed like mad hens and surrendered, permitting England to reopen her North Atlantic trade routes.

As the aura of French invincibility disintegrated, conquered peoples in Belgium, Luxembourg, Switzerland, and Italy rose in rebellion against French occupation. Russia organized a new alliance with Britain, Naples, Portugal, Sardinia, and the Turks to halt French expansion. An Anglo-Russian army landed in Holland, while another Russian force joined the Austrians to push the French out of the Bavarian and Italian Alps, Switzerland, and the Rhineland. In Tuscany, Italian patriots took up arms and expelled the French from their homeland, while farther south, the valiant king of Naples led his little army toward Rome to free the Holy See. In the Ionian Sea, a Turko-Russian fleet blockaded and isolated French-held islands, including Corfu. In the French Antilles, a slave rebellion all but stripped the French of authority on Saint Domingue and cut the vital flow of sugar to France. In France proper, Royalists staged a massive counterrevolution in the central provinces, and when the Directory tried to draft 200,000 more men to strengthen the army, one-third refused to report.

Besieged from all directions and stripped of revenues from foreign plunder, France faced economic collapse unless Talleyrand could restore the flow of supplies and foodstuffs from her former ally, the United States. In a typical turnabout, Talleyrand ordered immediate release of American seamen and other Americans from French prisons. He reopened French ports to American ships and ordered an end to French attacks on American shipping. He issued a formal invitation to peace talks that purposely adopted President Adams's own language in pledging that "whatever plenipotentiary the Government of the United States might send to France . . . would be undoubtedly received with respect due to the representative of a free, independent, and powerful nation."[50] On paper at least, Talleyrand seemed willing to write finis to the twenty-five-year-old French plot against America.

Napoléon, however, had other plans.

11

"I Renounce Louisiana"

Napoléon's flight from Egypt demoralized his armies in Europe as much as it emboldened his enemies. By mid-June, foreign troops had reached the borders of France, and French political leaders responded in habitual Gallic style with another coup d'état. The political upheaval left only the resilient Barras clinging to power, along with Lucien Bonaparte, one of Napoléon's younger brothers. They, in turn, dismissed every cabinet minister but Talleyrand. Unsure of the new government's stability, he resigned, jumped into his carriage, and sped off to Germany with carpetbags of extorted money to secrete in the banks of Hamburg—known then as England's private vault.

To unite the French against a foreign invasion, the Directors reverted to Jacobin tactics of 1793: they drafted all young men into the army and sent opponents of the regime to prison or exile. Strengthened by 120,000 new conscripts, the French Army in the North forced Anglo-Russian forces in the Low Countries to retreat northward.

On October 9, 1799, Napoléon landed secretly at Saint Raphael on the south coast of France near present-day Cannes, but word of his arrival spread quickly and set off joyful street demonstrations in Paris. He arrived a week later to cheering crowds that all but elevated him to power. The Directory had little choice but to welcome him as a hero and restore his supreme command in the military. He demanded more, however, and savagely accused the Directors of treasonous misrule during his absence.

"What have you done to the brilliant French nation I left in your hands?" he shouted. "I left you a nation at peace; I return to find her at war! I left you with nothing but victories, I return to find nothing but defeats!"[1] To end the political chaos that he believed underlay the nation's military reverses, he demanded the resignation of the Directors. Fearing for their lives, Barras and two others complied and left Paris for their country estates. Napoléon arrested the other two, then marched into the Council of Five Hundred and ordered troops to bar the doors with fixed bayonets.

"You are violating the sanctuary of the legislature," cried the angry assemblymen. "Leave the hall!" Bonaparte ignored the shouts and climbed to the tribune. "By coming in here, you are warring against your own people," shrieked a deputy. "Is it for this that you defeated our enemies?"[2]

As Napoléon tried to speak, angry council members shouted him down; a few rushed to the tribune, grabbed him by the arms and shoulders, and shook him; one attacked him with his fists. Four grenadiers rushed to the rescue. Clearly shaken, he turned to the troops and called out, "I appeal to you, my brave companions in arms. Remember that I march with the god of victory and the god of fortune." Then he snarled at the politicians and stomped out of the hall. The legislators called for his arrest, but his brother Lucien adjourned the session before they could vote.

Napoléon returned to his military garrison, declared the Council of Five Hundred "bold brigands . . . doubtless in the pay of England,"[3] and ordered their arrest. As troops stormed the council chambers, opposition members fled, ceding the hall to Bonapartists. They immediately overthrew the Directory in favor of a three-man consulate, which quickly became a one-man consulate after a rigged plebiscite approved life tenure for Napoléon as first consul by 3.5 million votes in favor, with only 8,000 opposed. Invested with the same title and powers as "Jules Caesar," Napoléon assumed four cabinet posts himself—Finance, Justice, Interior (police), and War (army and navy)—and ordered Talleyrand to resume his role as minister of foreign affairs and restore peace and normal trade relations with the

United States. Napoléon invited thousands of other noblemen who had fled the revolution to return to France—not to right the wrongs of the revolution but to rebuild the ranks of officers in the army and navy with experienced leaders. For centuries, the officers corps had been the exclusive preserve of the nobility, until the revolution forced them to flee into exile to escape slaughter by Jacobin soldiers. To lure them back into service, Napoléon restored their titles and returned their hereditary lands. To entice Talleyrand back to the Foreign Ministry for peace talks with the Americans, Napoléon restored his ancestral lands, named him grand chamberlain of France, and promised him the Papal State of Benevento, with the title Prince de Bénévent.

Napoléon had several motives for resuming peace talks with the United States. Renewal of Franco-American trade was paramount, but he also needed to end the quasi-war that had disrupted vital French commerce with her islands in the Carribean. A third reason for seeking peace with the Americans was to restore French control over Louisiana. Before his resignation, Talleyrand had all but convinced Spain to agree to secret retrocession of Louisiana to France, but rumors of the proposed retrocession had provoked Alexander Hamilton to threaten an American invasion of the territory. By restoring peace and free trade with America, Napoléon hoped to lure the United States into a sleepy prosperity that would let French transport ships slip through the Carribean and Gulf of Mexico to land troops in New Orleans and consummate retrocession. Slow but steady troop landings during the spring, summer, and autumn months, shipload by shipload, would gradually inject a powerful army into the territory before the United States became aware of the French presence—and too late to react.

Thus, Napoléon's orders to Talleyrand were unequivocal: make peace with the United States at almost any cost. To emphasize the importance of his directive, he appointed his personable brother Joseph Bonaparte, who spoke English fluently, to attend peace negotiations.

The United States was as eager for peace as Napoléon seemed to be. When the Corsican came to power, Anglo-American control of the seas had revived American ocean commerce; with shipping no longer subject to French raiders, insurance rates fell to 10 percent of cargo values, compared to 35 percent at the peak of the quasi war. After decades of conflict, almost every American—from the president to the common man, but especially merchants and farmers— wanted peace, and Talleyrand's overtures convinced President John Adams to appoint a new three-man peace commission to go to Paris. He picked Chief Justice Oliver Ellsworth, North Carolina governor William R. Davie, and the American minister in Holland, William Vans Murray.[4] Unlike the other commissioners, Murray spoke fluent French. He was also a close friend and confidant of John Quincy Adams, the president's son, who, as United States emissary in Berlin, served as the president's personal listening post in Europe.

As much as the president wanted peace, however, the XYZ affair had left him understandably wary of "the cloven footed Devil Talleyrand."[5] He therefore set strict preconditions for peace talks, demanding that France not only show his emissaries "the respect due to representatives of a free, independent, and powerful nation," but agree to compensate American merchants for nearly $60 million in losses during the quasi-war. Once France met these conditions, the American peace commissioners were to negotiate a new treaty of commerce to replace the Franco-American treaties of 1778. Like Washington, Adams believed that entangling foreign alliances would hinder the nation's future growth and prosperity, and he instructed peace commissioners to negotiate only a short-term, albeit renewable, agreement limited to commercial relations. To prevent repetition of the XYZ affair, his instructions prohibited discussing any loans or payments.

President Adams was convinced that America's surprising naval power had forced Talleyrand back to the peace table, and he ordered the navy to continue attacking the French in the Caribbean until the French foreign minister actually signed a peace agreement.

On February 1, 1800, the intrepid Captain Truxton, now commanding the thirty-eight-gun *Constellation*, spotted the fifty-four-gun French frigate *La Vengeance* and whipped his ship around to pursue. The French vessel carried a huge cargo of money from Guadeloupe to France—the island's entire profits from a month's trade—along with 80 military passengers, 36 American prisoners, and a crew of 320. It tried to flee, but the swifter *Constellation* closed in and raked it with cannon fire that left the deck in shambles and awash in Gallic blood. After five hours of brutal fighting, the French captain ordered the tricolor lowered and prepared to surrender. But darkness and smoke had enveloped both ships by then and obscured Truxton's vision. With American cannons still spitting fire, the wounded French ship turned and fled into the night. Although the *Constellation* suffered its fair share of damage, the savage punishment Truxton inflicted on the French frigate won him a congressional gold medal and completely demoralized the French fleet and its commanders.

"Whence comes this madness for killing," whined Jefferson's friend Pierre Samuel du Pont de Nemours, "when it is evident that both nations are reconciled or arbitrating?"[6]

On August 1, 1800, American Navy shelling of French forts on Saint Domingue ensured victory for rebel slaves and their leader, François Dominique Toussaint L'Ouverture. Although Toussaint stopped short of declaring independence, he nonetheless assumed political control and opened what had been an exclusive French preserve to American and British commerce as a gesture of gratitude for their help in the seven-year rebellion.

Before America's three peace commissioners reached Paris, Napoléon had cloaked his authoritarian rule in the trappings of republicanism to rally intellectuals and proponents of the Rights of Man to his side. He dictated a new constitution, which emphasized his respect for individual rights, for learning, science, the arts, and above all for peace and harmony in the world. Although brutal on the battlefield, Napoléon seemed anything but that in the halls of the Tuileries Palace or Fontainebleau.[7] Indeed, he was charming— certainly not the oafish brute from a Corsican cave that his enemies expected. Born to the island's highest nobility, he had graduated from a prestigious, royal school in Brienne, on mainland France, and from an equally renowned secondary school at Autun in Burgundy. He then earned degrees at the École Militaire in Brienne and in Paris, which prepared the most brilliant young officers for leadership in the French military. Well schooled in letters, arts, and sciences, he won membership to the National Institute along with the most learned thinkers, philosophers, and scientists of France.

But he was as sly as he was brilliant, and he had a remarkable gift for cloaking self-serving ambitions in the garb of altruism. After seizing power "to rescue the Republic from anarchy," he decreed "reforms" that invariably restricted individual liberties and expanded his own dictatorial powers. In the guise of protecting individual rights, Napoléon's constitution did away with universal suffrage and limited the legislature's powers to rubber-stamping his executive decrees. To end ministerial corruption, the constitution consolidated executive powers in his hands, giving him control over the most powerful ministries—War, Interior (police), Finance, and Justice. The new constitution conspicuously omitted mention of *liberté, égalité, fraternité,* and the Rights of Man.

"Power is my mistress," he boasted. "I am destined to change the face of the world."[8]

To restore order in France, he removed troublesome, unemployed young men from the streets with universal compulsory military service of five years for all twenty-year-olds. The draft swelled his military into the most powerful in European history and extended French dominion across western Europe, from the Mediterranean to the North and Baltic seas; from the Atlantic Ocean and English Channel to the Russian and Turkish borders. Napoléon accompanied restoration of empire with restoration of monarchy, including all its trappings—court etiquette, hereditary land grants and incomes, and hereditary titles such as duke, count, and baron. The trickle of exiled aristocrats returning to France turned into a torrent, with many of the Cent Familles returning to reclaim titles and properties. Such notables as Adrienne de Lafayette, wife of the marquis and a member of the great Noailles dynasty, returned to her ancestral château at La Grange, in the Brie region, seventy-five miles east of Paris.

Napoléon created a new imperial court and established his own hereditary dynasty to replace the Bourbons. Like Charlemagne, he seized spiritual as well as temporal control of France and western Europe—the former Holy Roman Empire. Under the Napoleonic "Law of Public Worship," the Catholic religion was subject to government and police regulation and Gallican religious principles, with government ownership of all churches, church buildings, and church lands and all clergy placed on government salaries within the civil service. Napoléon, not the Pope, appointed all French bishops, and to outshine Charlemagne, he forced the Pope not just to sanctify his coronation as emperor but to come from Rome to Paris for the ceremony. After the Pope anointed him, Napoléon crowned himself and his empress, Joséphine, before the altar in Notre-Dame Cathedral.

In the guise of eliminating illiteracy, Napoléon created public primary and secondary school systems that indoctrinated the young in the glories of Napoleonic France, the saintly qualities of her kings and military leaders, and the natural right of France to give the law to Europe and the world. It conditioned them to near worship and unquestioned obedience of the emperor. He designed the curricula himself, explaining, "As long as one is not taught from infancy whether to be republican or monarchical, Catholic or agnostic, the State will not form one Nation."[9] He redesigned church as well as lay instruction, rewriting the Catechism to include:

> Q. What should one think of those who would fail in their duties to our Emperor?
> A. According to the Apostle St. Paul, they would resist the order established by God himself, and would make themselves deserving of eternal damnation.[10]

To reduce unrest, Napoléon introduced a new code of laws—*le Code Napoléon*—that unified and simplified the nation's laws but put the burden of proof on the accused and allowed prosecutors to crush political opposition with unsubstantiated accusations against anyone protesting Napoleonic rule.

Shortly after he instructed Talleyrand to resume peace talks with the United States, the death of George Washington gave Napoléon a perfect opportunity to demonstrate his desire for reconciliation in the most extravagant fashion. Cloaked in republican garb and garble, he decreed ten days of official mourning; in his eulogy, he called Washington his personal idol and described the United States as "the wisest and most fortunate nation on earth." Calling himself the Washington of France, he solemnly intoned, "After great political crises, there often emerges an extraordinary man who by sheer power of character restrains the excesses of every faction and brings order out of chaos."[11]

With American peace commissioners on their way, Napoléon ordered a bust of Washington placed in the Grande Galerie—the great entrance hall—of the Tuileries Palace, and it was in place when Ellsworth, Davie, and Murray arrived on March 2, 1800.

Despite Napoléon's glorification of peace, it took the Americans six months to negotiate a treaty. The French said they could not afford to repay American merchants for losses in the quasi-war. In the interest of peace, the Americans relented and agreed to postpone questions of old treaties and indemnities. "It is our duty," Murray wrote in mid-September, "to try to settle something that shall end hostilities—and draw our Govt. out of the dispute." Recognizing that he and his colleagues had effectively ignored their instructions from the president, Murray added that "our whole negotiation has proceeded on the principle of No Open War—and our settling must go on that principle—we defer—not abandon indemnity. . . ." The French would never indemnify American merchants and ship owners for their losses.[12]

The final treaty contained benefits for both nations, however, including a declaration supporting freedom of the seas, as espoused by Europe's neutral nations and Russia. The treaty guaranteed neutral ships and their crews safe passage, safe harbor, and undisturbed refuge. But the most important clause—indeed, the opening clause of the document—ended hostilities between France and the United States.

The commissioners signed the peace treaty in Paris on September 30, 1800.

The following morning, Napoléon's emissary in Madrid signed a secret treaty with Spain that returned Louisiana to France in exchange for Etruria (now Tuscany and part of Umbria), a kingdom he had conquered in northern Italy. The Spanish queen's brother, the Duke of Parma, had, since boyhood, wanted to be a king, and his sister had badgered her husband, the Spanish king, to find him a kingdom. Etruria seemed a nice enough place—and an easy coach ride from the duke's home in Parma. By exchanging Louisiana for Etruria,

Napoléon I. The French emperor disguised plans to send an army of occupation to Louisiana by signing a treaty of peace and amity with the United States.

the Spanish king ridded himself of a costly American colony and put an end to his wife's nagging. The Spanish monarch boasted of exchanging "vast wildernesses of the Mississippi and Missouri . . . for the classical land of the arts and science . . . the beautiful home of Galileo, of Dante, of Petrarch and other great men of letters and science."[13]

For Napoléon, Louisiana gave him control of commerce on the Mississippi River and a huge territory that he envisioned developing as a bountiful granary for France and her West Indian islands. Initially, he planned to send 20,000 troops to fortify the territory, build roads, and prepare for mass colonization by French farmers, who would transform Louisiana into the motherland's primary source of grain, sugar, cattle, produce, cotton, and natural resources.

But reacquisition of Louisiana meant more than its natural resources: after nearly forty years of fruitless efforts by two French kings and a half-dozen nonroyal rulers, Napoléon would restore the glory of Louis XIV's French Empire. All that remained was to transport French troops into New Orleans fast enough to occupy the territory before the United States government learned of the transaction and tried to prevent it.

On October 3, American peace commissioners went to celebrate the treaty with France at Château Môrtefontaine, Joseph Bonaparte's lavish country estate some eighteen miles north of Paris. Fireworks lit the sky to welcome the celebrants, including Napoléon and his family, Talleyrand, and other high-level French officials. The Rabelaisian feast and entertainments raised festivities to legendary proportions and stamped the name of Château Môrtefontaine on the treaty. "Toasts to perpetual peace between France and the United States . . . and to the successor of Washington, were drunk to the sound of Cannon," Murray exulted to his friend John Quincy Adams.[14] After complimenting the American commissioners, Napoléon presented each with a Roman gold medal, which they reluctantly refused as contrary to their instructions forbidding gifts. Three weeks after the celebration, Napoléon appointed a new ambassador to the United States with instructions to assure the American government that France had abandoned all ambitions to reacquire Louisiana and the rest of New France.

When word of peace with France reached the United States, Congress was convening for the first time in the unfinished Capitol in the new federal city of Washington. Shortly before his death, Washington himself had participated in laying the cornerstone of the great monument to popular rule. The executive mansion stood off in the distance, only half-built, in a barren, isolated field near the Potomac River. "Around the Capitol," wrote Senator Albert Gallatin of Pennsylvania to his wife, "are seven or eight boarding-houses, one tailor, one shoemaker, one printer, a washing woman, a grocery shop, a pamphlets and stationery shop, a small dry-goods shop, and an oyster house. This makes the whole of the Federal city as connected with the Capitol."[15]

With peace, Americans turned their attention to the presidential elections, in which Republican vice president Jefferson had challenged incumbent John Adams. With the quasi-war and its domestic consequences still fresh in voter minds, Republicans declared themselves "friends of Peace" and assailed Federalists as "partizans [sic] of war. . . . With Jefferson we shall have peace, therefore the friends of *peace will vote* for Jefferson—the friends of war will vote for *Adams*. . . .[16]

To enhance Jefferson's election chances, Talleyrand took pains to avoid the errors of French ambassador Adet in the elections of 1796 by instructing French emissaries in America—and through them all French agents—to avoid "meddling in local questions" in the 1800 elections. He ordered them to show no "marked preference in . . . relations with the influential persons of one or the other party" and to assure United States officials that France had abandoned all ambitions to recover Louisiana or any other part of New France.[17]

Although a majority of Americans supported President John Adams for restoring peace with France, deep splits over domestic issues shattered Federalist party unity and gave Jefferson and the Republicans a narrow victory in the presidential and congressional elections. Only a few hundred votes in New York City would have reversed the results. As it was, plantation owners in the South won the election for the Republicans by casting slave votes—the Constitution allowed them to cast three votes for every five slaves they owned. Adams finished third behind Jefferson and Aaron Burr, each of whom garnered the same number of electoral votes.[18] In a tie, the Constitution called for the House of Representative to decide, and after thirty-three ballots, the House remained divided—and increasingly belligerent—until a Delaware Federalist switched his vote from Burr to Jefferson and gave the presidency to Jefferson.

Shrieks of joy echoed through the Tuileries Palace in Paris, where Napoléon and Talleyrand believed that Jefferson's witless reverence for all things French would permit swift and unimpeded French occupation of Louisiana. Once colonized by the French, the huge Louisiana territory—far larger than France herself—and the French Antilles would combine to dominate the United States economically, militarily, and perhaps politically.

Jefferson did little to make them question their evaluation at first. Indeed, more than 30 of the 150 guests he invited to his inauguration dinner were French. In a further sop to France, Jefferson named an outspoken Francophile, Robert R. Livingston, ambassador to France. The New York Republican leader had been the first American secretary of foreign affairs in the Confederation of American States.

Two weeks later, however—before Livingston left for France— rumors of the secret Louisiana retrocession grew too numerous to ignore. "There is considerable reason to apprehend that Spain cedes Louisiana and the Floridas to France," Jefferson wrote to James Monroe, who had served as ambassador to France in the last days of the Washington administration. "It is a policy very unwise to both, and very ominous to us." Secretary of State James Madison conveyed the president's anxieties to the French ambassador, who all but dismissed the allegation as "a thing entirely unlikely" and, "in any case . . . nothing more than the return of lost territory and of little importance to the United States."[19]

But Louisiana had become of great importance to the United States. The end of the Revolutionary War had unloosed a migratory tidal wave of Americans that some imaginative historians compare to the third-century sweep of Goths across Europe to the gates of Rome. Americans had outgrown their tiny family farms in the East, and with tens of thousands of immigrants arriving from Europe, the western borders of overcrowded eastern states burst open. Thousands of migrants rode or tramped across the Appalachian Mountains to exercise what they believed was a God-given "natural right" to claim and settle vacant lands. Many crossed the Mississippi; a few intrepid souls reached the Rockies and even the Pacific Ocean. "Our confederacy," Thomas Jefferson said, "must be viewed as the nest from which all America, North and South is to be peopled."[20] John Adams agreed that the United States "are destined beyond a doubt to be the greatest power on earth, and that within the life of man."[21]

Spain, of course, had ruled Louisiana since 1763, but her failure to populate the territory created a huge vacuum that Americans willingly filled. By 1801, American farmers, hunters, and merchants had settled the Ohio valley, the Illinois country, and upper Louisiana, and clogged the Mississippi River with hundreds of flatboats carrying whiskey, flour, and produce to New Orleans. The heavy river traffic had swelled the island town into a prosperous port city for trade between the North American midsection and the rest of the world. Secretary of State Madison described the importance of the Mississippi to westerners as "the Hudson, the Delaware, the Potomac, and all the navigable rivers of the Atlantic states, formed into one stream."[22]

Three thousand ships a year passed through New Orleans, more than half of them flying American colors. American merchants in eastern states financed and controlled more than half the port's commerce, and in rural areas beyond New Orleans, Americans made up more than half the white population, owned vast sugar and cotton plantations, and raised huge herds of cattle on lands stretching beyond the Mississippi across the west country in Texas, as far as the Mexican border. By 1802, the tide of American migrants had submerged Spain's influence in Louisiana and threatened her sovereignty in Texas and even Mexico. Talleyrand fed Spanish paranoia by warning of American and British plans for a joint assault on the French and Spanish West Indies and Louisiana. With Spain eager to accelerate retrocession, rumors of French Army landings in Louisiana united Americans as they had not been since the War of Independence. "Every eye in the U.S.," President Jefferson noted, "is now fixed on this affair of Louisiana. Perhaps nothing since the revolutionary war has produced more uneasy sensations through the body of the nation."[23] The French ambassador in America sent a warning to Talleyrand: "I am afraid they [the Americans] may strike at Louisiana before we can take it over."[24]

To the consternation of the French government, the "affair of Louisiana" made Jefferson forget his love for France. "There is on the globe," he warned his friend du Pont, "one single spot, the possessor of which is our natural and habitual enemy. It is New Orleans, through which the produce of three-eights of our territory must pass to market. The day that France takes possession of New Orleans fixes the sentence which is to restrain her forever within her low water mark. From that moment we must marry ourselves to the British fleet and nation."[25] Like Jefferson, du Pont was a "physiocrat" who believed land was the source of all wealth. An American citizen by then, he was returning to France to raise funds for his American enterprises. Deeply concerned that the two countries he loved might war with each other, he suggested buying Louisiana from France, and with Jefferson's consent, he promised to broach the subject when he got to Paris.

Du Pont took Jefferson's warning to Talleyrand, who had assured Napoléon of Jefferson's desire for commercial and even political union with France. To Talleyrand's dismay, Jefferson's sentiments had changed abruptly. Though still enamored with French culture, Jefferson now bristled at the prospects of France or any other foreign power assuming sovereignty over American territory. Like Washington and other Founding Fathers—indeed, like most Americans—Jefferson envisioned "distant times, when our rapid multiplication will expand . . . and cover the whole northern, if not the southern continent, with a people speaking the same language, governed in similar forms, and by similar laws. . . ." He told James Monroe that the United States could not "contemplate with satisfaction either blot or mixture on that surface."[26]

American ambassador Livingston arrived in Paris early in August 1802 with instructions to determine whether Spain had formally retroceded Louisiana to France. Napoléon told Talleyrand to delay meeting with the American as long as possible. "My intention is that we take possession of Louisiana with the least possible delay, that this expedition be made in the greatest secrecy, and that it have the appearance of being directed to St. Domingue."[27]

"The Minister will give no answer to any inquiries I make," Livingston complained to Madison. After two weeks with no substantive response from Talleyrand, Livingston all but abandoned efforts to negotiate. "There never was a government in which less could be done by negotiation than here. There is no people, no legislature, no counselors. One man is everything. He seldom asks advice, and never hears it unasked. His ministers are mere clerks."[28]

As Livingston fumed in frustration, 20,000 French troops were in Dunkerque awaiting transport to Louisiana, but the slave rebellion in Saint Domingue had unexpectedly evolved into a costly guerrilla war that forced Napoléon to divert supplies and ships from the Louisiana expedition. After Toussaint's victory earlier in the year, Napoléon's brother-in-law General Charles Victor Emanuel Leclerc had sailed to Saint Domingue and offered rebel slaves freedom under French rule if Toussaint pledged allegiance to France. Toussaint agreed, and Leclerc promptly arrested him and shipped him to prison in France, where he died a few months later.

Infuriated by the deception, the island's blacks descended on the French Army with terrifying vengeance, defying fierce rifle spray to hack their way through French army lines with machetes and knives, slashing, stabbing, and slaughtering until more than 10,000 French troops lay dead and mutilated. Then, like an avenging scourge from heaven, swarms of mosquitoes infected the white oppressors with yellow fever and claimed thousands more lives. By the end of September 1802, the island had claimed 24,000 French lives, including that of General Leclerc. To retain sovereignty over the island, Napoléon had no choice but delay the Louisiana expedition and send reinforcements to Saint Domingue.

Spanish authorities in New Orleans, meanwhile, grew fearful that increasing numbers of aggressive American sailors, frontiersmen, and traders might seize control of the city. In a startling policy shift, the Spanish administration revoked American rights to deposit cargoes. "The act justified war," James Monroe recalled in his autobiography, "and many were prepared to risk it by removing the obstruction by force."[29] The *Charleston Courier* declared, "We would be justified to ourselves and to the world in taking possession of the port in question and reclaiming, by force of arms, the advantages of which we have been unjustly deprived."[30] Secretary of State Madison issued a stern warning: "There are now or in less than two years will be not less than 200,000 militia on the waters of the Mississippi . . . [who] would march at a moment's warning to remove obstructions from that outlet to the sea . . . every man regards the free use of the river as a natural and indefeasible right and is conscious of the physical force that can at any time give effect to it."[31] Madison exaggerated American military strength just a bit. "We have in this part of the Territory," wrote Mississippi Territory governor William C. C. Claiborne from Natchez, "about two thousand Militia, pretty well organized, and with a portion of this force (say six hundred men) my opinion is, that New Orleans might be taken possession of provided there should be only Spanish troops to defend the place."[32]

Toward the end of 1802, President Jefferson ordered his secretary of war to prepare an assault on New Orleans. The latter sent three artillery and four infantry companies to Fort Adams, about forty miles south of Natchez, near the Spanish border. At the same time, Jefferson dispatched a small army of federal agents to buy as much land as possible from Indian tribes along the east bank of the Mississippi, from St. Louis to the juncture of the Yazoo River, the site of present-day Vicksburg. Jefferson intended to populate the area "with a hardy yeomanry capable of defending it."[33]

Before going to war, however, Jefferson borrowed a tactic from his two predecessors to demonstrate his commitment to peace: he appointed a special commissioner—his close friend and former ambassador to France James Monroe—to go to Paris and Madrid "with discretionary powers" to preclude war by purchasing New Orleans. Washington had sent Supreme Court Chief Justice John Jay to London on a comparable mission, and Adams had sent two peace commissions to Paris to end the quasi-war with France. Monroe's instructions authorized him to pay up to 5 million livres ($9,375,000) for New Orleans and Florida. If the French and Spanish governments refused, Monroe was to warn them that Americans believed "that they have a natural . . . right to trade freely through the Mississippi.

They are conscious of their power to enforce this right against any nation whatever."[34]

Even Federalists praised the mission: "This is certainly the best thing that can be done," said one. "It will save us from the expenses, hazards, and evils of a war."[35] The Federalist *New York Evening Post*, which Alexander Hamilton had helped found to undermine Jefferson, supported the Virginian's stand on "manifest destiny": "It belongs of *right* to the United States to regulate the future destiny of *North America*. The country is *ours*; ours is the right to its rivers and to all the sources of future opulence, power and happiness."[36]

As Monroe left for France, Jefferson told him, "All eyes, all hopes, are now fixed on you."[37]

Monroe's departure did not slow Jefferson's preparations for war. At the president's request, the Senate authorized a call-up of 50,000 militia to seize New Orleans. "Why not seize what is so essential to us as a nation?" Senator James Ross of Pennsylvania shouted. "When in possession, you will negotiate with more advantage."[38] But Congress was far from unanimous in favoring aggressive expansion. "Presently we shall be told we must have Louisiana," cried Virginia's Stevens T. Mason; "then the gold mines of Mexico . . . then Potosi—then St. Domingo, with their sugar and coffee and all the rest. . . . But what have we to do with the territories of other people? Have we not enough of our own?"[39]

In mid-January, Jefferson appointed Captain Meriwether Lewis to lead a military reconnaissance expedition through upper Louisiana and the northwest, to learn as much as possible about the people and terrain. Jefferson instructed him to find a route to the Pacific and determine whether white settlement of the area would be practicable. Where possible he was to establish relations with local Indian tribes and buy lands "to provide an extension of territory which the rapid increase of our numbers will call for."[40]

The growing public war frenzy frightened the Spanish ambassador in Washington. He warned Madrid that if Spain did not restore the American right of deposit in New Orleans "the impulse of public opinion . . . will force the President and Republicans to declare war."[41] At Napoléon's insistence, Spain yielded, and Jefferson exulted at accomplishing with four months of diplomacy what might have cost years of war, blood, and national treasure. Even as he savored his triumph, however, Pierre Clément de Laussat slipped quietly ashore in New Orleans to prepare the landing and occupation of Louisiana by Napoléon's army.

Delays in obtaining enough French ships for the Louisiana expedition had forced Napoléon to transfer the army from Dunkerque to Holland, where a fleet of Dutch transports awaited near Rotterdam. But by the time the troops reached their ships, an early blast of arctic air turned the port's waters into thick ice that froze the fleet in place for the winter. On January 7, 1803, Napoléon exploded in rage and despair at the succession of mishaps that were shattering his dreams of glory one by one: his brother-in-law and half the French Army in Saint Domingue were dead, rebel slaves had stopped shipping sugar and coffee to France, and Dutch ice blocked his army from reclaiming Louisiana.

"Damn sugar, damn coffee, damn colonies," Napoléon ranted.[42]

By the end of February, 15,000 French troops had massed at Brest to sail for Saint Domingue, while 20,000 more were boarding ships in Holland to sail for Louisiana. British spies, however, believed their destination was England. On March 2, 1803, George III warned Parliament that "considerable military preparations are carrying on in the ports of Holland and France. . . ." The British government responded by threatening war if the fleets left port and entered the English Channel. Rather than risk so many lives, Napoléon abandoned the Louisiana expedition and decided to sell the territory for cash to buy arms for what seemed inevitable war with Britain.

"I renounce Louisiana," Napoléon declared sadly. "I renounce it with the greatest regret. . . . I think of ceding it to the United States."[43]

"Through no effort of their own," the British ambassador in Paris said smiling, "the Americans . . . are now delivered. . . ."[44]

Knowing that Talleyrand had undermined previous peace negotiations by demanding bribes, Napoléon turned to Minister of the Treasury Marquis François de Barbé-Marbois, who had lived in America for six years, spoke English fluently, and had an American wife:

"I direct you to negotiate this affair with the envoys of the

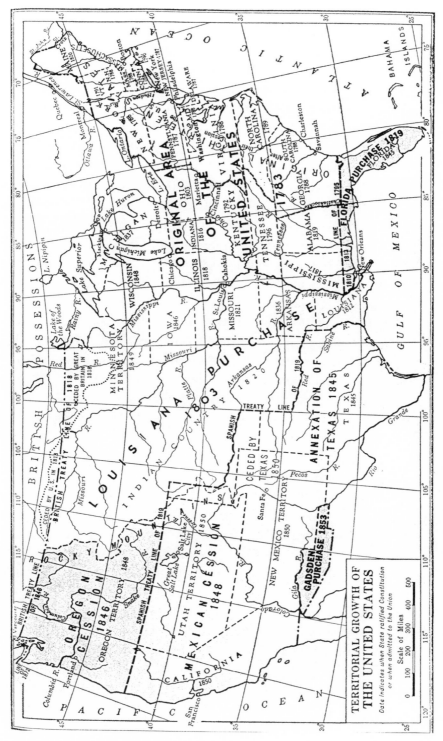

Territorial growth of the United States from the time of the Louisiana Purchase in 1803.

United States," Napoléon commanded. "Do not even await the arrival of Mr. Monroe: have an interview this very day with Mr. Livingston; but I require a great deal of money. . . . They only ask for me one town, but I consider the colony as entirely lost. . . . It is not only New Orleans that I will cede, it is the whole colony without any reservation. . . ."[45]

On April 10, 1803, James Monroe arrived in Paris to buy New Orleans. Livingston told him of Napoléon's intention to sell the entire Louisiana Territory, and three weeks later, after much haggling on price, the two Americans and Barbé-Marbois signed a treaty ceding Louisiana to the United States. The United States acquired almost 1 million square miles—an area larger than Great Britain, France, Germany, Spain, and Portugal combined—for $15 million. Having paid only pennies an acre, the Americans knew they had bested France; the price for an acre of federal lands at the time was $2.

"That the approaching war with England contributed to the cession there can be no doubt," Monroe explained, "but that it was his [Napoléon's] sole motive is not believed. We were satisfied, on the contrary, that the excitement produced in the United States by the suppression of our right of deposit at New Orleans and the menace of restoring it by force, which he knew that we could accomplish, and the measure adopted by the President to prevent a rupture and settle the affair by a friendly mission and amicable arrangements, gave . . . a decided impulse to make the cession."[46]

A few days after the cession, Napoléon invited Monroe to his château at St. Cloud, west of Paris, and, in a private conversation, admitted that he had ceded Louisiana to the United States "not so much on account of the sum obtained for it, as to preserve . . . friendship between the two republics. He had seen we entertained a jealousy of possession of that province which threatened to force us into measures which might prove equally injurious to both nations."[47]

When news of the Louisiana Purchase reached America, a few critics denounced it as too costly, but the vast majority of Americans—Federalists and Republicans alike—hailed it as a bargain that doubled the size of the nation without firing a single shot. "You have secured to us the free navigation of the Mississippi," a Tennessean wrote to President Jefferson. "You have procured an immense and fertile country: and all these great blessings are obtained without war and bloodshed."[48] What he did not—indeed, could not—add was that in procuring the immense and fertile country of Louisiana, Jefferson had also procured the future "Cotton Kingdom" of the lower Mississippi valley, which Eli Whitney's cotton gin would convert into the source of half the nation's dollar exports. As it turned out, the Louisiana Purchase also included the future oil fields of Oklahoma, the copper mines of the Dakotas, the gold of Colorado, and the world's richest fields of grain.

"We bought ourselves an Empire for four cents an acre," wrote a chronicler in an American magazine on the 150th anniversary of the Louisiana Purchase.[49]

Frontiersmen most affected by the territorial acquisition responded jubilantly. Tennessee's Andrew Jackson exulted in a letter to the president, "Every face wears a smile, and every heart leaps with joy."[50] Jefferson was beyond himself with joy. "The world will here see," he predicted, "such an extent of country under a free and moderate government as it has never yet seen."[51] Ever the Francophile, he told one of his French friends, "Your government has wisely removed what certainly endangered collision between us. I now see nothing which need ever interrupt the friendship between France and this country."[52]

The French would find a way to prove him wrong.

12

The American Menace

THE LOUISIANA PURCHASE drove the French off the North American continent for the second time in forty years but did little to dull insatiable French lust for foreign conquest or make French leaders question their "natural right" to give the law to the world. Napoléon, they argued, had sold Louisiana of his own volition; he had not lost it in war, and if the interests of France required its reacquisition, they believed he could simply take it back. It was his "natural right."

"God has given me the will and the force to overcome all obstacles," Napoléon declared seven years before he heard the name Waterloo.[1]

The Louisiana Purchase elevated Jefferson to hero status in America and ensured his reelection in 1804 by an overwhelming majority. Blinded by his own success to other possible factors behind Napoléon's decision, Jefferson believed his threats to seize Louisiana by force had intimidated the French emperor into ceding Louisiana peacefully rather than risk war with the United States. After his reelection, therefore, he threatened to send troops into Florida and Texas if Spain did not cede them peacefully as France had ceded Louisiana.

When Napoléon learned of Jefferson's arrogance toward his Spanish ally, he warned that France would send troops to defend Spanish territory if the Americans invaded. Not unexpectedly, the ever avaricious Talleyrand slipped his fingers into the diplomatic mix with a whisper to the American ambassador in Paris that he might be able to coax Spain into selling Florida for $6 million—plus a reasonable mediation fee for himself. Both Spain and America rejected Talleyrand's intervention.

Before Jefferson could mobilize a full-scale assault on Florida, the first of the Napoleonic Wars so disrupted American commerce on the Atlantic that it displaced expansionism on the list of presidential priorities, and Jefferson left office in 1809 without fulfilling any more territorial ambitions. His successor, James Madison, was equally expansionist, but the War of 1812 with Britain postponed acquisition of Florida until James Monroe took office. With Monroe's consent, General Andrew Jackson marched into Florida on April 7, 1818, and on February 22 the following year—George Washington's birthday—Spain ceded Florida to the United States in exchange for American renunciation of claims on Texas.

By then, of course, Napoléon had found the way to Waterloo, and more than a million troops—from England, Holland, Germany, Saxony, Prussia, Austria, Russia, and elsewhere—had overrun France and sent Napoléon to exile on a volcanic island off the West African coast. The allies sat fat old Louis XVIII on the French throne as puppet king, extracted 700 million francs in reparations from the French treasury, and left 150,000 occupation troops to crush the arrogance of the French and try to teach them to leave their neighbors alone and live within their own borders.[2]

In the three years that followed, startling economic gains produced such unexpected political and economic stability that the allies believed the French had, at last, learned the advantages of peace. In 1818, they withdrew their troops, and within two years, Louis XVIII reasserted the "natural right" of France to give the law to other nations. In 1820, Spain's South American colonies declared independence, and the Spanish military declared Spain a constitutional monarchy. When France threatened to restore the Spanish king's absolute power in South America, American president James Monroe warned that "the American continents are no longer subjects for any new European establishments." In October 1723, France backed

James Monroe. The fifth
president of the United
States, he articulated a
new foreign policy—the
Monroe Doctrine—that
closed the Western
Hemisphere to further
European colonization.

down and renounced her ambitions to invade or acquire former
Spanish American colonies.[3]

Less than a month later, the president, who had once embraced
American unity with France, announced a new foreign policy that
redefined the globe as an agglomeration of spheres of influence. "Our
policy in regard to Europe," Monroe declared "is not to interfere in
the internal concerns of any of its powers . . . to cultivate friendly relations with it, but submitting to injuries from none." Although the
doctrine bore the president's name, Secretary of State John Quincy
Adams drew up its salient elements, including a stern warning that

> the American continents, by the free and independent condition
> which they have assumed and maintain are henceforth not to be
> considered as subjects for future colonization by any European
> powers. . . . The political system of the allied [European] powers is
> essentially different from that of America. . . . We owe it, therefore,

to candor and to the amicable relations existing between the United
States and those powers to declare that we should consider any attempt on their part to extend their system to any portion of this
hemisphere as dangerous to our peace and safety.[4]

The Monroe Doctrine went on to pledge that the United States
would not interfere in Europe's internal affairs but warned Europe
not to interfere in the affairs of any independent government in the
Americas or further colonize any area of the Americas.

The first major test of the doctrine did not come for forty years—
when France once again eyed North America's treasures. Until then,
she had been too troubled internally to venture far beyond her borders. Louis XVIII had died without children in 1824; his younger
brother Charles X took the crown and imposed harsh dictatorial
measures that provoked a three-day revolution and establishment of
a constitutional monarchy under Louis Philippe I. He abided by the
constitution for five years before succumbing to the French urge to
conquer and sent French armies to seize Algeria. His increasingly ar-
bitrary rule at home, however, provoked revolution, and in 1848, he
lost his crown, and France her last monarch.

The oligarchs who enriched themselves under Louis Philippe
stepped from behind the throne after the revolution and wrote a new
constitution that again cloaked French expansionism under the banner of *liberté, égalité, fraternite*, and the Rights of Man. As in the
1700s, the makeup of the ruling oligarchy—the euphemistic Cent
Familles—had changed again. In the eighteenth century, a financial
revolution had mixed the blood of merchant-bankers from the *haute
bourgeoisie* with that of the *noblesse;* the nineteenth-century industrial revolution added manufacturers to the mix, and they proved as
eager as their predecessors for foreign conquest, to plunder raw materials for their factories in France. After establishing a Second French
Republic, French leaders elected Charles Louis Napoléon Bonaparte—Napoléon I's nephew—president of the republic for four
years, but after three years of constitutional restraints, they staged a
traditional Gallic coup d'état, dissolved the legislature, and replaced
republican government with the Second Empire. Louis Napoléon
took his place on the throne as Napoléon III.[5] Determined to outdo

his uncle and enrich the oligarchy that backed him, Napoléon III sent French armies spanning the globe. They swept across Europe to the Russian Crimea, then spilled over the Mediterranean to Africa as far south as Senegal. French armies went on to cross the Indian Ocean to conquer the entire Indochinese subcontinent and large areas of Polynesia.

Millions of tons of mineral ores, rubber, foodstuffs, and other resources from conquered territories flowed to France to feed the growing French industrial machine, but each conquest only whetted Napoléon III's appetite for more territory and glory. Now envisioning a globe-girdling empire, he looked westward to the boundless wealth of the Americas, where a populist Mexican president had suspended interest payments on his nation's loans from France, Spain, and Britain. Disguising his ambitions as a quest for economic justice, the French emperor convinced Britain and Spain to mount a joint invasion to collect overdue debts.

The invasion came as the United States was mired in a debilitating civil war and helpless to apply the Monroe Doctrine to protect Mexico. After landing on the southeast coast at Vera Cruz, the European invaders pushed toward the Mexican capital, only to suffer a humiliating defeat at Puebla, about a hundred miles inland. British and Spanish troops fled to their ships and sailed home, but the humiliation so infuriated Napoléon III that he doubled his expeditionary force and, in June 1863, sent 30,000 troops storming through Puebla to Mexico City.

Although American secretary of state William Seward invoked the Monroe Doctrine and warned France to withdraw, Louis Napoléon all but mocked the American statesman. He installed his own government in Mexico City and began planning reconquest of the vast Louisiana Territory. His scheme called for ensuring the breakup of the United States into two small countries, each too weak to block the French Army's march into Louisiana. He ordered French shipyards to build ironclads and cruisers for the Confederate Navy and prepared to recognize the Confederate States of America as an independent nation.

When Seward warned that recognition of Confederate independence would be tantamount to an act of war, Napoléon decided to delay recognition until he could ensure Confederate victory. Early in 1863, he acted to do just that by offering to mediate the American Civil War by sending French troops to establish a buffer zone between the two sides, thus physically ensuring de facto division of the United States. With near-unanimous support from an outraged Congress, Seward sent an angry rebuff that called the French emperor's proposal "foreign intervention."[6]

Unmoved by American rhetoric, Napoléon III consolidated French power in Mexico and waited for the right moment to strike at Louisiana. He assumed the moment had come in April 1865, when Confederate assassins stripped the Union of its spiritual as well as political leaders by killing President Abraham Lincoln and wounding Secretary of State William Seward. With nearly a million American soldiers dead or wounded in Civil War fighting, the French emperor assumed the United States lacked both the will and strength to defend its western territories and ordered his army to march to Louisiana.

In a startling response, President Andrew Johnson dispatched Civil War hero Major General Philip H. Sheridan to the Gulf Coast with 50,000 troops. When they reached the Mexican border early in 1866, Secretary of State Seward, still weak from his wounds, sent the French an ultimatum citing the Monroe Doctrine and demanding withdrawal of all French troops. With his forces facing annihilation by a much larger, battle-hardened American Army, Napoléon III yielded, and a year later, in the spring of 1867, the French Army quit American shores for the last time, leaving the hapless Austrian "emperor" of Mexico to face execution by Mexican partisans.

In 1870, Europe's conquered nations again rose against French rule and, as they had in 1814, sent their armies into France—and Napoléon III into exile. The national humiliation did nothing, however, to suppress French appetite for foreign conquest. The oligarchs who had put Napoléon III on the throne replaced the Second Empire with another republic—the third in less than a century—and rebuilt the French military. With the industrial revolution at its zenith, industrialized nations were competing to conquer every undeveloped area of the world to find natural resources for their factories. France joined the competition and by 1900 had created an empire larger than the one lost by the Bourbon monarchy in the eighteenth century. Already mistress over vast rubber plantations in Indochina, the Third Republic extended the French empire—and the farcical French "Rights of Man"—across Tunisia, Ivory Coast, Guinea, the Congo, Sudan, Djibouti, Mozambique, and Madagascar.

As in the 1750s, however, the multinational competition for empire in the 1890s expanded into a costly, four-year global war that cost 5 million European troops their lives—1.6 million of them French. Fought largely on French soil, World War I left 1 million French civilians crippled, 600,000 widowed, and 700,000 orphaned. Incredibly, French ambitions for foreign conquest remained as keen as ever. Under the terms of peace, France not only added the Rhineland to her continental territory, she incorporated Morocco into French North Africa and extended her colonial empire into the Middle East for the first time since the Crusades by acquiring Lebanon and Syria as French "protectorates."

The rise of Nazi Germany forced the French into temporary embrace of an unsought ally to preserve the French empire. They retroceded the Rhineland to Germany in 1936, then joined the English in useless peace negotiations with Germany that cost Austria, western Czechoslovakia, and Poland their independence without preventing the outbreak of World War II. After a month of token military resistance, the French government surrendered northern France to German military might but negotiated a treaty that allowed her to retain nominal political control of southern France and the overseas empire by forming a Franco-German military alliance and integrating the French economy with Germany's. Euphemistically calling themselves Free France—*l'État libre*—French rulers established a quasi-Nazi regime, sent 600,000 French workers to German factories and labor camps, and ordered French police to round up the nation's 500,000 Jews for transfer to German extermination camps. Firmly allied to Germany, Prime Minister Pierre Laval, twice a premier and foreign minister in the Third Republic, ordered the 100,000-man French Army to repel an Anglo-American invasion force on the beaches of French Algeria and Morocco in November 1942. After three days of fighting in which the French claimed more than 1,000 American lives, they surrendered.

Defeat and disgrace in World War II did little to dampen the ambitions of surviving French leaders for world power. As in the 1790s, however, what Talleyrand called "the American menace"—popular demands for liberty—stood in their way, provoking uprisings against colonial rule across the length and breadth of both French and British empires. "The effect of political equality," Talleyrand had warned, "invites every citizen, regardless of class, to acquire wealth that rightfully belongs to the aristocracy and monarchy."[7]

In 1946, French rulers repeated the errors of their monarchic predecessors by refusing to grant independence to Indochina. French rulers sacrificed the lives of 60,000 troops in a futile eight-year war that ended with the humiliation of the French Army at Dien Bien Phu—but did nothing to curb French government arrogance. When North Africans demanded independence, the French repeated the costly sacrifice of the nation's youth by sending another 100,000 to slaughter in a vain effort to keep Algeria under French bondage. In the spring of 1958, the humiliating disintegration of empire—and degrading efforts to preserve it—provoked another French coup d'état, which overthrew the Fourth Republic and elevated to power General Charles de Gaulle as president of a Fifth Republic. Rather than prolong costly colonial wars, de Gaulle tried to hold on to what was left of the empire by offering colonies a choice of independence or union with France with full citizenship. Only a few islands in the Caribbean and South Pacific chose union and are now *départements* that is, territorial and administrative divisions of France.

With the American Revolution of 1776 as their example, Algeria and most other French colonies chose independence and reduced the French empire to a relatively impotent segment of the European map—stripping her of the role she had played for more than a millennium as a world power. The charismatic de Gaulle tried in vain to recover that role and, not without reason, blamed the United States for his failure. The United States had not only dwarfed French military power and influence but had replaced her as the world's most influential economy, political system, and culture.

"During the twentieth century, Europe has lost its . . . leadership in the arts and sciences, geo-political and military policy and economic activity," explains French historian-philosopher Jean-François

Revel—one of the so-called "immortal" intellectuals in the exclusive Institut de France. "In France especially," he says,

> "the loss of world leadership—real or imagined—has caused the most profound bitterness as she has been forced to watch America become the first nation in history to merit the title of world super-power—a title that embraces leadership in four broad areas at the same time: economic, technological, military and cultural. . . . America's status as a superpower is the result of the determination and creativity of the American people and the cumulative failures of the rest of the world: the bankruptcy of communism, the socio-economic collapse of Africa, the divisions of Europe, and the slow development of democracy in Latin America and Asia. . . ."[8]

The great economic revolution of the twentieth century, Revel goes on to say,

> was not the Communist or Socialist revolution which quite clearly failed everywhere by 1970. The truly great economic revolution of the 20th century began in the United States, with the startling achievements of economic and industrial denationalization. Any suggestion that free American enterprise represents classic democracy, however, threatens the elite groups who control the wealth in socialist nations.[9]

Despairing of ever recapturing the French empire's lost territories, de Gaulle nonetheless sought to recapture its glory and influence. Recalling the words of Foreign Minister Vergennes to King Louis XVI— "France has the right to influence all the world's important matters"—de Gaulle launched a campaign to undermine American influence and restore French influence in world affairs, much as France tried to undermine English influence in the eighteenth century by supporting the American Revolution. To support de Gaulle, the "elite groups who control the wealth [in France]" underwrote a relentless propaganda campaign against the United States to demean American democracy and free enterprise and preserve the centuries-old system of statism that has remained unchanged since the Bourbon monarchs. Unlike leaders of the American Revolution, who dismantled centralized royal authority and dispersed it among the states, leaders of the French Revolution tightened central government authority over the economic and political system, replacing the "elite group" of aristocrats who controlled national wealth before the revolution with a new elite group of bourgeois—middle-class lawyers, merchants, and intellectuals—the ever-present Cent Familles. The Directory that followed and each of two emperors, three kings, and five sham republics replaced one elite group with another but, in the end, left France on the same statist foundations that existed under Louis XIV. *L'état c'est moi* ("I am the state") became *l'état c'est nous* ("we are the state"), but little else changed. Today's French constitution (the thirteenth since 1791) begins with "the principle that the nation is sovereign"—in sharp contrast to the opening words of the American Constitution: "We the People . . . do ordain and establish this Constitution for the United States of America." In effect, the French constitution establishes the state as the basic political unit, from which individuals derive their rights; the United States constitution establishes the individual as the basic political unit, with the state deriving its rights from the people.

"The engine that drives anti-Americanism—both on the right and left," Revel declares, "is simple hatred of democracy and the free economy it engenders."[10]

De Gaulle began the propaganda war against the United States to ensure his own accession to the presidency after World War II by inflating his insignificant contribution to French liberation and diminishing the American role. "In 1944," he complained to his biographer, Gaullist minister Alain Peyrefitte, "the Americans were no more concerned about liberating France than the Russians were about liberating Poland."[11] The absurdity of de Gaulle's contention stunned even some Frenchmen. Revel reacted with disbelief: "When one looks at the way the Russians treated Poland—slowing the Red Army advance to let Germans massacre the people of Warsaw and ensure Russian satellization of Poland—de Gaulle's statement must leave readers dumbbfounded by the comparison. Only spite or ignorance could generate such an absurd statement."[12]

Nor was that the end of de Gaulle's irrational libels. Ignoring the Japanese attack on Pearl Harbor and subsequent German declaration of war against the United States, de Gaulle called American intervention in World War II an attempt to recover profits from interrupted prewar trade with Europe. Indeed, the French president accused the United States of designing the Marshall Plan to convert France and western Europe into economic satellites.

Subsequent French presidents across the political spectrum from left (François Mitterand) to right (Jacques Chirac) have maintained the flow of anti-American vitriol—usually without regard to logic or rational thought. Foreign Minister Hubert Vedrine in Lionel Jospin's Socialist government vehemently condemned the United States in 1998 for unilaterally assuming a role as the world's policeman, only to reverse course that summer by assailing the United States for reverting to isolationism by refusing to intervene in fierce street fighting in Palestine.

Two years earlier, France—and the rest of Europe—had despaired of ending Serbian massacres in former Yugoslavia and pleaded for American intervention. After the American military ended the slaughter, the rightist Chirac government, like its Socialist predecessors, accused the United States of "naked imperialism"—only to change its collective mind again a few months later by reproaching Americans as "cowardly isolationists" for withdrawing in favor of a multinational European force.[13]

"It is a paradox," Revel points out, "that since the end of the Cold War, America's oldest ally despises and disapproves of the United States more than the Communists did during the Cold War."[14]

French publishers are key participants in the government propaganda war against America—and are often as absurd as their government coconspirators. *Le Monde*, the most respected daily newspaper in France, routinely publishes anti-American diatribes under the guise of objective journalism. When American unemployment jumped from 4.4 percent to 5.5 percent in the spring of 2001, *Le Monde's* front-page headline proclaimed: AMERICAN ECONOMIC DREAM SHATTERED.

The editors relegated to an inside page the revelation that French unemployment had climbed to 8.7 percent.[15]

"What a shame," Revel laughs, "that France cannot realize

America's shattered dream for herself. . . . If what the French press says is true, those poor Americans deserve pity instead of envy and less animosity than commiseration. What a remarkable people Americans must be to survive so disastrous a system. . . . One wonders how an economic system too terrible for the French government to adopt has been so powerful an engine for the economies of so many other nations?"[16] Revel goes on to wonder, "How did so many Europeans fall into that American hell and why didn't they warn their relatives not . . . to go to America? . . . If America is such a failure, it's a wonder that people are not flocking from the United States to more idyllic lives in Albania, Slovakia, or Nicaragua instead of the other way 'round."[17]

French book publishers reinforce distortions about American life in textbooks and nonfiction works distributed by the French government throughout the less developed world as well as in France. French history texts routinely focus on the immorality of American slavery without noting that, for nearly two centuries, all the slave-owning settlers in America were Europeans—French, English, Spanish, Dutch, Swedish, and German—and that they bought all their slaves from French, English, and other European slave traders. Ignored entirely is the role of Africans (mostly in French West Africa) who willingly sold their own people—often their own families—to French and English slavers.

Ignored, as well, are the roles of twentieth-century French and other European political, social, and *intellectual* leaders in provoking history's two worst social, military, and economic cataclysms and creating communism and naziism—the two most barbaric political ideologies ever imposed on the human race. In contrast to France, where coups d'état have produced four monarchs, two emperors, and five different republics, the United States has survived more than two centuries without ever turning to a dictator. Yet French anti-American propaganda continues to infect the collective French psyche by portraying "the United States as a repressive, unjust, racist, imperialist state. . . ."[18]

The pervasive reach of such propaganda begins in the earliest years of school. Once the purview of the Catholic Church, education remained centralized after the French Revolution, when the government nationalized the church and put teaching priests in the civil service. Like monarchs before them, subsequent French rulers have maintained a tight hold over education—and, indeed, every other institution that affects the lives, thoughts, and behavior of the French people. In addition to the armed services and national finance, the central government runs all public schools and universities in France, every police station, courtroom, and even every church, with all church lands and buildings *government owned*. The central French government controls employment, with more than one-quarter of the French working population on government pay and the rest "protected" by government-imposed workplace regulations that determine the number of hours and years employees may work and the pay, benefits, and pensions they receive.

With de Gaulle's blessing, a new generation of oligarchs— so-called *enarchs*—emerged after World War II to take control of national wealth and political power. His foresight put *enarchs* in the presidency and cabinet ministries, the legislature, the supreme court, and the diplomatic corps. *Enarchs* are all graduates of an elite supra-postgraduate training school, the École Nationale d'Administration (ENA+ the Latin/Greek suffix *arch*, or "chief" = *enarch*)—a school first described in Plato's *Republic* to prepare national rulers and chief government administrators. From its founding in 1945, ENA's stated mission has been "to provide interministerial training . . . for State senior public servants," a small group of carefully selected applicants.[19] Once graduated, "**students can select their job assignments** [their bold-faced type] in accordance with their class rank: the State Council . . . Public Finances, the Prefectorial and Diplomatic Corps, Civil administrators for different ministries . . . administrative tribunals and Appeals courts."[20] ENA graduates form a tightly knit club whose members control every major government and nongovernment political and economic institution in France. While *enarchic* government concentrated power in relatively few hands, it all but emasculated individual populists and extremist parties and ensured political and economic continuity and stability, whether left, right, or center. All *enarchs* have the same training and share the same interests. As Socrates explained to a student in a dialogue in Plato's *Republic*: "Our state, like every other, has rulers and subjects.

> Student: What is the name people give to their rulers . . . ?
> Socrates: Generally they call them masters, but in democratic states they call them rulers.
> Glaucon: And what do *they* [the rulers] call the people?
> Socrates: Servants.[21]

To prevent social unrest and ensure their grip on political and economic power, *enarchs* cling to a form of socialism that restricts free enterprise with cumbersome regulations and start-up taxes but swathes French workers in enough social benefits to dull personal ambition and add enormous risks to individual initiative. Under pretense of promoting industrial efficiency, the French government maintains government monopolies and government-regulated private monopolies that concentrate the nation's wealth but swaddle workers in slumber-inducing social dependency on government allowances and services: free education, child care, transportation, utilities, health care, paid sick and maternity leave, pensions, limited weekly work hours, guaranteed retirement at an early age, extended paid vacations, more than a dozen paid holidays a year, and a plethora of costly minor benefits such as paid lunches at work. To protect jobs, the government all but forbids employee layoffs in public and private enterprises and subsidizes a wide range of private enterprises (and uses a maze of customs regulations) to protect companies and their workers from foreign competition.

Dominque de Villepin, an *enarch* foreign minister and minister of interior under the center-right presidency of *enarch* Jacques Chirac, admits France is "elitist and stratified—a prisoner of the phantoms of Versailles, policed by the military and ruled by the aristocracy and clergy."[22] Like monarchs at Versailles, *enarchs* like de Villepin conceal in their socialist ministries unsuspected opulence that matches the extravagances of former royal residences—gilt ceilings and furnishings, magnificent handwoven tapestries, and other adornments in sprawling palatial apartments that the French Republic maintains for cabinet members and their families at a cost of hundreds of millions of euros a year. All ministries are closed to the public—as are the National Assembly, the Senate, and the Palais Elysée, or executive mansion. "Certain places exude magic, mystical power," de Villepin admits. "The Elysée [is] an enchanted garden . . . where the souls of heroes gathered"[23]—but never the souls of taxpayers who fund it. More than two centuries ago—two years before the French Revolution of 1789—the marquis de Lafayette assailed King Louis XVI and his cabinet with words that still apply in France: "The millions being dissipated come from taxes, which cannot be justified to meet the real needs of the state. The millions absconded to plunder and greed are the fruit of sweat, tears and blood of the people, and the number of people sacrificed to misery to amass the sums so carelessly wasted shames . . . [our] sense of justice and goodness. . . ."[24]

Plus ça change, plus c'est la même chose—the more things change, the more they remain the same.[25]

In using socialism to preserve and concentrate national power and wealth, *enarchs* have badly undermined the French economy by discouraging free enterprise, limiting investments in creative genius and modern invention, stunting expansion of the arts and sciences, and discouraging individual initiative. Harvard University's endowment alone, for example, is more than double the combined annual budgets of *all* universities in France. As *Wall Street Journal* drama critic Terry Teachout points out, "It has been a very long time since a Frenchman wrote a symphony or a novel, or choreographed a ballet, that the rest of the world found compelling or memorable."[26] It has also been a very long time since a Frenchman has significantly advanced the sciences or technology. Revel calls France a nation "that only taxes and redistributes earnings, has the world's blindest political and intellectual leadership and encourages her people to work less and less, in the belief that they can increase earnings by studying and working less."[27]

Although they persist in pursuing policies of obstructionism in international organizations and in knee-jerk opposition to American foreign policies, *enarchs* remain frustrated in their efforts to defeat the "American menace"—and restore the glory and power of France. Although their propaganda has propagated anti-Americanism around the world—especially in statist societies ruled by dictators—it has not, ironically, extended French influence. Indeed, the opposite appears true: after the French assailed American intervention in Iraq—largely because *enarchs* were profiting from illicit arms-for-oil deals with Saddam Hussein—the United States government systematically excluded its "oldest ally" from foreign-policy deliberations and all but locked France out of the corridors of world power. "No one listens to her anymore," complains de Villepin. Revel responds that the substitution of shrill animosity for sage, behind-the-scenes counsel, "has condemned [France] to impotence in world affairs and nourished the strength of the American superpower she claims to despise."[28]

Impotent or not, France and the French continue to plot against America. As de Villepin boasts, "France is obsessed with power . . . galvanized by conquest. It is a national disease passed down through the ages . . . we have never learned to live in partnership . . . France is still aflame with the passions of her past, the passions of a great nation, fervently defending her rightful place in history."[29]

Notes

Introduction: The Seeds of Treachery

1. Charles F. Adams, ed., *The Works of John Adams* (Boston, 1850–1856, 10 vols.) III:303.

2. Francis Wharton, *The Revolutionary Diplomatic Correspondence of the United States, Edited under Direction of Congress, with preliminary index, and notes historical and legal. Published in conformity with Act of Congress of August 13, 1888.* (Washington, D.C.: Government Printing Office, 6 vols., 1889), 6:48.

3. G. de Bertier de Sauvigny, *Histoire de France* (Paris: Flammarion, 1977), 45.

4. Both Crusades of (Saint) Louis IX were disasters. In the first, he landed his army on the sands along the Nile River near Cairo, only to have the Egyptians open the sluice gates of nearby reservoirs and convert the French encampment into a barren island. Without water or food, Louis agreed to pay an enormous ransom to sail away. Once in Palestine, he managed to obtain what he insisted was the Crown of Thorns, which is stored in the treasury of Notre-Dame Cathedral and displayed annually in the Sainte-Chapelle in Paris on Good Friday. Louis led the eighth and last Crusade to Tunisia in 1270 but died shortly after landing, and the French Army returned home. Until recently Arab vendors in the old market of Jerusalem were still selling thorns.

5. The approach to the palace at Versailles for visiting statesmen was not through the gates visitors use today but along the vast Great 100-Step Staircase, along the north side of the Orangerie. The half-mile climb is so steep that its summit reveals nothing but sky and radiant light of the sun from the east. Only after ninety exhausting steps does the huge palace suddenly appear through the blinding rays of sunlight on the hilltop—a marvel enough to stagger visitors already faltering from the climb.

6. Henri Doniol, *Histoire de la Participation de la France à l'Établissement des États-Unis d'Amérique* (Paris: Imprimerie Nationale, 5 vols., quarto, 1886), I:24.

7. Michel Poniatowski, *Talleyrand aux États-Unis, 1794–1796* (Paris: Presses de la Cité, 1967), 75.

8. Edward S. Corwin, *French Policy and the American Alliance of 1778* (Princeton, N.J.: Princeton Univ. Press, 1916), 375–376.

Chapter 1: The War in the Wilderness

1. *Journal et Mémoires du Marquis d'Argenson* (Paris: Ratheray, 1859), I, 325–326; 371–372; IV, 131.

2. Jacques Brosse, ed., *Mémoires du Duc de Choiseul*, (Paris: Mercure de France, 1987), 192–193.

3. Ibid, 198.

4. Ibid., 63.

5. Isaac J. Cox, ed., *The Journeys of René Robert Cavalier, Sieur de La Salle* (New York, 1922, 2 vols.), I:167, cited in Alexander DeConde, *Entangling Alliance* (Durham, N.C.: Duke Univ. Press, 1958), 7.

6. Fairfax Downey, *Louisbourg: Key to a Continent* (Englewood Cliffs, N.J.: Prentice-Hall, 1965), 14; Harold Underwood Faulkner and Tyler Kepner, *America, Its History and People* (New York: Harper & Brothers Publishers, 1942), 54.

7. Douglas Southall Freeman, *George Washington: A Biography* (New York: Charles Scribner's Sons, 6 vols., 1954), I:292.

8. Ibid., I:304.

9. Richard Harwell, *Washington, An abridgment in one volume of the seven-volume George Washington by Douglas Southall Freeman* (New York: Charles Scribner's Sons, 1968), 48.

10. Ibid.

11. Ibid., 55.

12. John Ferling, *John Adams: A Life* (New York: Henry Holt and Company, 1992), 126.

13. Freeman, I:405.

14. Ibid., I:377.

15. Jared Sparks, ed., *The Writings of George Washington* (Boston: Tappan and Dennet, 1834–1837, 12 vols.), II:463–465.

16. Freeman, I:423–424.

17. Ibid., II:64.

18. Jared Sparks, *The Life of George Washington* (Boston: Tappan and Dennet, 1843), 63.

19. Ibid., 64.

20. Freeman, II:76.

21. John C. Fitzpatrick, ed., *The Writings of Washington* (Washington, D.C.: Government Printing Office, 39 vols., 1931–44), 29:44.

22. Freeman, II:78.

Chapter 2: Shattered Glory

1. Harwell, 101; Washington to Dinwiddie, April 27, 1756.

2. Ibid., 103.

3. Michel Denis and Noël Blayau, *Le XVIIIe Siècle* (Paris: Armand Colin/VUEF, 2002), 98.

4. Corwin, 35n.

5. Choiseul, 21.

6. Ibid., 162.

7. Corwin, 35.

8. Ibid., 58.

9. Ibid., 38.

10. Choiseul, 162.

11. Corwin, 40.

12. Harlow Giles Unger, *John Hancock: Merchant King and American Patriot* (New York: John Wiley & Sons, 2000), 82. New England merchants were smuggling 1.5 million gallons of molasses for rum production each year and avoided paying the £37,500 in duties by bribing customs officials with £2,000. The merchants argued disingenuously that duties would double the price of rum and leave colonists unable to afford a drop of their favorite drink. In truth, pure greed lay behind their objection to duties. They distilled a gallon of molasses, costing 16 pence, into a gallon of rum that they sold for 192 pence—a profit of 1,100 percent. In all, New England merchants paid about £100,000 a year for molasses and earned gross revenues of about £1.25 million, on which they refused to pay a mere 3 percent—£37,500—in taxes.

13. Ferling, 126.

14. James Otis, *Boston Gazette*, April 4, 1763, in Unger, *Hancock*, 75.

15. Corwin, 41.

16. Ibid., 40.

17. Robert Douthat Meade, *Patrick Henry: Patriot in the Making* (Philadelphia and New York: J. B. Lippincott Company, 1957), 171.

18. Unger, *Hancock*, 97.

19. Corwin, 42.

20. Friedrich Kapp, *The Life of John Kalb, Major-General in the Revolutionary Army* (New York: Henry Holt and Company, 1884), 47.

21. Ibid., 64.

22. Ibid., 55.

23. Unger, *Hancock*, 126.

24. Doniol, I:6.

25. Choiseul, 190.

26. Ibid., 198.

Chapter 3: The Treacherous Alliance

1. Edmund Randolph, *History of Virginia* (Charlottesville: Univ. Press of Virginia, 1970), 176–178.

2. Moses Coit Tyler, *Patrick Henry* (New Rochelle, N.Y.: Arlington House, 1898), 115.

3. Harwell, 141.

4. Ibid., 179.

5. For complete details of Washington's transformation of Mount Vernon, see Alan and Donna Jean Fusonie, *George Washington: Pioneer Farmer* (Mount Vernon, Va.: Mount Vernon Ladies Association, 1998).

6. Freeman, III:189.

7. Harwell, 200.

8. Unger, *Hancock*, 185.

9. Ibid., 186.

10. Doniol, I:2–4.

11. Ibid., I:6.

12. Although unidentified, the notes of the mysterious agents, or "French Traveler," as historians call him, are in the archives of the Ministère de la Marine, Paris, under the curious section called *Service Hydrographique*. The *American Historical Review* (vol. 26: 745–746), cites a *"French Visitor's Diary"* that is identical to the notes of the "French Traveler" in the French Ministère de la Marine.

13. Meade, *Patriot in the Making*, 334–335.

14. William Wirt, *The Life of Patrick Henry* (New York, 1852), 120–123. The speech as quoted was reconstructed by Henry's adoring grandson thirty years later. Although Henry never wrote out his speeches, and there are no authentic manuscripts of his orations, there is little doubt that he uttered the words "liberty or death," which became a popular slogan for patriots, who sewed the words on their shirts. The French agent who overheard the speech from the vestibule of St. John's Church sent a summary to Vergennes, along with assurances that Henry was now firmly in the French camp.

15. Tyler, 145.

16. *Essex Gazette*, April 25, 1775.

17. Gage to Lord Dartmouth, April 22, 1775.

18. Harwell, 219.

19. Ibid., 266.

20. Richard B. Morris, ed., *Encyclopedia of American History* (New York: Harper & Brothers, 1953), 88.

21. Doniol, I:84.

22. Ibid., 233.

23. The Rossini opera based on the Beaumarchais play came years later, in 1816, with a libretto by Cesare Sterbini. The premier in Rome was a disaster, but a number of revisions quickly turned it into one of the most popular comic operas of the repertoire.

24. Wharton, *Correspondence of the United States*, I:366.

25. Georges Lemaître, *Beaumarchais* (New York: Alfred A. Knopf, 1949), 265. D'Eon returned to France and lived and dressed as a woman until 1783, when he returned to England, where he died in 1810. An examination of his remains determined that he had "male organs of generation perfectly formed in every respect."

26. Meade Minnigerode, *Jefferson—Friend of France* (New York: G. P. Putnam & Sons, 1928), 33.

27. Doniol, I:240–248.

28. Ibid.

29. Ibid.

30. Ibid., I:149.

31. Wharton, I:367.

32. Ibid., I:371.

33. Beaumarchais's firm, Roderigue Hortalez et Cie of Paris, operated for seven years, from 1776 to 1783, and earned gross revenues 21,095,515 livres against outlays of 21,044,191 livres, for a net profit of 51,234 livres.

34. Pierre Augustin Caron [de Beaumarchais], *Le Mariage de Figaro, ou la folle journée*, as translated by Jacques Barzun in Robert Lowell and Jacques Barzun, *Phaedra and Figaro: Robert Lowell Racine's Phèdre and Jacques Barzun Beaumarchais's Figaro's Marriage* (New York: Farrar, Straus and Cudahy, 1961), 193. (Lorenzo da Ponte's libretto for Mozart's opera *Le Nozze de Figaro* is based only on the Beaumarchais play and omits harshly political aspects of the original. The play was first presented in Paris 1784; the opera was first presented in Vienna, in 1786.)

35. Doniol, I:151.

36. Harwell, 259.

37. Morris, 91.

38. Minnigerode, 25.

39. Doniol, I:585.

Chapter 4: "So Many Spies in Our Midst"

1. Doniol, I:519–20. In an effort to participate in the French arms traffic to America, Dubourg responded to Beaumarchais's snub by sending a letter to Vergennes accusing Beaumarchais of "keeping girls" in his home. Brushing aside the accusations, Vergennes sent the Dubourg letter to Beaumarchais with a humorous note. Beaumarchais immediately wrote to Dubourg: "I do not believe keeping young girls in my home will interfere with my [arms] business, Monsieur. I do admit that I have been keeping them, Monsieur, for the last twenty years. There are five of them, my four sisters and my niece. I can only imagine what you would think if you know of the greater scandal of my keeping young, rather good-looking boys—two nephews—and the unfortunate father who brought this shameless keeper of girls into the world?"—Lemaître, *Beaumarchais*, 193.

2. Harlow Giles Unger, *Lafayette* (Hoboken, N.J.: John Wiley & Sons, 2002), 15.

3. Freeman, 4:180.

4. Ibid., 4:198.

5. Ibid., 4:212.

6. Doniol, I:616.

7. Corwin, 86.

8. Kapp, 96.

9. Kalb to Deane, December 17, 1776; Wharton, 1:77–78.

10. Doniol, I:646.

11. Wharton, 1:395.

12. Deane to Congress, November 6, 1776; Wharton, 2:190–191.

13. Wharton, 2:190–191.

14. Ibid., 2:145.

15. Ibid., 1:397.

16. Vergennes to the marquis de Noailles, French ambassador to England, April 11, 1777, in Doniol, II 402.

17. George Morgan, *The Life of James Monroe* (Boston: Small, Maynard and Company, 1921), 54.

18. A distant cousin of George Washington, Colonel William Washington so respected his namesake that after he was promoted to general, he insisted on being called " 'colonel,' because there can be but one *General* Washington in America." (Freeman, 7: 599n.).

19. Wharton, 2:218.

20. Ibid., 2:220.

21. Unger, *Lafayette*, 21.

22. *Correspondences et Manuscrits du Général Lafayette, publiés par sa famille* (Bruxelles: Société Belge de Librairie, Etc., Hauman, Cattoir et Compagnie, 2 vols., 1837), I:12.

23. Washington to the president of Congress, February 20, 1777; Sparks, *Writings*, 4:327.

24. Washington to Richard Henry Lee, May 17, 1777; Sparks, *Writings*, 4:423.

25. Greene to [Adams?], May 28, 1777; G. W. Greene, *The Life of Nathanael Greene, Major-General in the Army of the Revolution* (New York, 1871, 3 vols.), I:417.

26. Deane to Congress, November 29, 1776; Wharton, 2:202–203.

27. Deane to M. Gérard, April 1, 1777; Doniol, II:386.

28. Franklin and Deane to Congress, May 25, 1777; Wharton, 2:324.

29. *Diary of Chevalier du Buysson*, in Doniol: III:18.

30. Kapp, 127.

31. Doniol, II:644; III:140.

32. Ibid., III:576.

33. Kapp, 127.

34. Ibid., 137, 145.

35. Unger, *Lafayette*, 64.

36. *Correspondences*, I:33.

37. Kapp, 137–141.

38. Lafayette to Washington, February 19, 1778, in Unger, *Lafayette*, 65.

39. Conway returned to France at the outbreak of the French Revolution, and in 1793, he was exiled as a royalist. He disappeared from public life and is believed to have died in 1800.

40. *Journals of Congress*, December 5, 1778.

41. John R. Alden, *A History of the American Revolution* (New York: Alfred A. Knopf, 1969), 391–393.

Chapter 5: The French Invasion

1. Corwin, 247n; Doniol, III:8.

2. *The Adams Papers, Diary & Autobiography of John Adams*, L. H. Butterfield, ed. (New York: Atheneum, 1961, 4 vols.), IV:246.

3. *Webster's American Biographies* (Springfield, Mass.: Merriam-Webster, 1984), 365.

4. Ferling, 203, 185.

5. Corwin, 277.

6. The pianoforte is "an early form of the piano originating in the eighteenth and early nineteenth centuries and having a smaller range and softer timbre than a modern piano."—*Merriam-Webster's Collegiate Dictionary, 11th ed.*

7. Corwin, 275.

8. The king of France to Congress, March 28, 1778; Wharton, 2:521–522.

9. Official Report of the comte d'Estaing to the secretary of the French Navy, Doniol, III:374–382.

10. Greene, II:117.

11. Unger, *Lafayette*, 83.

12. Greene to d'Estaing, Boston, September 23, 1778; Doniol, III:392–393.

13. Unger, *Lafayette*, 89.

14. Washington to Henry Laurens, November 14, 1778; Sparks, *Life*, 289.

15. Doniol, III:464–466.

16. Unger, *Lafayette*, 81.

17. Doniol, III:422.

18. *Correspondences*, I:31.

19. *Adams Papers*, IV:246–247.

20. Ibid, IV:251.

21. Ibid., IV:246.

22. John Bartlett, *Bartlett's Familiar Quotations*, 16th ed. Justin Kaplan, general ed. (Boston: Little, Brown and Company, 1992), 348:10.

23. Unger, *Lafayette*, 107.

24. Maurice Renard, *Rochambeau: Libérateur de l'Amérique* (Paris: Fasquelle Editeurs, 1951), 147.

25. Doniol, IV:415.

26. Corwin, 252–253.

27. Ibid., 261.

28. Doniol, IV:418.

29. Corwin, 290n.

30. Unger, *Lafayette*, 117.

31. Doniol, III:158.

32. Ibid., IV:488.

33. Doniol, IV:611.

34. Ibid., IV:602.

35. Wharton, 1:466; IV:505.

36. Doniol, IV:611.

37. Corwin, 307n.

38. Unger, *Lafayette*, 143.

39. Renard, 147.

40. George Washington to Noah Webster, July 14, 1788; Harlow Giles Unger, *Noah Webster: The Life and Times of an American Patriot* (New York: John Wiley & Sons, 1998), 149.

41. Letter by George Washington, July 26, 1777; Thomas Powers, "The Literature of Secrets," the *New York Times Magazine*, December 28, 2003.

42. *Correspondences*, I:98.

43. Ibid., I:136n., ff.

44. Washington to Lafayette, September 7, 1781; Stanley J. Idzerda, ed., *Lafayette in the Age of the American Revolution: Selected Letters and Papers, 1776–1790* (Ithaca, N.Y., Cornell Univ. Press, 1981, 5 vols.), IV:390–391.

45. Unger, *Lafayette*, 156.

46. Ibid., 154.

47. Sparks, *Life*, 340.

48. Freeman, V:377.

49. On the field of surrender, Rochambeau openly acknowledged that Washington had devised the strategy for victory at Yorktown, but to avoid censure by Vergennes, his formal report claimed that he and Washington had developed the strategy together and that, contrary to Washington's assertions, he had been party to Washington's secret from the beginning. See his fifteen-page monograph, *Relation, ou, Journal des opérations du Corps Français sous le commandement du Comte de Rochambeau, depuis le 15 d'Août, 1781* (Philadelphie: Imprimerie de Guillaume Hampton).

50. Freeman, V:394.

51. Unger, *Lafayette*, 162.

52. Corwin, 272.

Chapter 6: Winners and Losers

1. Minnigerode, 64–65.

2. At the end of the sixteenth century, heirs to the French throne bore official sobriquets: Dauphin (sometimes, Grand Dauphin), the king's oldest son and heir apparent; Monsieur, the second oldest son and heir to the throne in the event the dauphin died before ascending the throne or died without sons of his own to succeed him.

3. Unger, *Lafayette*, 167.

4. Wharton, 5:321.

5. Ibid., 5:740.

6. Adams, *Works*, III:303.

7. Wharton, 5:849.

8. Adams to James Warren, April 16, 1783, in Unger, *Lafayette*, 176.

9. Wharton, 5:849.

10. Jay to Livingston, November 17, 1782; Wharton, 6:28.

11. Wharton, 6:48–49.

12. Ibid.

13. Jefferson to Madison, January 30, 1782; Wharton 1:351.

14. Corwin, 413.

15. Doniol, V:192.

16. Ibid., 188.

17. The actual treaty was signed in Paris on September 3, and Congress ratified it on January 14, 1784.

18. Freeman, V:477.

19. Corwin, 363.

20. Ibid., 367.

21. *Annual Register*, in Corwin, 375–376.

22. Ibid., 376.

23. Poniatowski, *Talleyrand aux États-Unis*, 350.

24. John Locke (1632–1704), *Two Treatises on Government*, 1690.

25. Unger, *Lafayette*, 237.

26. Jefferson to Richard Price, January 8, 1789, in Dumas Malone, *Jefferson and the Rights of Man* (Boston: Little, Brown and Company, 1951), 214.

27. Ibid., xvii. Of the hundreds of thousands slaughtered in the French Revolution, only 2 percent were aristocrats and clergy—allegedly the targets of revolutionaries. Many of those killed were ordinary citizens who happened to be in the way of a surging mob or, more often, people involved in family or neighborhood feuds and small merchants suspected of cheating neighbors.

28. Ammon, 20; Tulard, 349.

29. Unger, *Lafayette*, 293.

30. Jean Tulard, Jean-François Fayard, and Alfred Fierro, *Histoire et Dictionnaire de la Révolution Française, 1789–1799* (Paris: Robert Laffont, 1998), 602.

31. Ammon, 7.

32. Ibid., 12.

33. Minnigerode, 133.

34. *Le Petit Robert des Noms Propres* (Paris: Dictionnaires Le Robert, 1999), 1253.

35. Ibid., 92.

36. DeConde, *Entangling Alliance*, 181.

37. Ibid., 181n.

38. Alexander Hamilton, writing pseudonomyously as "Pacificus" in *Gazette of the United States* (Philadelphia), July 3, 1793.

39. DeConde, *Entangling Alliance*, 221.

40. Dumas Malone, *Jefferson and the Ordeal of Liberty* (Boston: Little, Brown and Company, 1962), 97.

41. Jefferson to Madison, January 30, 1778, in Malone, *Jefferson and the Rights of Man*, 46.

42. John C. Miller, *The Federalist Era, 1789–1801* (New York: Harper & Brothers, 1960), 127.

43. John Alexander Carroll and Mary Wells Ashworth, *George Washington, Volume Seven, First in Peace, completing the Biography by Douglas Southall Freeman* (New York: Charles Scribner's Sons, 1957), 36.

44. Harwell, 622.

45. Miller, *The Federalist Era*, 132.

46. Archives des Affaires Etrangères, Ministère des Affaires Etrangères, Dossier *Genet* (hereafter abbreviated as "AAE-Genet").

47. Jefferson to Vergennes, November 20, 1785, in Frederick A. Schminke, *Genet: The Origins of His Mission to America* (Toulouse: Imprimerie Toulousaine Lion et Fils, 1939), 31, citing Papers of the Continental Congress, no. 107, I, 171–173 Library of Congress, Washington, D.C.

Chapter 7: The Appetite of Despotism

1. *Boston Columbian Centinel*, January 30, 1793, reporting on the minister's sermon at the Plymouth, Massachusetts, parish church. After the sermon, the choir sang "Down with these Earthly Kings; No King but God."

2. *Delaware Gazette* (Wilmington), July 16, 1792.

3. *Boston Gazette*, January 21, 24, 28, 1793.

4. All will be well, will be well, will be well;
   Send the aristo[crat]s onto the gallows;
   All will be well, will be well, will be well;
   We are going to hang the aristocrats.

5. Minnigerode, 168.

6. *Philadelphia National Gazette*, April 20, 1793. Louis XVI was both Bourbon and Capetian. The Capetian dynasty succeeded the Carolingians in 967, with the accession of Hugues Capet to the throne of France. The marriage of Robert de Clermont, son of Louis IX (Saint Louis), to Béatrice de Bourbon in the mid-thirteenth century linked the Bourbon and Capetian families to each other, although the first Bourbon monarch, Henry IV, would not ascend the throne until 1589.

7. Minnigerode, 167.

8. *Boston Gazette*, November 19, 1792.

9. *Connecticut Journal* (New Haven), July 6, 1791.

10. *New-York Journal*, January 13, 1798.

11. Minnigerode, 221.

12. *Boston Gazette*, April 29, 1793.

13. Minnigerode, 221.

14. Ibid., 207.

15. Ibid.

16. French Jacobin leaders purposely discarded *culottes*, or knickers, which were standard aristocratic dress at court.

17. Minnigerode, 190.

18. Genet to Minister of Foreign Affairs, June 19, 1793; Malone, *Ordeal of Liberty*, 104.

19. *Kentucky Gazette* (Lexington), April 5, 1794.

20. Paul Leicester Ford, *The Writings of Jefferson* (New York: Putnam, 1892–1899, 10 vols.), VI, 245–246.

21. AAE-Genet.

22. Ibid., 191

23. *New York Spectator*, November 16, 1798.

24. Unger, *Webster*, 186.

25. DeConde, *Entangling Alliance*, 207.

26. Minnigerode, 201–202.

27. To emphasize his republican complexion, Genet abandoned his private carriage before reaching Chester and took a public coach to his lodgings in Philadelphia, accidentally bypassing the reception waiting to escort him into town. The reception committee at Chester caught up with him later to greet him officially and set off the celebration of cannon fire and church bells.

28. Minnigerode, 191.

29. *Philadelphia National Gazette*, June 5, 1793.

30. John Adams to Thomas Jefferson, June 30, 1813, in Lester J. Cappon, ed., *The Adams-Jefferson Letters: The Complete Correspondence Between Thomas Jefferson and Abigail and John Adams* (Chapel Hill: Univ. of North Carolina Press, 1959), 346–347.

31. AAE-Genet.

32. Without correspondents or other links to major cities, the nation's press simply copied articles from Philadelphia, New York, Boston, and Baltimore newspapers to keep readers in smaller communities informed. It was "an era of scissors-and-paste journalism," according to Henry Ammon, 141.

33. Minnigerode, 219.

34. *New York Spectator*, November 16, 1798.

35. DeConde, *Entangling Alliance*, 254.

36. Ibid., 254–255.

37. Thomas Jefferson to Jack Eppes, May 12, 1993, in Malone, *Ordeal of Liberty*, 81.

38. Minnigerode, 205.

39. Malone, *Ordeal of Liberty*, 97.

40. Thomas Jefferson to James Madison, May 19, 1793, in Malone, *Ordeal of Liberty*, 97.

41. Ibid., 210, 202.

42. Ibid., 418.

43. Ibid., 282–283.

44. Minnigerode, 208; Ammon, 67.

45. Ford I: 238–240.

46. Unger, *Webster*, 183.

47. Ibid., 71.

48. *Philadelphia National Gazette*, July 15, 1793.

49. Ibid., July 21, 1793. (Genet sent a copy to the French Foreign Ministry and it remains in vol. 38, Dossier *Correspondence Consulaire*.)

50. Ammon, 70.

51. Minnigerode, 223.

52. *Instructions to Citizen Genet, Minister Plenipotentiary from the French Republic to the United States from The Executive Council*, French Foreign Ministry, vol. 38, Dossier *Correspondence Consulaire*.

53. Ammon, 83–84.

54. Ford, I: 236.

55. Ibid., 265.

56. Donald H. Stewart, *The Opposition Press of the Federalist Period* (Albany: State Univ. of New York Press, 1969), 132.

57. Ibid., 312.

58. AAE-Genet.

59. Minnigerode, 236.

Chapter 8: "Down with Washington!"

1. Ammon, 91; Ford, VI:340, n1.

2. Minnigerode, 265.

3. AAE-Genet. The terms "democrat" and "republican" were synonymous references to political philosophies rather than political parties.

4. Harwell, 697.

5. George Washington to Governor Henry Lee, September 17, 1793, in Carroll and Ashworth, *George Washington*, 131.

6. Ammon, 97.

7. Minnigerode, 421; Ammon, 97.

8. Ibid., 267.

9. Minnigerode, 210.

10. Ibid., 196.

11. Unger, *Webster*, 185.

12. Ibid.

13. *Greenleaf's New York Journal*, August 28, 1793.

14. Minnigerode, 193.

15. *Boston Columbian Centinel*, August 17, 1793.

16. Ibid., 215.

17. Adams to Jefferson, June 30, 1813; *The Adams-Jefferson Letters*, 346.

18. *The Diary; or Loudon's Register* (New York), August 12, 1793.

19. *New York Daily Advertiser*, August 6, 1793.

20. *Philadelphia Federal Gazette*, November 9, 1793; *State Gazette of North Carolina*, Edenton, December 14, 1793.

21. DeConde, *Entangling Alliance*, 288.

22. Jefferson to Genet, August 16, 1793, in DeConde, *Entangling Alliance*, 288.

23. Ammon, 108.

24. Walter Lowrie and Matthew St. Clair Clarke, eds., *American State Papers, Foreign Relations* (Washington, D.C., 1832), I:172–174 passim.

25. Jefferson to Madison, August 11, 1793, DeConde, *Entangling Alliance*, 289.

26. Minnigerode, 287.

27. DeConde, *Entangling Alliance*, 304.

28. Ammon, 58–62.

29. DeConde, *Entangling Alliance*, 284, 306–310.

30. Jefferson to Madison, July 7, 1793, Ford, VI, 338–339.

31. DeConde, *Entangling Alliance*, 306–307.

32. Ibid.

33. British ambassador to the United States George Hammond to British foreign secretary Lord Grenville, Philadelphia, February 22, 1794.

34. Adams to his wife, Philadelphia, February 23, 1794, in C. F. Adams, ed., *Letters of John Adams Addressed to His Wife*, II, 143, cited in DeConde, *Entangling Alliance*, 305.

Chapter 9: Toasts to Sedition

1. Madison to Jefferson, March 9, 1794, in DeConde, *Entangling Alliance*, 397n.

2. Washington to Richard Henry Lee, April 15, 1794, in DeConde, *Entangling Alliance*, 398.

3. John C. Hamilton, ed., *The Works of Alexander Hamilton* (New York: 1850–1851, 7 vols.), V:346–347.

4. Madison to Jefferson, March 2, 1794, in DeConde, *Entangling Alliance*, 394.

5. Fauchet to Randolph, February 22, 1784, AAE, Correspondence Consulaire, vol. 3.

6. Washington to Henry Lee, August 26, 1794, Caroll and Ashworth, 181–182; DeConde, *Entangling Alliance*, 262.

7. Miller, *Federalist Era*, 161.

8. Genet became a U.S. citizen and the father of six children by Cornelia Clinton. One of his great-great-grandsons, Edmond Charles Clinton Genet, was the first American aviator killed in World War I—shot from the sky over France fighting with the Lafayette Escadrille, a group of American fliers who volunteered with the Allies before the United States entered the war.

9. Miller, *Federalist Era*, 169–170.

10. DeConde, *Entangling Alliance*, 267. The quotation is not that of Osgood but Professor DeConde paraphrasing Osgood's words.

11. DeConde, *Entangling Alliance*, 415.

12. Harwell, 673.

13. Unger, *Lafayette*, 37.

14. Harwell, 677.

15. Randolph's letter of resignation included the assertion "I here most solemnly deny that any overture ever came to me which was to produce money to me, or any others for me; and that in any manner, directly or indirectly, was a shilling ever received by me. Nor was it ever contemplated by me that one shilling should be applied by Mr. Fauchet to any purpose relative to the insurrection." The Fauchet letter created a bitter rift between the two Virginians that would never heal. Randolph later published a 103-page pamphlet entitled "A Vindication," which proved his innocence but so insulted the president that it failed to restore Randolph in the public trust. (For a full discussion, see Harwell, 678–689.)

16. DeConde, *Entangling Alliance*, 416.

17. *Nouvelle Biographie Générale depuis les Temps les Plus Reculés jusqu'a Nos Jours*, I:278–279; *Dictionnaire de la Biographie Française*, I:574–576.

18. DeConde, *Entangling Alliance*, 427.

19. Malone, *Ordeal of Liberty*, 267.

20. Ibid, 267–268.

21. Archives des Affaires Etrangères, Ministère des Affaires Etrangères, Paris, *États-Unis*, vol. XLV.

22. Ibid.

23. Minnigerode, 347.

24. Harwell, 701–702.

25. Ibid.

26. DeConde, *Entangling Alliance*, 474.

27. Ibid., 473.

28. Adet to Secretary of State Timothy Pickering, November 15, 1796, *American State Papers, Foreign Relations*, I:579–583.

29. John Quincy Adams to Joseph Pitcairn, November 13, 1796 in Worthington C. Ford, ed., *Writings of John Quincy Adams*, (New York, 1913–1917, 7 vols.), II:42.

30. Malone, *Ordeal of Liberty*, 288.

31. Miller, *Federalist Era*, 196–197.

32. *American Minerva*, April 11, 1794.

33. DeConde, *Entangling Alliance*, 476.

34. Malone, *Ordeal of Liberty*, 290.

35. DeConde, *Entangling Alliance*, 488.

36. Ibid., 490–491.

Chapter 10: The War with France

1. "Directoire," *La Grande Encyclopédie* (Paris: Librairie Larousse, 1973, 20 vols.), 3895.

2. Babeuf was also called "Gracchus," after Tiberius Semprionus Gracchus (163–133 B.C.), who sponsored proposals in ancient Rome to raise the lot of peasant farmers by redistricting lands and restricting the acreage each citizen could occupy.

3. *La Grande Encyclopédie*, 3895; Felix Maurice Hippiel Markham, *Napoleon* (New York: The New American Library of World Literature, 1963), 27.

4. Markham, 27.

5. Ibid., 29.

6. Poniatowski, *Talleyrand aux États-Unis*, 375.

7. Ibid., 164.

8. Maurice Denuzière, *Je Te Nomme Louisiane: Découverte, colonisation et vente de la Louisiane* (Paris: Éditions Denoël, 1990), 385.

9. Markham, 44.

10. Ibid., 42.

11. Jean Tulard, et al., 244.

12. Poniatowski, *Talleyrand aux États-Unis*, 75.

13. Alexander DeConde, *This Affair of Louisiana* (New York: Charles Scribner's Sons, 1976), 87.

14. Alexander DeConde, *The Quasi-War: The Politics and Diplomacy of the Undeclared War with France 1797–1801* (New York: Charles Scribner's Sons, 1966), 114.

15. Ibid., 23.

16. Poniatowski, *Talleyrand aux États-Unis*, 353–355.

17. Michel Poniatowski, *Talleyrand et le Directoire, 1796–1800* (Paris: Librairie Académique Perrin, 1982), 555.

18. Ibid., 554.

19. Albert J. Beveridge, *The Life of John Marshall* (Boston: Houghton Mifflin, 1916–1919, 4 vols.), II:267.

20. Poniatowski, *Talleyrand et le Directoire*, 559.

21. Ibid., 562.

22. Ibid., 563.

23. Ibid.

24. DeConde, *The Quasi-War*, 53.

25. Beveridge, *Marshall*, II:327.

26. DeConde, *The Quasi-War*, 58.

27. Ibid., 145.

28. Malone, *Ordeal of Liberty*, 372–373.

29. DeConde, *The Quasi-War*, 75.

30. Knox to Oliver Wolcott, May 2, 1798, Massachusetts Historical Society.

31. *Boston Columbian Centinel*, July 4, 1798.

32. DeConde, *The Quasi-War*, 88.

33. Markham, 46.

34. *Philadelphia Porcupine's Gazette*, June 7, 1898.

35. DeConde, *The Quasi-War*, 85.

36. Ibid., 95.

37. *Works of Hamilton*, V:184.

38. *Philadelphia Porcupine's Gazette*, July 1797.

39. Robert Goodloe Harper, June 19, 1798, *Annals of Congress*, VIII.

40. Harrison Gray Otis, June 19, 1798, *Annals of Congress*, VIII.

41. DeConde, *The Quasi-War*, 108.

42. Miller, *Federalist Era*, 215.

43. *Works of Hamilton*, VI:390.

44. John Adams to Timothy Pickering, October 3, 1798, Adams, *Works*, X:146–149.

45. DeConde, *The Quasi-War*, 139.

46. Ibid., 129.

47. Miller, *Federalist Era*, 217.

48. DeConde, *The Quasi-War*, 129.

49. Markham, 52.

50. DeConde, *The Quasi-War*, 160.

Chapter 11: "I Renounce Louisiana"

1. Tulard et al., 262.
2. *La Grande Encyclopédie*, 7:3898–3899.
3. Markham, 61–62.
4. Murray's official title was American minister resident to the Batavian Republic.
5. DeConde, *The Quasi-War*, 179.
6. Ibid., 210.
7. The Tuileries Palace was built by Catherine de Medici as a royal residence in Paris. Destroyed by French Communards in 1871, it stretched across the existing Tuileries Gardens, connecting the two pavilions at the ends of the projecting arms of the Louvre Palace. Louis XIV virtually abandoned it in favor of Versailles, which became the seat of government until the French Revolution, although he used the Tuileries Palace as a royal pied-à-terre when he and his family were in town for a special function. Uninterested in Versailles, Napoléon restored the Tuileries Palace to its status as primary royal residence, although his favorite residence was the Château de Fontainebleau, which François I began building southeast of Paris in 1527.
8. Markham, 42.
9. Ibid., 149.
10. Ibid.
11. "Éloge funèbre de Washington," *Le Moniteur Universel* (Paris), February 19, 1800.
12. *American State Papers, Foreign Relations*, II:339.
13. DeConde, *Louisiana*, 96.
14. William Vans Murray to John Quincy Adams, October 5, 1800, in DeConde, *The Quasi-War*, 257.
15. Ibid., 283.
16. *Philadelphia Aurora*, October 4, 1800.
17. DeConde, *The Quasi-War*, 302.
18. At the time, presidential candidates ran independently, with the winner named president and the second-place finisher named vice president, regardless of political party affiliation.
19. Ford, *The Writings of Thomas Jefferson*, VIII:58.
20. DeConde, *Louisiana*, 49.
21. Adams to John Jay, May 8, 1785, *Works of John Adams*, VIII:246.
22. Madison to Pinckney, November 27, 1802, in DeConde, *Louisiana*, 122.
23. Jefferson to Livingston, April 18, 1802, in DeConde, *Louisiana*, 114.
24. Louis André Pichon to Talleyrand, October 15, 1801, AAE, Correspondence Politique, États Unis.
25. Ford, *The Writings of Thomas Jefferson* IX: 363–368.
26. DeConde, *Louisiana*, 111.
27. Ibid., 103.
28. Ibid., 117–118.

29. James Monroe, *The Autobiography of James Monroe*, Stuart Gerry Brown, ed. (Syracuse, N.Y.: Syracuse Univ. Press, 1959), 153.

30. *Charleston (SC) Courier*, January 11, 1803.

31. DeConde, *Louisiana*, 124.

32. Dumas Malone, *Jefferson the President: First Term, 1801–1805* (Boston: Little, Brown and Company, 1970), 273.

33. Ibid.

34. Ibid., 136.

35. Ibid., 139.

36. *New York Evening Post*, January 28, 1803.

37. Ford, *The Writings of Thomas Jefferson*, IX:418–419.

38. *Annals of Congress*, February 16, 1803.

39. Ibid., February 25, 1803.

40. DeConde, *Louisiana*, 137.

41. Ibid., 142.

42. Ibid., 151.

43. Denuzière, 393.

44. DeConde, *Louisiana*, 154.

45. Denuzière, 393.

46. James Monroe, *Autobiography*, 167.

47. Ibid., 173.

48. DeConde, *Louisiana*, 189.

49. Jean-Louis Aujol, *L'Empire Français du Mississipi* [sic] (Paris: Collection "à tire d'ailes" G.F.P.E.), 5.

50. Jackson to Jefferson, August 7, 1803, in Malone, *Jefferson the President*, 348.

51. Malone, *Jefferson the President*, 348.

52. DeConde, *Louisiana*, 180–181.

Chapter 12: The American Menace

1. *La Grande Encyclopédie*, 3895.

2. Louis XVIII became the legitimate heir to the French throne as eldest uncle to Louis XVII, the eight-year-old son of Louis XVI, whom revolutionaries beheaded in 1793. Ripped from his mother's arms in their prison cell, he was abducted and never seen again.

3. Morris, 161, 162.

4. Faulkner and Kepner, *America*, 624.

5. With the defeat of Napoléon I, the Austrians essentially kidnapped his three-year-old son, Napoléon II, to prevent his accession to the French throne from becoming a rallying point for French Bonapartists. He died a virtual prisoner in Austria at the age of twenty-one.

6. Morris, 240.

7. Poniatowski, *Talleyrand aux États-Unis*, 75.

8. Ibid., 15–16.

9. Ibid., 30–2.

10. Ibid., 16.

11. Alain Peyrefitte, *C'était de Gaulle* (Paris: De Fallois-Fayard Éditions, Tome II, 1947), cited in Revel, 23.

12. Ibid. Spite may well have motivated de Gaulle's statement. On President Franklin Roosevelt's orders, American leaders gave de Gaulle only two days notice of Normandy invasion plans in June 1944 and refused to allow him to participate for fear he would be unwilling to obey orders from the supreme allied commander, American general Dwight D. Eisenhower.

13. Ibid., 43.

14. Revel, 45.

15. *Le Monde* (Paris), February 15, 2001.

16. Revel, 45, 61.

17. Ibid., 175.

18. Ibid., 40.

19. Total annual enrollment is about a hundred French students and forty foreign students (largely from French-speaking former colonies), for a program lasting twenty-seven months and divided into a fifteen-month study program and a twelve-month internship. Seven months of the internship are spent with a prefect, or state governor, and five months in a diplomatic post or international organization. Civil servants with five years' work experience constitute 45 percent of each class, and 5 percent are professionals with eight years' experience outside the public sector. Course work includes public law, economics, budget and financial planning, public administration, international and European affairs, human resources development, and a range of foreign languages. (Taken from descriptive leaflet, issued by the République Française, Premier Ministre, École Nationale d'Administration, www.ena.fr.)

20. Ibid.

21. *The Works of Plato: The Republic*, Book V (New York: Simon and Schuster, Irwin Edman, ed., 1928), 417.

22. Dominique de Villepin, *Le Cri de la Gargouille* (Paris: Éditions Albin Michel, 2002), 19

23. Ibid., 213.

24. Unger, *Lafayette*, 221.

25. Alphonse Karr (1808–1890), *Les Guêpes*, January 1849 (John Bartlett, *Bartlett's Familiar Quotations* 16th ed., 443).

26. *Wall Street Journal*, March 2, 2004.

27. Revel, 40, 268.

28. Ibid., 300.

29. De Villepin, *Cri*, 17–18; 210.

Selected Bibliography

Adams, Charles F., ed. *The Works of John Adams* (Boston: Little Brown 1850–1856, 10 vols.).

Adams, James Truslow. *Revolutionary New England, 1691–1776* (Boston: The Atlantic Monthly Press, 1923).

Adams, John. *The Adams-Jefferson Letters: The Complete Correspondence Between Thomas Jefferson and Abigail and John Adams*, Lester J. Cappon, ed. (Chapel Hill: Univ. of North Carolina Press, 1959).

Alden, John R. *A History of the American Revolution* (New York: Alfred A. Knopf, 1969).

Ammon, Henry. *The Genet Mission* (New York: W. W. Norton & Company, 1973).

d'Argenson, Marquis. *Journal et Mémoires du Marquis d'Argenson* (Paris: Ratheray, 1859).

Augur, Helen. *The Secret War of Independence* (New York: Duell, Sloan and Pearce, 1955).

Aujol, Jean-Louis. *L'Empire Français du Mississipi* [sic] (Paris: Collection "à tire d'ailes" G.F.P.E., undated).

Berthier, Jean. *Aide-Mémoire d'Histoire de France* (Paris: Larousse Bordas, 1998).

Beveridge, Albert J. *The Life of John Marshall* (Boston: Houghton Mifflin, 1916–1919, 4 vols.).

Bonnel, Ulane. *La France, Les États-Unis et la guerre de course (1797–1815)* (Paris: Nouvelles Editions Latines, 1961).

Brosse, Jacques, ed. *Mémoires du Duc de Choiseul* (Paris: Mercure de France, 1987).

Budd, Henry. *Citizen Genet's Visit to Philadelphia* (Philadelphia: City History Society of Philadelphia, 1918).

Butterfield, L. H., ed. *The Adams Papers, Diary & Autobiography of John Adams* (New York: Atheneum, 4 vols., 1961).

Carroll, John Alexander, and Mary Wells Ashworth. *George Washington, Volume Seven, First in Peace, completing the Biography by Douglas Southall Freeman* (New York: Charles Scribner's Sons, 1957).

Corwin, Edward S. *French Policy and the American Alliance of 1778* (Princeton, N.J.: Princeton Univ. Press, 1916).

Cox, Isaac J., ed. *The Journeys of René Robert Cavalier, Sieur de La Salle* (New York: 1922, 2 vols.).

Cunliffe, Marcus. *The Nation Takes Shape, 1789–1837* (Chicago: The University of Chicago Press, 1959).

DeConde, Alexander. *This Affair of Louisiana* (New York: Charles Scribner's Sons, 1976).

———. *Entangling Alliance* (Durham, N.C.: Duke University Press, 1958).

———. *The Quasi-War: The Politics and Diplomacy of the Undeclared War with France 1797–1801* (New York: Charles Scribner's Sons, 1966).

Denis, Michel, and Noël Blayau. *Le XVIIIe Siècle* (Paris: Armand Colin/VUEF, 2002).

Denuzière, Maurice. *Je Te Nomme Louisiane: Découverte, colonisation et vente de la Louisiane* (Paris: Éditions Denoël, 1990).

Doniol, Henri. *Histoire de la Participation de la France à l'Établissement des États-Unis d'Amérique* (Paris: Imprimerie Nationale, 5 vols., quarto, 1886).

Downey, Fairfax. *Louisbourg: Key to a Continent* (Englewood Cliffs, N.J.: Prentice-Hall, 1965).

Edman, Irwin, ed. *The Works of Plato* (New York: The Modern Library, 1928).

Faulkner, Harold Underwood, and Tyler Kepner. *America, Its History and People* (New York: Harper & Brothers Publishers, 1942).

Ferling, John. *John Adams: A Life* (New York: Henry Holt and Company, 1992).

Fitzpatrick, John C., ed. *The Writings of Washington* (Washington, D.C.: Government Printing Office, 39 vols., 1931–1944).

Ford, Paul Leicester. *The Writings of Thomas Jefferson* (New York: Putnam, 1892–1899, 10 vols.).

Ford, Worthington C., ed. *Journals of the Continental Congress* (Washington, D.C.: 34 vols., 1904–1936).

———, ed. *The Writings of John Quincy Adams* (New York: 1913–1917, 7 vols.).

Freeman, Douglas Southall. *George Washington: A Biography* (New York: Charles Scribner's Sons, 6 vols., 1954).

Fusonie, Alan and Donna Jean. *George Washington: Pioneer Farmer* (Mount Vernon, Va.: Mount Vernon Ladies Association, 1998).

Genet, Citizen [Edmond-Charles]. *The Correspondence between Citizen Genet, Minister of the French Republic to the United States of North America, and the Officers of the Federal Government; to which are prefixed the Instructions from the Constituted Authorities of France to the Said Minister* (Philadelphia: Benjamin Franklin Bache, 1793).

Genet, George Clinton. *Washington, Jefferson, and "Citizen" Genet, 1793* (New York, privately published, 1899).

Gipson, Henry Lawrence. *The Coming of the Revolution, 1763–1775* (New York: Harper & Brothers, 1954).

Greene, G. W. *The Life of Nathanael Greene, Major-General in the Army of the Revolution* (New York: 1871, 3 vols.).

Hamilton, John C., ed. *The Works of Alexander Hamilton* (New York: 1850–1851, 7 vols.).

Harwell, Richard. *Washington, An abridgment in one volume of the seven-volume*

George Washington by Douglas Southall Freeman (New York: Charles Scribner's Sons, 1968).

Henry, William Wirt. *Patrick Henry: Life, Correspondence and Speeches* (New York: Charles Scribner's Sons, 3 vols., 1891).

Hicks, John D. *A Short History of American Democracy* (Cambridge, Mass.: Riverside Press, 1946).

Higginbotham, Don. *The War of American Independence: Military Attitudes, Policies, and Practice, 1763–1789* (New York: Macmillan Company, 1971).

Idzerda, Stanley J., ed. *Lafayette in the Age of the American Revolution, Selected Letters and Papers, 1776–1790* (Ithaca, N.Y.: Cornell Univ. Press, 1981, 5 vols.).

Jefferson, Thomas. *The Adams-Jefferson Letters: The Complete Correspondence Between Thomas Jefferson and Abigail and John Adams*, Lester J. Cappon, ed. (Chapel Hill: Univ. of North Carolina Press, 1959).

Jensen, Merrill. *The New Nation: A History of the United States During the Confederation, 1781–1789* (New York: Alfred A. Knopf, 1950).

Kapp, Friedrich. *The Life of John Kalb, Major-General in the Revolutionary Army* (New York: Henry Holt and Company, 1884).

Kirchhoff, Elisabeth. *Histoire de France* (Paris: Molière, 1997).

Knollenberg, Bernhard. *Origin of the American Revolution: 1759–1766* (New York: The Free Press, 1961).

———. *Growth of the American Revolution, 1766–1775* (New York: The Free Press, 1975).

Koch, Adrienne, and William Peden, eds. *The Selected Writings of John and John Quincy Adams* (New York: Alfred A. Knopf, 1946).

Lafayette, George-Washington. *[Gilbert Motier, Marquis de Lafayette] Mémoires, Correspondences et Manuscrits du Général Lafayette, publiés par sa famille* (Paris: H. Fournier, ainé, 1837, 6 vols.; Bruxelles: Société Belge de Librairie, Etc., Hauman, Cattoir et Compagnie, 2 vols., 1837).

Lancaster, Bruce. *From Lexington to Liberty, The Story of the American Revolution* (Garden City, N.Y.: Doubleday & Company, 1955).

Lebédel, Claude. *Chronology of the History of France* (Rennes: Éditions Ouest-France, 1999).

Lemaître, Georges. *Beaumarchais* (New York: Alfred A. Knopf, 1949).

McCullough, David. *John Adams* (New York: Simon & Schuster, 2001).

Malone, Dumas. *Jefferson and the Ordeal of Liberty* (Boston: Little, Brown and Company, 1962).

———. *Jefferson the President: First Term, 1801–1805* (Boston: Little, Brown and Company, 1970).

———. *Jefferson and the Rights of Man* (Boston: Little, Brown and Company, 1951).

Markham, Felix Maurice Hippiel. *Napoleon* (New York: The New American Library of World Literature, 1963).

Marston, Daniel. *The Seven Years' War* (Oxford: Osprey Publishing Limited, 2001).

Meade, Robert Douthat. *Patrick Henry: Patriot in the Making* (Philadelphia and New York: J. B. Lippincott Company, 1957).

————. *Patrick Henry: Practical Revolutionary* (Philadelphia and New York: J. B. Lippincott Company, 1969).

Miller, John C. *Crisis in Freedom: The Alien and Sedition Acts* (Boston: Little, Brown and Company, Boston, 1951).

————. *The Federalist Era, 1789–1801* (New York: Harper & Brothers, 1960).

Minnigerode, Meade. *Jefferson: Friend of France* (New York: G. P. Putnam & Sons, 1928).

Monroe, James. *The Autobiography of James Monroe*, Stuart Gerry Brown, ed. (Syracuse, N.Y.: Syracuse Univ. Press, 1959).

————. *The Writings of James Monroe, including a collection of his public and private papers and correspondence now for the first time printed*, Stanislaus Murray Hamilton, ed. (Brookland, D.C.: Government Printing Branch, Department of State, 1898).

Morgan, George. *The Life of James Monroe* (Boston: Small, Maynard and Company, 1921).

Morris, Richard B., ed. *Encyclopedia of American History* (New York: Harper & Brothers, 1953).

Nabonne, Bernard. *La Diplomatie du Directoire et Bonaparte d'après les Papiers Inédits de Reubell* (Paris, La Nouvelle Édition, 1951).

Péronnet, Michel. *Le XVIIIe Siècle (1740–1820), Des Lumières à la Sainte-Alliance* (Paris: Hachette Livre, 1998).

Poniatowski, Michel. *Talleyrand aux États-Unis, 1794–1796* (Paris: Presses de la Cité, 1967).

————. *Talleyrand et le Directoire, 1796–1800* (Paris: Librairie Académique Perrin, 1982).

Raddin, George Gates, Jr. *Caritat and the Genet Episode* (Dover, N.J.: Dover Advance Press, 1953).

Randolph, Edmund. *The History of Virginia* (Charlottesville: Univ. Press of Virginia, 1970).

Renard, Maurice. *Rochambeau, Libérateur de l'Amérique* (Paris: Fasquelle Editeurs, 1951).

Revel, Jean-François. *L'obsession anti-américaine: Son fonctionnement, ses causes, ses conséquences* (Paris: Plon, 2002).

de Sauvigny, G. de Bertier. *Histoire de France* (Paris: Flammarion, 1977).

Schachner, Nathan. *Thomas Jefferson: A Biography* (New York: Appleton-Century-Crofts, 2 vols., 1951).

Schminke, Frederick A. *Genet: The Origins of His Mission to America* (Toulouse: Imprimerie Toulousaine Lion et Fils, 1939).

Smith, Page. *John Adams* (Garden City, N.Y.: Doubleday & Company, 2 vols., 1962).

Sparks, Jared. *The Life of George Washington* (Boston: Tappan and Dennet, 1843).

————, ed., *The Writings of George Washington* (Boston: Tappan and Dennet, 1834–1837, 12 vols.).

Stewart, Donald H. *The Opposition Press of the Federalist Period* (Albany: State Univ. of New York Press, 1969).

Tagg, James. *Benjamin Franklin Bache and the Philadelphia Aurora* (Philadelphia: Univ. of Pennsylvania Press, 1991).

Tulard, Jean, Jean-François Fayard, and Alfred Fierro. *Histoire et Dictionnaire de la Révolution Française, 1789–1799* (Paris: Robert Laffont, 1998).

Tyler, Moses Coit. *Patrick Henry* (New Rochelle, N.Y.: Arlington House, 1898).

Unger, Harlow Giles. *John Hancock: Merchant King and American Patriot* (New York: John Wiley & Sons, 2000).

———. *Lafayette* (Hoboken, N.J.: John Wiley & Sons, 2002).

———. *Noah Webster: The Life and Times of an American Patriot* (New York: John Wiley & Sons, 1998).

Ver Steeg, Clarence L. *The Formative Years, 1607–1763*, in *The Making of America*, ed. David Donald (New York: Hill and Wang, 1964).

de Villepin, Dominique. *Le Cri de la Gargouille* (Paris: Éditions Albin Michel, 2002).

Vivent, Jacques. *Barras, le "Roi" de la République, 1755–1829* (Paris: Librairie Hachette, 1946).

Wenzler, Claude. *The Kings of France* (Rennes: Éditions Ouest-France, 1995).

Wharton, Francis. *The Revolutionary Diplomatic Correspondence of the United States, Edited under Direction of Congress, with preliminary index, and notes historical and legal. Published in conformity with Act of Congress of August 13, 1888.* (Washington, D.C.: Government Printing Office, 6 vols., 1889).

Wirt, William. *The Life of Patrick Henry* (New York: 1852).

Wrong, George M. *The Conquest of New France: A Chronicle of the Colonial Wars* (New Haven, Conn.: Yale Univ. Press, 1918).

Periodicals

American Minerva
Boston Columbian Centinel
Boston Gazette
Connecticut Journal
Delaware Gazette (Wilmington)
The Diary; or Loudon's Register (New York)
Essex Gazette
Gazette of the United States
Kentucky Gazette (Lexington)
Le Monde
New York Daily Advertiser
New-York Journal
New York Times Magazine
Philadelphia Aurora
Philadelphia Federal Gazette
Philadelphia National Gazette
Porcupine's Gazette (Philadelphia)
Spectator (New York)

Reference Works

American State Papers, Foreign Relations
Annals of Congress
Bartlett's Familiar Quotations
Biographie Universelle
Dictionary of American Biographies
Dictionary of National Biographies
Dictionnaire de la Biographie Française
Dictionnaire Napoléon
Encyclopaedia Universalis
Encyclopedia of American Education
Encyclopedia Britannica, 10th ed.
Funk & Wagnall's New Encyclopedia
La Grande Encyclopédie
Journals of Congress
The New Cambridge Modern History
Nouvelle Biographie Générale depuis les Temps les Plus Reculés jusqu'a Nos Jours
Le Petit Robert des Noms Propres
Webster's American Biographies
Webster's New Biographical Dictionary

Manuscript Collections

American State Papers, Foreign Relations
Archives des Affaires Etrangères, Ministère des Affaires Etrangères, Paris (abbreviated as AAE in notes)
Archives du Ministère de la Marine, Paris
Bibliothèque de l'Institut de France, Paris
Bibliothèque Historique de la Ville de Paris, Paris
Bibliothèque Nationale de France, Paris
Library of Congress, Washington, D.C.
New York Public Library, New York, N.Y.

Index

Act Concerning Aliens, 209
Act Respecting Alien Enemies, 209–210
Adams, Abigail, 206, 207
Adams, Fort, 230
Adams, John
    American Revolution, 66, 87, 105
    election of 1800, 225–226
    France, 1, 2, 5, 88–89, 97, 114, 122,
        144, 199–200, 201, 203, 204, 207,
        208, 211, 212, 214, 218
    Genet, Edmond Charles, 151–152, 167
    Great Britain, 127, 210–211
    Holland, 103, 115, 118
    Lafayette, marquis de, 121
    military power, 207–209, 211, 212
    peace negotiations, 107, 120–122,
        230
    presidency of, 191
    Talleyrand-Périgord, Charles-Maurice
        de, 217
    Vergennes, Charles Gravier, comte de,
        89, 97–98, 103, 106
    XYZ affair, 205–206
Adams, John Quincy, 89, 189, 218, 224,
    239–240
Adams, Samuel, 34
Adet, Pierre August, 185, 187–190, 225
Africa, 241, 243
Agence France Presse, 1
Aix-la-Chapelle, Treaty of, 7, 24
Albemarle, Earl of, 19

Algeria, 244
Alien and Sedition Acts, 209–210
American Revolution, 244. See also
    British Army; United States
    Breeds Hill and Bunker Hill battles,
        50–51
    British economy, 124–125
    Canada, 57–58, 61
    Clark, George Rogers, 137
    debt assumption, 145
    Declaration of Independence, 60
    France, 2, 5, 125–126
    France assists, 48, 53, 55–57
    Lexington, Battle of, 48–49
    peace negotiations, 118–120
    Philadelphia, Pennsylvania, 80
    southern campaign, 96
    Trenton, Battle of, 72–73
    Yorktown, Battle of, 112
Amherst, Jeffrey, 27
Ammon, Henry, 172–173
anti-Americanism, France, 1, 2, 246–252
Anti-George (French privateer), 146
arms trade, Beaumarchais, Pierre
        Augustin Caron de, 55–56, 58–59,
        60, 81
Army (British). See British Army
Army (U.S.), strength of, 208–209. See
    also American Revolution;
    Continental Army
Arnold, Benedict, 57, 83, 104, 107, 184

Arouet, François-Marie (Voltaire), 27, 65, 203
Articles of Confederation, political instability, 126–128
Athanasius II (pope of Rome), 2
Augusta, Georgia, capture of, 96
Austria
  American Revolution, 104
  France, 28, 195
  French Revolution, 135–136
  Seven Years War, 25, 29
  War of the Austrian Succession, 7, 24
Ayen, duc d', 77

Babeuf, François Noël, 194
Bache, Benjamin Franklin, 205
Barbé-Marbois, François de, 232, 234
Le Barbier de Séville (Beaumarchais opera), 53, 65
Barras, Paul, 193–196, 197, 198, 199, 200, 213, 215, 216
Barry, Guillaume du, 38
Barry, Jeanne du, *nee* Bécu (Comtesse du Barry), 37–38, 44
Bastille, storming of, 129, 139
Beauharnais, Joséphine de, 193
Beaumarchais, Pierre Augustin Caron de, 203, 205
  arms trade by, 55–56, 58–59, 81
  career of, 53–54
  Dean, Silas, 64
  espionage by, 54–55
  politics of, 59–60, 65
Beaumont, Charles Geneviève de, 54–55
Bécu, Jeanne. *See* Barry, Jeanne du, *nee* Bécu (Comtesse du Barry)
Belgium, France, 132, 133, 193, 213
Bellamy, Monsieur, 200–203, 205
black cockade, 206
Bonaparte, Charles Louis Napoléon. *See* Napoléon III (Louis-Napoléon, emperor of France)
Bonaparte, Joseph, 217, 224
Bonaparte, Lucien, 215
Bonaparte, Napoléon (emperor of France). *See* Napoléon Bonaparte (emperor of France)

Boniface VIII (pope of Rome), 3
Bonvouloir, Archard de, 52, 57
Boston (British frigate), 165–166
Boston Massacre, 38, 41
Boston Port Bill, 43, 44
Boston Tea Party, 43
boycotts
  Continental Congress (First), 44
  Washington, George opposes, 41
Braddock, Edward, 19–22, 23, 50
Breeds Hill, Battle of, 50–51
Brissot, Jacques Pierre
  execution of, 171–172
  French Revolution, 131, 132–133
  United States, 133–135, 137
Britain. *See* Great Britain
British Army. *See also* American Revolution; Continental Army
  Boston evacuated by, 60–61
  Breeds Hill and Bunker Hill battles, 50–51
  Burgoyne, John surrenders, 81
  Lexington, Battle of, 48–49
  Philadelphia, Pennsylvania, 80
  skills of, 58
  southern campaign, 96
  successes of, 101
  Trenton, Battle of, 72–73
Broglie, Charles François, comte de. *See* de Broglie, Charles François, comte
Bunker Hill, Battle of, 51, 53
Bureau of Interpreters (France), 31, 32, 35, 37, 38, 49. *See also* espionage; France
Burgoyne, John, 81
Burke, Edmund, 5, 124–126
Burr, Aaron, 225–226

Cadwalader, John, 85–86
Campan, Henriette, 116
Canada
  American Revolution, 57–58, 61, 66, 84, 94–96, 108, 114, 115, 117
  France, 136, 141, 186, 197
  Genet, Edmond Charles, 147
  Great Britain conquers, 27, 30
  peace negotiations, 122
  Quebec Act, 43

Catherine II (the Great, empress of
    Russia), 135
Cent Associés (One Hundred Associates,
    France), 11
Cent Familles (One Hundred Families,
    France), 11, 28, 58, 128–129, 130,
    220, 240, 246
Champlain, Samuel de, 11
Charlemagne (Charles the Great, king of
    the Franks, Holy Roman Emperor),
    2–3, 220
Charles IV (king of Spain), 135
Charles X (king of France), 240
Charleston, South Carolina
    defense of, 61
    fall of, 101
    recapture of, 112–114, 124
China trade, 126
Chirac, Jacques, 247, 250
Choiseul, Étienne François, duc de, 44,
    68, 197
    Barry, Jeanne du, *nee* Bécu (Comtesse
        du Barry), 38
    career of, 28
    dismissal of, 38, 44
    Louis XV, 10
    Louis XVI, 44
    North America, 5, 27, 33, 34–35, 37,
        46, 47, 49, 61
    powers of, 30–32
    Seven Years War, 29–30
Church, Benjamin, 52
church-state relations, France, 2–4
Citizen Genet (French privateer), 146
Civil War (U.S.), 241–242
Claiborne, William C. C., 230
Clark, George Rogers, 137, 147, 159–160
Clarke, Elijah, 147
class structure, monarchy, 24–25
Clavière, Etienne, 133
Clinton, Cornelia, 168
Clinton, George, 124, 167, 181
Clinton, Henry, 109, 110
Clovis (king of the Franks), 2
Cobbett, William, 209
Code Napoléon, 221
Coercive Acts, 43–44, 90
Cold War, 247

communism, 149, 248
Compagnie de la Nouvelle-France
    (Company of New France), 11
Concord, Massachusetts, 48–49
La Concorde (French frigate), 166
Confederate States of America, 241
Congress (U.S.). *See also* Continental
    Congress (First); Continental
    Congress (Second)
    Alien and Sedition Acts, 209–210
    France, 212
    military strength, 207–209
Constellation (U.S. warship), 211, 212,
    218–219
Constitutional Convention, United
    States, 128
Constitution (France), 131–132, 220, 240
Constitution (United States), 132, 140,
    225–226
Constitution (U.S. warship), 211
Continental Army, 49–52, 59, 63, 65–66,
    68–69. *See also* American
    Revolution; British Army
    conditions in, 105
    French commissions in, 69–71, 72–73,
        75–76, 78
    Lafayette, marquis de, 110
    mutinies in, 101
    Newport, Rhode Island, 91
Continental Congress (First), 43–44,
    47–48
Continental Congress (Second)
    army, 49–52, 59, 66–67, 71, 75, 78
    Canada, 57
    composition of, 105
    d'Estaing, Charles Henri, comte, 93
    devaluation by, 101–102
    flight of, 68
    France, 87–88, 115
    Instructions to the Commissioners for
        Peace, 106–107
    Lafayette, marquis de, 78, 80, 84, 115
    peace treaty ratified by, 124
    territorial ambitions of, 102–103, 105
    trade, 61
    Washington, George, 94–95
Convention of 1800 (Môrtefontaine,
    Treaty of), 222, 224–225

Conway, Thomas (comte de Conway),
    76–77, 83–86, 88
Cornwallis, Charles, 61, 108, 109, 110,
    111–112, 115, 117
Corwin, Edward S., 125, 126
Crusades, France, 3, 74
Cuba, 30
Cumberland, Duke of, 65
Cumberland, Fort, 22

Dallas, Alexander J., 158
Dalmatia, 195
Damiens, Robert, 27
Davie, William R., 218, 222
Deane, Silas
    arms trade, 59
    Congress, 77, 88
    French mission of, 63–65, 67, 68–71,
        73–74, 75, 76, 81, 87, 89
    Lafayette, marquis de, 77–78, 80
de Broglie, Charles François, comte,
    33
    Adams, John, 121
    American Revolution, 65, 68–70,
        73–75, 77, 97
    Great Britain, 47
    Kalb, Johann (Baron de Kalb), 80, 83,
        84–85
    Lafayette, marquis de, 78
    Seven Years War, 35
Declaration of Independence, 60, 61, 64,
    65, 66, 129
"Declaration of Rights and Grievances of
    the Colonists in America," 34
Declaration of the Rights of Man, 129,
    130, 193, 219, 240, 243
"Declaration of the Causes and
    Necessities of Taking Up Arms,"
    51–52
DeConde, Alexander, 173, 174
de Gaulle, Charles, 244, 245, 246–247,
    249
de Grasse, François. *See* Grasse, François
    de
de Jumonville, Sieur, 17, 19
Delecroix, Charles, 186, 189
Democratic Societies, 149, 154, 158, 164,
    165, 178, 181, 182, 184, 188, 209

d'Estaing, Charles Henri, comte. *See*
    Estaing, Charles Henri, comte d'
devaluation, Continental Congress
    (Second), 101–102
Diderot, Denis, 65
Dien Bien Phu, Battle of, 244
Dinwiddie, Robert, 15, 17, 18, 24, 25
Drake, Francis, 120
du Barry, Madame. *See* Barry, Jeanne du,
    nee Bécu (Comtesse du Barry)
Dubourg, Barbeu, 63–64, 70–71
du Coudray, Philippe Trouson, 73, 76,
    77
du Pont de Nemours, Pierre Samuel, 219,
    228
Du Quesne, Ange de Menneville (French
    governor of Canada), 12, 14, 16
Du Quesne, Fort, 16, 19–21, 22,
    26–27
Dwight, Timothy, 206

École Nationale d'Administration
    (ENA), 249
Édon, Charles Geneviève de Beaumont
    d', 54–55
Egalité, Phillipe (Louis-Philippe-Joseph,
    duc d'Orléans), 130, 196
Egypt, 198, 207, 213, 215
Ellsworth, Oliver, 218, 222
l'Embuscade (French frigate), 146–147,
    150, 151, 166
enarchs, 249–252
England. *See* Great Britain
espionage
    Beaumarchais, Pierre Augustin Caron
        de, 54–55
    by France, 31, 33, 36–37, 38, 48,
        49, 52–55, 57, 76, 78, 87, 117,
        178–179
    by Great Britain, 52–53, 55, 60, 68, 86,
        108–109, 232
Estaing, Charles Henri, comte d', 103
    Continental Congress, 93
    failures of, 90–92, 96, 98, 99, 111,
        120
    "Papist" proclamation, 95–96
    Washington, George, 93–94
    West Indies expedition, 98–99

Family Compact. *See* Pacte de Famille (France)
Fauchet, Jean Antoine Joseph
  arrival of, 175
  career of, 178
  espionage by, 178–179, 183–184, 190
  food purchases by, 179–180
  Genet, Edmond Charles, 181
  neutrality, 177–178
  Whiskey Rebellion, 182
First Continental Congress. *See* Continental Congress (First)
First Provincial Congress (Concord), 43
Flaubert, Gustave, 60
Fleury, Cardinal, 7, 10
Florida
  France, 136, 141, 199
  Genet, Edmond Charles, 147, 160
  Jefferson, Thomas, 237–238
  Spain cedes to United States, 238
  United States, 209
Forbes, John, 26
Fort Adams, 230
Fort Cumberland, 22
Fort Du Quesne, 16, 19–21, 22, 26–27
Fort Moultrie, 61
Fort Necessity, 17–18
Fort Niagara, 14
Fort Pitt, 27
Fort St. John, 57
Fort Ticonderoga, 57
Fourth Republic (France), 244
France. *See also* Navy (French)
  Adams, John, 88–89
  Africa, 241, 243
  Algeria, 244
  American Revolution assisted by, 48, 53, 55–57, 64–65, 68–71, 95–96, 100–101, 103–104
  anti-Americanism in, 1, 2, 246–252
  Belgium, 193
  Canada, 136, 141, 186, 197
  church-state relations, 2–4, 144, 221, 248–249
  Constitutional Convention (U.S.), 128
  Constitution of, 131–132, 220, 240
  court of, 28, 29

economy and society, 24–25, 125, 131, 133, 172, 195, 212–214, 240, 241, 245–246, 249–251
education in, 248–250
espionage by, 31, 33, 36–37, 38, 48, 49, 52–55, 57, 76, 87, 117, 178–179
famine in, 179–180
Great Britain, 2, 3, 4–5, 12–13, 32, 33, 61–62, 64, 77, 81–82, 89, 117–118, 135–136, 153, 163, 186, 194, 197–198, 207, 232
Indochina, 241, 243, 244
Iraq, 252
Louisiana, 136–137, 179, 180
Louisiana relinquished by, 232–235
Louisiana retrocession to, 217, 222, 224, 226, 227, 232
Mexico invaded by, 241
military strength of, 220
monarchy, 3–4, 129
Monroe, James, 238–239
North American ambitions of, 2, 4, 5, 10–13, 30, 32, 38, 46–47
peace negotiations, 104–107, 118–120, 123–124
peace treaty, 124
politics in, 125–126, 128–129, 193–194, 240–241, 242
revolution in, 5, 129–134, 139, 143–144, 178, 182–183, 196, 245–246
revolution of 1848, 240
Robespierre, Maximilien, 171–172
Santo Domingo, 229
Seven Years War, 25, 28–30
Spain, 145, 180, 186, 195, 199, 209, 217
United States, 138–139, 141–142, 143–144, 172, 174–175, 184–191, 197, 199–208, 210, 214, 218–219, 245–246
United States peace commissions to, 200–204, 218, 222, 230–231
Washington, George, 137–138, 163, 165, 172, 189, 190, 207
World War II, 243–244
XYZ affair, 205–206
Francis I (emperor of Austria), 44

Franco-American Treaties of 1778, 137–141, 184, 185, 186, 188, 218
Franco-German military alliance, 243
Franklin, Benjamin
    American Revolution, 66, 81, 105
    France, 87–88, 89, 97, 100, 115
    Lafayette, marquis de, 78, 80
    peace negotiations, 118–120, 122
Freemasonry, 65, 78, 80
French and Indian War, 2. *See also* Seven Years War
    escalation of, 23–24
    Washington, George, 15–22, 25–27
French immigrants, 206, 209, 210
French Revolution. *See* France, revolution in
fur trade, 12, 13, 14

Gallatin, Albert, 225
Gallican Catholic Church, 3–4
Gates, Horatio, 59, 81, 82, 83–84, 85
Gaulle, Charles de, 244, 245, 246–247, 249
Genet, Edmé
    Adams, John, 89
    American Revolution, 57, 59, 73, 76, 105
    career of, 31–32
    death of, 115–116
    espionage, 33–34, 35, 52, 76
    Lafayette, marquis de, 78
    New France, 38, 48
    Vergennes, Charles Gravier, comte de, 46, 47, 81
    Washington, George, 50, 83
Genet, Edmond Charles, 177, 190
    arrest of, 175, 178
    asylum granted to, 179
    bankruptcy of, 169
    career of, 116–117, 134
    Democratic Societies, 149
    education of, 89, 116
    French Revolution, 134–135
    instructions to, 141–142, 174–175
    Jefferson, Thomas, 139, 149, 154–155, 156–157, 158, 160–161, 164–165, 169–171, 172

    military adventures of, 146–147, 150, 153, 155–162, 168
    personality of, 173–174
    politics, 149, 172–173, 174–175
    popularity of, 145–146, 148, 151–152, 167–168
    propaganda campaign by, 152–153, 161–162
    Robespierre, Maximilien, 172
    Vergennes, Charles Gravier, comte de, 115–116
    Washington, George, 147, 149–150, 152, 155–156, 157–158, 161–162, 163–165, 167, 170–171, 178, 181
Genet, Henriette, 32
George II (king of England), 13, 65
George III (king of England)
    American Revolution, 52
    France, 232
    Olive Branch Petition, 51–52
    Rochford, Lord, 55
Gérard de Rayneval, Conrad Alexandre, 87, 96–97, 101–102, 104, 105
Germany, World War II, 243
Gerry, Elbridge, 200, 202, 204
Gibralter, 120
Girondins, 130–131, 133, 134, 138, 160, 171
Gloucester, Duke of, 65, 74
Grasse, François de
    British defeat of, 117–118
    Charleston, South Carolina, 112–113
    Chesapeake Bay, 109–112
    preparations of, 108
Great Britain. *See also* Navy (British)
    Canada conquest, 27, 30
    Coercive Acts, 43–44
    economy of, 124–125
    espionage by, 52–53, 55, 60, 68, 86, 108–109, 232
    France, 2, 3, 4–5, 12–13, 32, 33, 61–62, 64, 77, 81–82, 89, 117–118, 135–136, 153, 163, 186, 194, 197–198, 207, 232
    Ireland, 150
    Jay Treaty, 183
    Mexico invaded by, 241

North American loyalty to, 34, 36, 51–52, 57–58, 71, 200
North American settlement by, 11–12, 14
peace efforts, 104–105, 118–120
peace treaty,. 124
Seven Years War, 24, 25
Spain, 120, 122, 210–211
taxation by, 32–35
United States, 127–128, 138, 140, 145–146, 150, 153–154, 155–156, 180, 200, 210–211
Virginia colony, 41–42
Washington, George, 41
Great War for Empire. *See* Seven Years War
Greene, Nathanael, 52, 76, 92, 93, 113, 184
Grenville, William Wyndam, 150
Gustave III (king of Sweden), 46

Half-King (Oneida chief), 15, 17, 18, 19
Hamilton, Alexander, 188, 231
armed forces, 209, 211
Democratic Societies, 165
Fauchet, Jean Antoine Joseph, 178
Franco-American Treaty of 1778, 138, 140
Genet, Edmond Charles, 149, 154, 160–161, 169
Louisiana, 217
Whiskey Rebellion, 180–182
Hammond, George, 150, 175
Hancock, John, 63
American Revolution, 91, 92
Continental Congress, 43, 52
d'Estaing, Charles Henri, comte, 93–94
taxation, 33
haute bourgeoisie, class structure, 24, 240
Hauteval, Lucien, 201, 202
Henry, Patrick, 41
career of, 39–40
France, 48
taxation, 34
Hessians
New York City, 66
Trenton, Battle of, 72
Holland. *See* Netherlands

Hortalez, Roderigue, 58–59
Hortalez et Cie, 58–59, 203
Hottinguer, Jean Conrad, 200–202, 205
Howe, William, 68
Hussein, Saddam, 252

impressment, of seamen, 138
India, 198
Indians. *See also* French and Indian War
border attacks by, 145, 147, 157
France and, 12–13, 15
Louisiana, 231
Indochina, France, 241, 243, 244
Institut de France, 245
Instructions to the Commissioners for Peace, 106–107
Insurgente (French frigate), 212
Ionian Islands, 195
Iraq, 252
Ireland, 197, 198, 199, 207, 213
Irish immigrants, 150, 206, 209, 210
Italy, 133, 195, 213–214

Jackson, Andrew, 235, 238
Jacobin Democratic Society, 158
Jacobins, 130–131, 132, 147, 149, 161, 165, 166–167, 171, 172, 178, 182–183, 193, 196, 215
Jamaica, 120
Jay, John, 167
France, 1–2, 5, 87, 105, 106, 122
Great Britain, 140, 145–146, 180, 183, 200, 230
Lafayette, marquis de, 121
peace negotiations, 107, 120–121, 122–123
Spain, 115, 118
Jay Treaty, 183, 184, 185–186, 187–188, 200
Jeanne d'Arc, 8, 74
Jefferson, Thomas, 118, 179, 219
American Revolution, 67
Florida, 237–238
France, 106, 134, 142, 154, 159, 160, 172, 187, 190, 204, 226
Franco-American Treaty of 1778, 138–139
Freemasonry, 65

Jefferson, Thomas (*cont.*)
   French Revolution, 130, 139
   Genet, Edmond Charles, 149, 154–155,
      156–157, 158, 160–161, 163,
      164–165, 169–171, 172, 173–174
   Louisiana, 227–228, 230–231, 237
   Madison, James, 178
   Mazzei, Philip, 185–186
   politics of, 129
   presidency, 225–226
   resignation of, 165, 175
   vice presidency, 191
   war powers, 140
   Washington, George, 165
   XYZ affair, 205
Johnson, Andrew, 242
Jones, John Paul, 90, 97, 98–99
Jospin, Lionel, 247
Jumonville, Sieur de, 17, 19

Kalb, Johann (Baron de Kalb)
   American Revolution, 68–70, 73, 74,
      75, 77, 84–85, 148
   career of, 35
   de Broglie, Charles François, comte, 80
   espionage by, 36–37, 78
   loyalty of, 83
   retirement of, 38
King, Rufus, 210
Kléber, Jean Baptiste, 213
Knights of St. John, 207
Knox, Henry, 160, 165, 205, 207

Lafayette, Adrienne de, 220
Lafayette, George-Washington, 100
Lafayette, marquis de
   Canada, 94–95
   commission of, 73–74, 78–80
   de Broglie, Charles François, comte,
      78
   d'Estaing, Charles Henri, comte, 93–94
   experience of, 74–75
   family of, 74
   French Revolution, 130–131
   Louis XVI (king of France), 97, 251
   Newport, Rhode Island, 91–92
   peace negotiations, 118, 120–122
   politics of, 65, 129

   popularity of, 96–97, 115
   Washington, George, 84, 96, 99–100,
      104, 107–110
La Luzerne, Anne César, chevalier de,
   105–107
land speculation, 105, 133, 145
La Salle, René-Robert Cavalier Sieur de,
   11, 13, 15
Laussat, Pierre Clément de, 232
Laval, Pierre, 243
Lebanon, 243
Leclerc, Charles Victor Emanuel, 229
Lee, Arthur, 67
Lee, Charles, 107, 184
   British capture of, 71
   Continental Army, 50, 60, 61, 63,
      67–68
   court-martial of, 86
Lee, Henry, 181–182
Lee, Richard Henry, 41, 60
Lee, Thomas, 13
Leo III (pope of Rome), 2–3
Leopold II (emperor of Austria), 135
Lewis, Meriwether, 231
Lexington, Battle of, 48–49, 50, 64
Lincoln, Abraham, 242
Little Sarah (British ship), 158–159
Livingston, Robert, 115, 120, 122–123,
   226, 229, 234
Locke, John, 65, 129
Louis IX (king of France), 3
Louis XIII (king of France), 4, 11
Louis XIV (king of France), 4, 7, 8, 11,
   224, 246
Louis XV (king of France), 4, 5, 65
   Barry, Jeanne du, *nee* Bécu (Comtesse
      du Barry), 37–38
   Beaumarchais, Pierre Augustin Caron
      de, 53, 54
   Beaumont, Charles Geneviève de, 55
   Choiseul, Étienne François, duc de, 38
   death of, 44
   Maupeou, René-Nicolas de, 44
   reign of, 7–10, 27–28
Louis XVI (king of France), 4, 28, 48, 245
   American Revolution, 82, 87, 92
   ascension of, 44–46
   execution of, 135, 137–138, 144

French Revolution, 129–130
Genet, Edmond Charles, 116
Lafayette, marquis de, 97, 251
Vergennes, Charles Gravier, comte de, 46, 117
Louis XVIII (king of France), 116, 238, 240
Louisiana. *See also* Mississippi River; New France; New Orleans, Louisiana
    France, 134, 136–137, 141–142, 179, 180, 186, 199, 217, 241, 242
    French sovereignty, 11
    Genet, Edmond Charles, 147, 159–161
    retrocession to France, 217, 222, 224, 226, 227
    Spain, 30, 180, 183, 199, 227
    United States, 209, 226–232
    United States purchase of, 232–235, 237
Louis Philippe I (king of France), 240
Lovell, James, 78

Madison, James, 238
    Fauchet, Jean Antoine Joseph, 178, 179
    Jefferson, Thomas, 155, 171, 173–174, 226
    Livingston, Robert, 229
    Louisiana, 230
Malta, 198, 207
Mangourit, Michel Ange, 147
manifest destiny, 231
Manifesto of Equality (France), 194
Maria Theresa (empress of Austria), 44
Marie-Antoinette (queen of France), 28, 32, 44, 46, 117, 134, 135
Marine Corps (United States), 208
Le Marriage de Figaro (Beaumarchais opera), 60
Marshall, John, 200–204, 208
Marshall Plan, 247
Mason, Stevens T., 231
Massachusetts colony
    boycott recommended by, 41
    Breeds Hill and Bunker Hill battles, 50–51
    British fleet called to, 37

Lexington, Battle of, 48–49
    rebellion in, 48
    rioting in, 34, 38, 43
Maupeou, René-Nicolas de, Louis XV (king of France), 44
Maurepas, comte de, 46, 77
Mazarin, Cardinal, 4
Mazzei, Philip, 185–186
Mercer, George, 26, 40–41
merchant bankers, class structure, 24
Mexico, France invades, 241
Michaux, André, 159–160
Middle East, France, 243
Mifflin, Thomas, 84–85, 151
Minutemen
    Lexington, Battle of, 48–49, 50
    medical treatment of, 52
Miranda, Francisco de, 134, 210
Mississippi River, navigation on, 136–137, 149, 177, 179, 183, 224, 227, 230–231, 234. *See also* Louisiana; New Orleans, Louisiana
Mitterand, François, 247
monarchy
    class structure, 24–25
    France, 3–4, 129
    succession struggles, 24
Monroe, James, 72, 165, 226, 229–230, 231, 234, 238–239
Monroe Doctrine, 238–240, 241, 242
Montgomery, Richard, 57, 83
Montreal, French surrender of, 27
Morroco, France, 243
Môrtefontaine, Treaty of (Convention of 1800), 222, 224–225
Moultrie, Fort, 61
Moultrie, William, 145, 148, 171
Murray, William Vans, 218, 222, 224

Naples, Italy, 213–214
Napoléon Bonaparte (emperor of France)
    Barras, Paul, 193, 194
    Council of Five Hundred, 216
    exile of, 238
    Florida, 237–238
    Louisiana relinquished by, 232–235
    Louisiana retrocession, 217, 222, 224, 228–229, 232

Napoléon Bonaparte (emperor of France)
        (*cont.*)
    military conquests of, 194–196,
        197–199, 206–207
    personality of, 219–220
    politics of, 219–221
    popularity of, 215–216
    power seized by, 216–217, 220
    reverses to, 213–214, 215
    Spain, 231
    United States, 217–218, 226
    Washington, George, 221–222
Napoleonic Wars, 238
Napoléon III (Louis-Napoléon, emperor
        of France), 240–242
National Convention (France), 131–132,
        135, 182, 193
nativism, 209
Naturalization Act, 209
natural resources, depletion of European,
        25
Navy (British). *See also* British Army
    American Revolution, 61
    French Navy and, 165–167, 213
    mutiny in, 197
    strength of, 37
Navy (French)
    British Navy and, 179–180, 213
    Choiseul, Étienne François, duc de,
        37
    mutiny in, 169
    Philadelphia arrival of, 162
Navy (Spanish), strength of, 37
Navy (U.S.), 207, 208, 211–212
Nazi Germany, World War II, 243
naziism, 149, 248
Necessity, Fort, 17–18
Nelson, Horatio, 213
Netherlands, 103, 133, 195
neutrality
    Fauchet, Jean Antoine Joseph, 177–178
    United States, 140–141, 148–150, 153,
        157, 159, 186, 187
"Neutrality Proclamation," 149–150, 153,
        157, 159
New France. *See also* Canada; Louisiana
    Choiseul, Étienne François, duc de, 37
    extent of, 10–14

    fortification of, 14
    Genet, Edmé, 38, 48
    loss of, 30
    Vergennes, Charles Gravier, comte de,
        124
New Orleans, Louisiana, 227, 228,
        229–232, 234. *See also* Louisiana;
        Mississippi River
Newport, Rhode Island, 91, 103
New York City
    British evacuation of, 124
    British garrison in, 66
    British Navy, 61
    French Army, 122
    French Navy, 165–167
    Washington, George, 66–68, 109
    yellow fever, 168–169
New York colony
    French and Indian War, 23–24
    rioting in, 34
Niagara, Fort, 14
Noailles, vicomte de, 65, 75, 77
North Africa, 243

O'Hara, Charles, 112
Ohio Company, 13, 14, 15
oligarchs, 128–129, 240, 241, 242
Olive Branch Petition, 51–52
One Hundred Families. *See* Cent Familles
Oneida people, 15, 18
Orléans, Battle of, 74
Orléans, Louis-Philippe-Joseph, duc d'
        (Philippe Egalité), 130, 196
Osgood, David, 182
Otis, Harrison Gray, 209
Otis, James, 33, 34

Pacte de Famille (France), 30, 58
Paine, Thomas, 135, 202
La Paix ou la Guerre (Beaumarchais), 55
"Papist" proclamation, d'Estaing, Charles
        Henri, comte, 95–96
Paris, Treaty of, 30, 46, 64
Pearl Harbor attack, 246
Pépin the Short (king of the Franks), 2
Petite Démocrate (French privateer),
        159
Peyrefitte, Alain, 246

Philadelphia, Pennsylvania, American
    Revolution, 80, 109
Philip IV (king of France), 3, 195
Philippines, 30
Pickering, Timothy, 189, 199, 202, 205
Pinckney, Charles Coatesworth, 146, 189,
    200–201, 203–204, 210
Pitt, Fort, 27
Pitt, William, 25, 27, 30, 210
Pius VI (pope of Rome), 195
Plato, 249, 250
Poisson, Jeanne-Antoinette. *See*
    Pompadour, Madame de
Poland
    succession struggles, 24
    World War II, 246
Pompadour, Madame de (Jeanne-
    Antoinette Poisson), 10, 28, 32
Pontleroy, Sieur, 33, 34, 48
Portugal, 30
Prussia
    French Army, 132–133, 144
    French Revolution, 135–136
    Seven Years War, 25

Quebec, Canada, 27, 57
Quebec Act, 43

Randolph, Edmund, 175
    American Revolution, 66
    attorney general, 158
    career of, 184
    Fauchet, Jean Antoine Joseph, 183–184
    Genet, Edmond Charles, 179
    Virginia, 39
    Washington, George, 184
    Whiskey Rebellion, 182
Rayneval, Gérard de. *See* Gérard de
    Rayneval, Conrad Alexandre
Reed, Joseph, 66
the Reign of Terror, 183, 196. *See also*
    France, revolution in
Republican (French privateer), 146
Revel, Jean-François, 244–245, 246,
    247–248, 251, 252
Revere, Paul, 43, 49, 52
Revolutionary War. *See* American
    Revolution

Rhineland, 195, 213, 243
Rhode Island colony, rioting in, 34
Richelieu, Cardinal, 4, 11
Robespierre, Maximilien, 196
    Brissot, Jacques Pierre, 131
    execution of, 182–183, 193
    Fauchet, Jean Antoine Joseph,
    178
    power seized by, 171–172
Rochambeau, Jean-Baptiste-Donatien de
    Vimeur, comte de, 116, 118, 134
    career of, 100–101
    tactics of, 103–104, 114
    troops of, in U.S., 122
    Washington, George, 104, 108, 112
Rochford, Lord, 52, 55
Rolfe, John, 13
Ross, James, 231
Rousseau, Jean-Jacques, 65
"Rules Governing Belligerents," 156
Russia
    American Revolution, 104
    France, 195, 213–214
    French Revolution, 135
    Poland, 246
    Seven Years War, 25
Rutledge, John, 146

St. John, Fort, 57
Sans-Culotte (French privateer), 146
Santo Domingo, slave uprisings in, 169,
    214, 219, 229, 232
Savannah, Georgia, capture of, 96
seamen
    French treatment of, 185, 190–191,
    197
    impressment of, 138
    release of, 214
Second Babylonian Captivity, 3
Second Continental Congress. *See*
    Continental Congress (Second)
Second Empire (France), 240, 242
Second Republic (France), 240
le Secret du Roi, 7–8, 31, 33, 55
Sedition Act, 210
Ségur, comte de, 65, 75, 77
Serapis (British ship), 98–99
Serbia, 247

Seven Years War, 26, 33, 35, 36, 50, 54,
    64, 101, 105, 125, 197. *See also*
    French and Indian War
  causes of, 25
  costs of, 30
  French losses in, 28–30
  Great Britain, 24
  Vergennes, Charles Gravier, comte de,
    46
Seward, William, 241–242
Shelby, Isaac, 160
Sheridan, Philip H., 242
Shirley, William, 15
slavery, 207, 214
smallpox, 98
Smith, William Loughton, 188
socialism, 250–251
Socrates, 250
Spain
  American Revolution, 58–59, 81–82,
    95, 97, 98, 102, 104, 118
  border attacks by, 145
  Florida, 237–238
  Florida ceded to United States,
    238
  France, 145, 180, 186, 195, 199, 209,
    217
  French Revolution, 135–136
  Genet, Edmond Charles, 147, 160
  Great Britain, 120, 122, 210–211
  Louisiana, 30, 134, 136–137, 141–142,
    149, 180, 183, 199, 217, 227,
    231
  Louisiana retrocession to France, 217,
    222, 224, 226, 227
  Mexico invaded by, 241
  peace negotiations, 122, 124
  peace treaty, 124
  Seven Years War, 29–30, 50
  South American colonies, 238–239
  succession struggles, 24
  United States, 128, 177, 209
  Vergennes, Charles Gravier, comte de,
    120
Spanish Armada, 120
Staël, Anne-Louise-Germaine de
    (Madame de Staël), 196, 197
Stamp Act, 33–34, 68, 145

Stephen II (pope of Rome), 2
succession struggles
  monarchy, 24
  War of the Austrian Succession, 7
Sullivan, John, 66, 91–93
Switzerland, 195
Syria, 243

Talleyrand-Périgord, Charles-Maurice de,
    5, 198, 224, 232
  Adams, John, 217
  career of, 196
  Florida, 238
  Jay Treaty, 200
  Louisiana, 227, 228
  Napoléon, 216–217, 221
  politics, 199, 244
  resignation of, 215
  United States, 196–197, 212, 214, 225,
    226
  United States peace commission,
    200–205
taxation. *See also* France, economy and
    society
  France, 251
  Great Britain, 32–35, 90
  United States, 145, 180–181, 208
Tea Act, 90
Teachout, Terry, 251
the Terror, 183, 196. *See also* France,
    revolution in
Texas, 237, 238
Third Republic (France), 243
Ticonderoga, Fort, 57
tobacco trade, 13, 41, 42, 126
Toussaint L'Overture, François Dominque,
    219, 229
Townshend, Charles, 35
Townshend Acts, 35
trade
  Continental Congress, 61
  France, 125, 217
  French attacks on, 197
  fur trade, 12, 13, 14
  Great Britain, 41, 44, 138
  Napoleonic Wars, 238
  United States, 126, 217–218
Trenton, Battle of, 72–73

Trumbull, John, 202
Truxton, Thomas, 212, 218–219

United States. *See also* American
    Revolution
    Alien and Sedition Acts, 209–210
    Bonaparte, Napoléon, 217–218
    Civil War, 241–242
    Constitutional Convention, 128
    Constitution of, 132, 140, 225–226
    election of 1800, 225–226
    France, 172, 174–175, 184–191, 197,
        199–208, 210, 214, 218–219,
        245–246
    Franco-American Treaty of 1778,
        137–141
    French Revolution, 137–138, 143–144,
        153, 168
    Great Britain, 127–128, 138, 140,
        145–146, 150, 153–154, 155–156,
        180, 200, 210–211
    Louisiana, 209, 226–235
    military strength of, 207–209, 211–212,
        218–219, 230
    peace commissions to France, 200–204,
        218, 222, 230–231
    politics in, 126–128, 144
    Spain, 128, 177, 209
    Talleyrand-Périgord, Charles-Maurice
        de, 196–197
    trade, 126
    XYZ affair, 205–206
United States (U.S. warship), 211

Valley Forge encampment, 84–85, 151
Vedrine, Hubert, 247
Venezuela, 134
La Vengeance (French frigate), 218
Venice, Italy, 195
Vergennes, Charles Gravier, comte de,
    114, 245
    Adams, John, 89, 97–98, 103, 106
    American Revolution, 52, 53, 56–57,
        58, 60, 61–62, 65–66, 68, 71, 72,
        81–82, 83, 94, 100, 102–103,
        105–106, 133–134
    Canada, 95–96, 108
    career of, 46

Dean, Silas, 64
    death of, 126
    devaluation, 101–102
    espionage, 55
    Genet, Edmond Charles, 115–116, 117,
        134
    Lafayette, marquis de, 77, 97
    monarchy, 4
    peace negotiations, 104–107, 118, 122,
        124
    Rayneval, Conrad Gérard de, 87
    revolutionary politics, 126
    Spain, 120
    Washington, George, 101
    Yorktown, Battle of, 115
Vietnam. *See* Indochina
Villepin, Dominique de, 250, 252
Villette, Madame de, 203
Virginia colony, 13–14
    complacency in, 39
    French and Indian War, 23
    Great Britain, 41–42
    society in, 40
Voltaire (François-Marie Arouet), 27, 65,
    203

Ward, Artemis, Continental Army, 50
War of 1812, 238
War of the Austrian Succession, 7, 24
Warren, James, 121
Warville, Jacques Pierre Brissot de. *See*
    Brissot, Jacques Pierre
Washington, D. C., 225
Washington, George, 63, 65, 126, 225
    American Revolution, 61, 66, 67–68,
        71–73
    career of, 40–43
    Charleston, South Carolina, 112–114
    commander in chief of armed forces,
        209
    Constitutional Convention, 128
    Continental Army, 50–51, 52, 59
    Continental Congress, 94–95
    Conway, Thomas (comte de Conway),
        83–86
    death of, 221–222
    de Grasse, François, 112–113
    d'Estaing, Charles Henri, comte, 93–94

Washington, George (*cont.*)
  education of, 14
  Fauchet, Jean Antoine Joseph,
    177–178, 183–184
  France, 5, 68, 69–70, 73, 75–77, 78,
    82–83, 94, 104, 163, 165, 172, 189,
    190, 207
  Franco-American Treaty of 1778,
    137–141
  Freemasonry, 65
  French and Indian War, 15–22, 24,
    25–27
  French Revolution, 137–138
  Genet, Edmond Charles, 147, 149–150,
    152, 155–158, 161–162, 163–165,
    167, 169, 170–171, 179
  Great Britain, 41
  Hamilton, Alexander, 138
  Jefferson, Thomas, 165
  Kalb, Johann (Baron de Kalb), 83
  Lafayette, marquis de, 84, 96, 99–100,
    107, 110
  Lee, Charles, 50, 86
  Newport, Rhode Island, 91, 92–93
  Ohio Company, 13
  presidency of, 145, 149–150, 153, 157,
    158–159, 163–165, 172
  Randolph, Edmund, 184
  resignation of, 124
  retirement of, 186–187, 191
  Rochambeau, Jean-Baptiste-Donatien
    de Vimeur, comte de, 104
  tactics of, 107–109
  Talleyrand-Périgord, Charles-Maurice
    de, 196–197
  taxation, 33
  Vergennes, Charles Gravier, comte de,
    101
  Whiskey Rebellion, 181–182
  Yorktown, Battle of, 112
Washington, John, 13
Washington, Lawrence, 13, 14
Washington, Martha Dandrige Custis, 40,
  42
Washington, William, 72
Wayne, Anthony, 109
Webster, Noah, 150, 152, 189–190
West Indies, 94, 96, 99, 117, 120, 136,
  212, 213, 217, 219, 229, 232
westward migration, 180, 199, 226–227.
  See also Louisiana
Whiskey Rebellion, 180–182
Whitney, Eli, 235
Wolfe, James, 27
World War I, 243
World War II, 243–244, 246–247

XYZ affair, 210, 218
  peace commission to France, 200–204
  reactions to, 205–206

yellow fever, 168–169
Yorktown, Battle of, 112, 115, 117
Yugoslavia, 247